HITLER'S BASTARD

'Be strong, boy, be strong! If you're not strong, you're as good as dead!'

– Eric Pleasants' father on his son's
departure from home

'Stinking Englishman – you were never born – some whore pissed you against a brothel wall and the sun hatched you out!'

– Fellow inmate in the Gulag slave mine

'I had grown to like Germany.'

– Ex-SS trooper Eric Pleasants on his final
release from prison camp

'It's governments who declare war – but the people who have to fight it.'

– Eric Pleasants

hitler's bastard

THROUGH HELL AND BACK IN NAZI GERMANY AND STALIN'S RUSSIA

ERIC PLEASANTS

Edited by
Ian Sayer and Douglas Botting

MAINSTREAM
PUBLISHING

EDINBURGH AND LONDON

First published in Great Britain in 2003 by
MAINSTREAM PUBLISHING COMPANY (EDINBURGH) LTD
7 Albany Street
Edinburgh EH1 3UG

ISBN 1 84018 743 3

Typeset in Modern Blackletter and Times New Roman

Printed in Great Britain by Mackays of Chatham plc

CONTENTS

ABOUT THE EDITORS

Ian Sayer and Douglas Botting are co-authors of three previous major documentary accounts of hitherto unknown aspects of the Second World War and the Third Reich – the bestselling *Nazi Gold: The Story of the World's Greatest Robbery*, *America's Secret Army* and *Hitler's Last General: The Case Against Wilhelm Mohnke*. These books have been published in the UK, USA and across Europe, and remain the definitive histories of their subjects. In the USA there is also considerable current interest in making a movie based on *Nazi Gold*, for, as the *New York Times* reviewer wrote: 'It is one of the most fascinating stories of fabulous wealth and greed I've ever read, with a mystery that unravels deliciously page by page. I had to remind myself that it's a true story.'

Ian Sayer is a businessman and the founder and owner of the world's most extensive private document archive and library on the Second World War and the Third Reich. He was publisher and editor of the monthly magazine *World War Two Investigator* and maintains ongoing research connections overseas, especially in the USA and Germany. It was his extensive research that cracked the mystery of the disappearance of the Reichsbank gold and currency reserves at the end of the Second World War, and it was his discovery and acquisition of the hitherto unknown papers of Walter Wagner, the mystery man at

Hitler's wedding, which was the start-point of this present book.

Douglas Botting has a Masters degree from Oxford University and is a Member of the Royal Institute of International Affairs and a Life Member of the National Counter Intelligence Corps Association of America. He was formerly a special correspondent for the BBC and *Time-Life* and has written a number of highly praised histories and biographies in his own right (several on twentieth-century German themes, among them *From the Ruins of the Reich*, Crown/New American Library), published in the UK, USA, Japan, Russia, Brazil and most European countries, including the following current titles:

Dr Eckener's Dream Machine (HarperCollins/Holt & Co., London/New York, 2002) – 'a fascinating, lively and meticulously researched story' – *New York Review of Books*.

Gerald Durrell: The Authorised Biography (HarperCollins/Carroll & Graf, London/New York, 2002) – 'a captivating, deeply moving and surprisingly candid biography – an extraordinary saga' – *Publishers Weekly* (starred review); 'the best biography I have read in years' – *The Scotsman*. Runner-up, BP Natural World Book Prize.

The Saga of Ring of Bright Water: The Enigma of Gavin Maxwell (Neil Wilson Publishing/HarperCollins, Glasgow/London, 2000) – 'an immaculate, masterly, enthralling biography' – *Spectator*.

EDITORS' PREFACE

SOME THOUGHTS ABOUT *HITLER'S BASTARD*

Recently Ian Sayer and Douglas Botting acquired the typed manuscript of a book written by a retired Norfolk judo instructor and PE teacher by the name of Eric Pleasants, now deceased. Though Mr Pleasants had been a highly regarded model member of his local community, living a quiet, respectable, useful life with his wife in his modest thatched country cottage, his book – *Hitler's Bastard* – revealed a sensationally different past life. The subtitle we have given to his book – *Through Hell and Back in Hitler's Germany and Stalin's Russia* – is not hyperbole, it is exact.

Few other Englishmen can have undergone this particular kind of extraordinary picaresque nightmare or endured seemingly unendurable constraints as Eric Pleasants did in the 16 fantastical but indomitable years he describes in this book – from a country childhood in rural Norfolk, flirtation with the British Communist Party, then a brief membership of the British Fascist Party and, finally, of the pacifist Peace Pledge Union, followed by a vagabond life in Nazi-occupied Jersey, forced labour in Nazi correction camps in France, a life on the run in occupied Paris, recruitment into the British Free Corps of the Waffen-SS – a tongue-in-cheek organisation, it has to be said, which was not responsible for any deaths in battle – love and marriage (amid the ruins of Berlin) with a young German woman to whom he was devoted, the bombing of Dresden, a failed escape along the sewers of Berlin, a bizarre gipsy life as a strong man in a travelling circus in Communist East Germany, arrest by the Soviet KGB, two years' solitary confinement, then trial by a Soviet court and a sentence of 25 years' slave labour as a coal miner in the notorious 'hard regime' Vorkuta complex of forced labour camps in Arctic Russia.

If the first half of Pleasants' remarkably well-written book reads like an Englishman's version of Maxim Gorki's *Lower Depths*, the second half reads like a blow-by-blow vision of hell from Solzhenitsyn's *Gulag Archipelago*. Only with Stalin's death in 1953 is Pleasants finally released from his unique kind of purgatory, when he begins the long slow train journey from Arctic Russia to the English Channel coast. Though every minute brings him closer to 'England, home and beauty', he still carries the long-inured mindset of the slave confined below ground. Unable to bear the terrifying view of the unconstrained expanse of sea and sky and freedom he can see from the deck of the cross-Channel steamer, he seeks refuge in the only environment he can now understand – the close confinement of the engine room and the hard labour of shovelling coal.

And then at last he lies down to sleep in his narrow iron bed in his mother's Norfolk cottage – the bed in which he had last slept 16 eventful and nightmarish years ago – paradise regained. He is free at last and finally disburdened of the ultimate rule of survival – more common among jungle animals than the citizens of an island democracy – 'kill or be killed'.

In a sense, Pleasants' odyssey takes the form of a version of the hero-quest myth in which a young petty crook cum anti-war renegade and turncoat undergoes a sea-change under the impact of real war (Dresden, Berlin) and true love (his young and devoted German girlfriend, later his wife), and becomes more hero than villain. This is redemption through pain, especially once he enters the vortex of the Russian slave camps – the culmination of nearly half a lifetime of peripatetic nightmare endured with cunning, opportunism, courage and primordial stoicism.

All in all, *Hitler's Bastard* is an extraordinary testament to one man's adherence to an imperishable instinct – the will to survive – under circumstances few of us can even bear to imagine.

This autobiography was originally put together by Eric Pleasants with the assistance of Christine Ramble, whom the editors have been unable to trace. The editors have, however, taken every care to check and, if necessary, correct all verifiable facts in so far as this is possible.

Ian Sayer
Douglas Botting
September 2003

PROLOGUE BY ERIC PLEASANTS

This is the true story of an English national, a conscientious objector who, during the Second World War, was voluntarily recruited to the ranks of that bastard child of the German SS, the British Free Corps.

That is not a contradictory statement. The fact that I joined Hitler's army has no political or moral significance for me. Why should it have? In a war forced upon me I was on nobody's 'side' except my own, neither traitor nor partisan, and I never fought for anybody except myself. I was neither anti-British nor anti-German, not anti-Semitic or anti-Russian.

I most certainly was, and still am, anti-war and anti-establishment. There is no such thing as a war conducted according to the rules of common decency and humanity. To throw people into an arena and then expect them to behave as they would in time of peace is as reasonable as applying the Queensberry rules to a street brawl, the most illogical double-think of all time.

Nevertheless, in all the 'historical' accounts of the British Free Corps that I have read the narrative has been highly coloured by the author's personal, uninformed interpretation and sanctimonious judgement of character and motivation. These histories have been 'researched' largely from scant documentation and transcripts of post-war trials, where the writer has not always checked the authenticity of the evidence given. Mistakes are excusable – everyone makes those. But pious moralising upon the actions of people of whom one has no personal knowledge is not. It is no part of a historian's business to prejudice posterity by his own emotional bias.

This book does not attempt to be a history of the British Free Corps any more than it is a definitive account of the Russian penal system. It is simply my own story: it actually happened to *me*. Maybe I was a rebellious opportunist, but I made my own, highly individual way through the war and the years immediately following. I make no apology; and I have no regrets.

Eric Pleasants

Chapter 1

THE JERSEY JACKALS

When we arrived, the grave was dug and ready. I had the feeling that it had been there waiting since the time we first met him, more than 30 years ago. A pauper's grave, a shabby three-ply coffin, a name on a brass plate: Francis Caesar Jegou.

Jegou was brutally murdered in December 1976, his stabbed and mutilated body huddled by a bench in a quiet Maidstone park. No one knows why he was killed, or, if they do, they're not saying. But then Jegou always was a mystery man, as the sensational newspaper headlines aptly described him at the time. Even the police knew nothing of his background until John Leister and I volunteered to fill it in for them. The detectives went away and made their investigations. Two months later they came back and tried to convince us that the murdered man wasn't Jegou at all but someone totally unknown to us and so, they said, there was no need for us to attend his funeral.

But we went all the same; maybe they had forgotten we had positively identified the dead man from the photographs they had shown us. Even after 30 years we recognised the face, and the distinctive tattoos left no room for doubt.

Collars turned up against the driving February rain, we watched the mud obscure the name on the brass plate. Only two wreaths were laid on the grave – one from the police and one from us. The note on ours read: 'With deepest sympathy. To our friend Jegou, the only man who gave us shelter when most others were against us. [signed] John Leister and Eric Pleasants.'

Something about that murder, that funeral, nagged at us. Something was wrong somewhere. Why had he been murdered? The police discounted obvious motives like robbery. Yet there must be a reason. Maybe it had its roots in German-occupied Jersey during the Second World War.

I could still see those tattoos on Jegou's arms as he sat, sleeves rolled up, in the waterfront café where I first laid eyes on him. A loner, Jegou was sitting sullenly by himself, fenced in by a sort of silent surliness. He was remarkably unclannish as Jersey people go, shunning islanders, English and Germans alike. He had been born and raised on the island and spoke Jersey French as his mother tongue. In one of his rare confidential moods he told us that he was, or had been, in the English Merchant Navy – hence the tattoos, no doubt – and watching his habits and mannerisms sometimes I could well believe this.

He was all right, for a Jerseyman. I didn't think much of the rest of his race. But then maybe 1940 wasn't the time to see Jersey and its inhabitants in the best light. I'd only arrived there myself (along with my young wife) in May 1940 to take up non-combatant agricultural work under the auspices of the Peace Pledge Union. I was, quite honestly, trying to avoid the war. Not to escape it, because there is no escape from a world war and its effects, but to avoid being forced into active combat with people with whom I had no personal quarrel.

I'll say this now and get it clear from the start because this whole story turns on it. War is wrong. If I hadn't believed with every last breath in me that all wars are always wrong, none of this would have happened. I don't need a whitewash label saying 'pacifist' or 'conscientious objector'. I'm a fighter, by nature, temperament and physical ability. But I've also got a reasonably good brain.

I know that the first two casualties in any war are truth and reason. Robbed of these two things by militant propaganda, people soon forget about compassion and the sanctity of human life (with the leaders of organised religion in the front line nevertheless proclaiming God on their side), rushing headlong into temporary insanity and the

16

opportunity to indulge their basest instincts. But no fine words can alter the fact that to kill human beings methodically on calculated orders, whether impersonally from an aeroplane, or on the gallows in the guise of punishment, is wrong. To fight and kill, to carry out deeds of daring in the heat of battle is relatively easy, much easier than standing by your own unpopular convictions. Scientist and philosopher Albert Einstein put it very neatly: 'Heroism by order, senseless violence and all the pestilent nonsense that goes by the name of patriotism – how I hate them! War seems to me a mean, contemptible thing. I would rather be hacked in pieces than take part in such an abominable business.'

I wasn't exactly hacked in pieces over the ensuing years because I refused to play the game, but I came pretty close to it sometimes. Certainly I suffered a lot more misery and hardship than I would if I'd joined up meekly from the start. But I couldn't see any justification for killing people with whom I had no personal argument merely because I was ordered to do so by a person or authority who, so far as I could see, had no moral right to make me do anything of the kind. Life – especially my own – is a very precious thing to me and I was not going to throw away mine or anyone else's just to maintain the world's economic see-saw, which is what all wars are about at rock bottom. If the majority of people wanted to do that, then let them get on with it without my help, but all the same their war was a downright inconvenience to me.

There was I at 29 years of age, a fine specimen of manhood. Professional boxer, wrestler, weightlifter, well-travelled circus and cabaret performer, and qualified physical culture instructor with a great future ahead of me. And blast if this damn fool war didn't go and bury it all in a potato patch in Jersey! I hated the bloody place.

I reckon that that was the first time I'd worked for a 'guvnor' on a regular basis since I was about 17, which was when my father wisely gave up trying to get me apprenticed to a steady trade. I liked it even less now than I had then, mostly because the Peace Pledge Union had found me work with one of the Jersey farmers who treated their hired hands about the same as they treated their cattle.

Some of the conscientious objectors placed by the Peace Pledge Union with island farmers in need of labour were in fact satisfactorily housed, fed and paid. But the majority were exploited as cheap labour, treated with ridicule and contempt and housed and worked in worse conditions than the farm animals they tended. Complaints were supposed to be made to the PPU and its island officials, chief among whom was an eccentric named Flynn, who was finally recognised even by the government authorities – who tend to turn a blind eye to such things – as a warped, unscrupulous individual who used for his own ends the unfortunate people who passed through his hands. Anyone having the gall to complain to Flynn was bullied into submission by him with threats of official reprisal, but his tactics did not always work against the more intelligent and better-educated members. They simply left the PPU and found work for themselves where they were of good service to their employers while still maintaining their principles.

By June it became apparent that there was every possibility that the German advance would carry them right into the Channel Islands. The unperturbed complacency of the islanders was shaken. The trickle of the wealthy, who had already started leaving, became a panic-stricken popular flood. They queued by the harbour day and night, many with crammed suitcases and hastily tied bundles, to try and obtain tickets for a passage on the two ships leaving for England.

I didn't particularly want to stay either and hung around the harbour at St Helier hoping to make the acquaintance of some of the seamen and get taken on with the crew of one of the boats leaving the island. One day, as I stood on the street corner opposite the queue of would-be evacuees outside the harbour master's office, I saw a young man stagger out of the crowd and collapse face down in the gutter. To my amazement, not one person moved a muscle to help him, so afraid were they of losing their place in the line. I ran over to where he had fallen and turned him over to examine him. He wasn't just drunk: in a little while he would probably have been dead drunk from alcohol poisoning, judging by the smell of him and the ghastly pallor of his face. I hoisted him onto my shoulder and carried him to hospital where they went to work on him with a stomach pump.

The next day I found myself thinking about him, wondering who he was and how he was doing, and being at a loose end as usual I went to see him. I was glad to find that he was recovering with the resilience of the young and healthy and when he realised that it was I who had brought him to hospital his boyish face broke into that disarmingly innocent smile that I came to know so well. I took a good look at him and I liked what I saw, for John Leister was a strikingly good-looking youth of 17, blond, blue-eyed; but the open innocence of his smile concealed a rebellious, independent nature and reckless high spirits very like my own.

Like me, he had come to Jersey with the PPU; his father had been German and John had no desire to fight for one side or the other. He had been in London when the war broke out, apprenticed as a baker in the family business run by his grandmother, who was once again experiencing the prejudice and ill-feeling of the First World War when perfectly normal people who had patronised the shop for years suddenly boycotted it, and windows were smashed and slogans daubed on its walls. John got sick of it all one fine day and rather than be interned he had simply left to find non-combatant work through the PPU, but now he, like me, had also become disillusioned with the organisation and was trying to find some way out.

It seemed that despite the difference in our ages we had a lot in common. We took to each other immediately and when John left hospital he quit the group he had been working with and threw in his lot with mine.

We were not the only PPU members who wanted to get away from the island and the German threat. But it was at this point that Flynn made himself most objectionable and unreasonable. He refused to grant anyone with the PPU permission to leave, saying they were under contract and threatening government reprisal. More to the point, he withheld money due to members and hung on to such of their property as he had in his possession. There were growls of dissatisfaction and discontent in our ranks so, after a bit, he changed his tack, promising a special boat to evacuate all those who were his responsibility.

We swallowed this for a while until it became clear that there was no boat and no special arrangements. In my usual forthright manner I walked into his office one day and demanded the passage promised to me and my wife. I cut across his blustering threats and gave him two hours to come up with the tickets. In those two hours he had me arrested for, I think, threatening behaviour or something of the sort. I couldn't pay the fine of £5 because Flynn had my money, so I did 14 days in Jersey's Gloucester Street Prison, one of many incarcerations. By the time I got out of prison, transport to and from Jersey was non-existent, but if the incident had any effect it was to make me a minor hero among the PPU members for standing up to Flynn, whose prestige was beginning to look a bit battered.

On 1 July 1940, a lone fighter flew low across the island dropping the terms of the German ultimatum to the people of Jersey. There was to be no resistance. A white cross was painted on the market square and public buildings sprouted a crop of white flags. Every house quickly sported some emblem of surrender; in their eagerness to comply, the islanders even draped dog kennels and chicken coops with white sheets.

The first German soldiers on the streets of Jersey were peaceful and polite, taking over for the first time in history a portion of the United Kingdom, and they all appeared to be extremely conscious of this fact. But, like all members of an army of occupation, they were the bosses. Since then I have experienced being under the occupation of four different nationalities and in them all I have seen the same cold official cruelty, the same arrogance, the same flashes of spontaneous humanity, kindness and curiosity.

It wasn't long before the Germans formed their own opinion of the people over whom they now ruled: they didn't seem to like them very much. Not having any patriotic prejudices myself, I soon got to know several of the German soldiers. They made no secret of their preference for an Englishman from the mainland; Jerseymen, as one of them said to me, were 'all potatoes and tomatoes and no backbone'.

Personally I felt that if there had been more potatoes and tomatoes life would have been a lot easier because soon the food shortage, which followed upon the invasion, began to gnaw at our stomachs. Food for the civilian population was in very short supply. Extra rations could be got by stealing somebody else's – theft was rife among the islanders – or by working for the occupational government, helping to build sea walls, gun emplacements and defences, which was what most people eventually did.

Most people, but not me. I had nothing against the Germans, but I wasn't going to work for them in their war effort either, even though by this time I had left my PPU employers because of the conditions under which they expected me and my wife to live and work. At first I tried to earn a living as a wrestler, but engagements were few and far between and I could have starved to death at that rate.

So I stole. I stole impartially from the Germans and from the wealthier islanders. Nationality didn't mean much to me at the best of times, least of all when I was hungry. Certainly I was a thief, but I wasn't after the quick easy money most criminals go for – just food. I was a young, healthy athlete and my body simply demanded food. It was impossible for me to feel satisfied or well nourished on the meagre rations supplied legally. Fortunately there was a quickly growing illegal source of supply: the black market. Many of the islanders had their private rackets and who could blame them. Certainly I didn't, since I myself didn't do too badly out of my own little deals with the German soldiers, some of whom I got quite friendly with. Fur coats – from the houses of the wealthy evacuees – were always in demand for the Frau or Fräulein back home and had a good exchange rate in German foodstuffs.

Not that the Germans were the only ones with a store of goodies. John and I formed our own intelligence network of people who on the surface led respectable lives but who would ferret out for us the places where privileged people had hidden secret supplies of food and fuel. We would plunder these caches after curfew, rewarding our informants with a share of the spoils. But one of our best hauls we discovered, quite by accident, for ourselves.

John and I had just broken into what before the German occupation must have been a busy fried fish shop. The three bowls of fat we had found there and taken away and hidden in the garden of an evacuated house would bring us a small fortune on the black market. We felt in high spirits as we made our way home through an elite quarter of St Helier with 20 minutes to go before curfew, when from one of the house doorways we heard a despairing groan followed by somebody throwing up the contents of an objecting stomach. It splattered noisily on the step. Then came the sound of a door opening and a twittering female voice comforting the drunk in ludicrous German. Without the attempt at German it could have been a late-night episode in St John's Wood but this was starving teetotal Jersey groaning under the German heel. And the house was that of the island governor. It seemed it would be worth looking the place over.

Every night for two weeks after that one of our friends would prowl about the area and bring us information on all the comings and goings, the staff cars, the braided officers and well-dressed women, the governor's absence and return. If this was all official business it was conducted under attractive circumstances. Then one night John and I slipped socks over our shoes and crouched in a nearby garden waiting for evening curfew and the German night patrol to stamp by. We had been told the house could be empty that night and after watching it for a bit and seeing no sign of life we made our way round the back. We carefully broke a pane and unlatched the window. John climbed through to open the door and let me in.

We found ourselves in a large kitchen that smelt deliciously of food. I wedged the door shut in case we were disturbed and with the speed of long practice we searched the place. The stress of breaking into other people's houses has an unfortunate effect on the bladder and bowels and you don't hang around any longer than you need. Experience had taught us the best places to look and sure enough we found cupboards stacked with tins of German meat, French wine, cheeses, sugar, tins of biscuits and several bottles of German brandy. In three leg-aching, back-sweating trips we had cleared the contents to the garden of a neighbouring empty house, where we settled down for the rest of the night. It was worth the long cold wait to the lifting of morning curfew when our day shift arrived in working overalls and complete with builder's barrow and equipment to carry the load home to the Panama boarding house.

A second-class, gently decaying boarding house it may have been, but to us crowd of 'Jersey Jackals' the Panama was home. The place seemed to attract types as headstrong and independent as myself. Stan Craig, it seemed, was a British swimming representative of the 1936 Olympic Games, a wrestler and a pacifist – although he did enjoy a good fight. An ardent Marxist, he was a born orator and could unconsciously command attention for hours on end. Back in London, shortly before the war started, he would speak at a meeting of the

National Socialist Party of Great Britain on Mondays and Wednesdays, but his heart was in the gatherings for Tuesdays and Thursdays, when he would speak for the Communist Party. He received 15 shillings a night, four nights a week, although he would cheerfully have spoken on Tuesdays and Thursdays for free!

Max Martin Schultz, who was, like John, of part-German descent, was apparently European light-heavyweight wrestling champion. Joe Anderson, a breezy London mechanic, wasn't exactly the athletic type, but he had taken a lot of trouble to train his mind and the extent of his knowledge and thoughtful reading were incongruous with his background and accent. It was more what one would have expected to find in Paul Steward, a quiet, amiable schoolmaster who said very little and silently went his independent way.

Little Bognor, who didn't join us until much later, was the odd man out. That wasn't his real name, but that's what we called him then (he came from Bognor Regis) and we'll keep to it now because it's unlikely that the reverend gentleman who is his father and the rest of his respectable family would appreciate reading about his youthful escapades. For one thing Bognor was very young, even younger than John, and his frightfully upper-class accent and attitude were in complete contrast to the rest of us. John and I picked him up wandering about St Helier with no place to sleep and little to eat. His extreme youth and obvious difficulty in coping with his circumstances appealed to our better natures, so we adopted him. His other nickname was Oliver Twist, because he had that lad's sort of naive trust, and perhaps it was this which made us, unlike Fagin, try to avoid involving him in any of our dubious activities. Eventually he became aware of our attitude to him and, to our amazement, he objected strongly. On several occasions he tried to show us that he too had little regard for the law by bringing home a bottle of milk stolen from a doorway or a chicken from a nearby farm until, eventually, I became alarmed for our collective safety and made him promise not to do anything without telling us. He kept his word and there was at least one occasion later on when he was really useful to us – even though that particular episode did land us in jail.

This motley collection soon achieved notoriety with the authorities as the 'Panama Group', with John and me known as the foremost members of the quasi-criminal fraternity. Brooding protectively over us all, however, was Mother Seawood, proprietor of the Panama, a lively, rascally old Irish Catholic lady. She didn't exactly encourage 'her boys' (as she called us) to steal, but she turned a benevolently blind eye. She knew very well that we would sometimes hide our loot in her room, as it was the one place in the house where the local police would never dare search, such was her reputation. There was one particular occasion when she did, quite literally, save our bacon.

The Germans, making their contribution to increasing food resources, decided to breed pigs, choosing a strip of cultivated land on top of Mount Bingham for the purpose and importing their breeding stock. It was Joe Anderson, temporarily employed on the Jersey food production project, who brought us news of the first arrivals. He, like the rest of us at the time, was feeling the pangs of hunger and no doubt knew what the result of this piece of information would be. His supposition was correct.

That same evening, two hours before curfew, John, Anderson and I set out for Mount Bingham on the outskirts of St Helier. I was equipped with a well-greased pyjama cord and, as always, a sharp pocket knife. Anderson carried an empty rucksack and John a hacksaw and a piece of bread. Armed with this curious collection of implements we set out singly and in different directions because any combined excursion by the Panama Group quickly came to the notice of the island police. It was dark when we met but Anderson was able to point out the sty which housed a litter of young pigs.

John's hacksaw dealt effectively with the several padlocks securing the premises and, leaving Anderson on guard outside, we sneaked in among the grunting, rooting piglets. Enticed by the piece of bread in John's hand, one unsuspecting piglet wandered over to us. With the dexterity of an oriental thug, I slipped the noose of the waxed pyjama cord over its head and pulled it tight while John lay on the poor struggling little beast until it was still, strangled into unconsciousness, when I quietly slit its throat and bled it. The other piglets continued their snuffling with complete unconcern.

We put the carcass into the rucksack and gave it to Anderson to carry home while the two of us disappeared back to the Panama to await his arrival. His notoriety not being a patch on ours, he would be less conspicuous with a rucksack than we would.

As soon as Anderson came in, the still-warm carcass was rushed into Steward's bathroom and dumped in the bath. I set to work with my pocket knife and a small chopper, produced magically from somewhere, to deal with the more robust bits. We dealt with the pig as skilfully, smoothly and speedily as though we had done nothing but slaughter pigs all our lives. I sliced, chopped and cut systematically, putting the offal straight in the lavatory pan, where Steward stood ready to pull the chain and flush each lot away. The edible portions I handed to John, who piled them into a mincing machine borrowed from Mrs Seawood's kitchen. In less than 30 minutes we were finished, the bathroom and the instruments completely clean. There was nothing to show of the piglet or how he met his end except a washbowl of minced pork, which we put in the kitchen. Satisfied with the night's work, we all went to bed.

Next morning we had reason to be thankful that we had done the job so thoroughly as the expostulating voice of Mrs Seawood woke us out of a deep sleep. The law had arrived in the shape of 6 ft 2 in. Police Constable Le Jontier, complete with outsize feet and nose, and a few other policemen. Obviously they had no definite information to work on, just suspicion, because they picked first on John, no doubt hoping (in vain as usual) that he, being the youngest, would let something slip. They never did learn that John's youth and apparent innocence covered a wiliness far beyond his years. John, with his customary air of bland naivety, kept them occupied long enough for us to dive into the kitchen to rescue the basin of mince. To our utter dismay, it had disappeared – where to, we had absolutely no idea. We all sat in there with our heads in the serving hatch, hearing perfectly the progress of the questioning in the dining room as, one by one, we were all hauled in. The police, of course, had no idea that the hatch was open. Pottering about the dining room doing the chores, dear old Mrs Seawood decided that the hatch needed dusting and accidentally she left it slightly ajar. She kept up a constant scolding as she dusted and polished the dining room, grumbling about them rascally young boys for causing the lovely policemen so much bother.

'May the good Lord forgive them young rascals, sir, if they have been up to anything wicked, but they're not really bad, the little devils. And would you good gentlemen be wanting a nice cup of tea now while you be asking all these questions?' adding, before they had time to accept or refuse, 'I'll make one now, it really do help, you know.'

With my head in the serving hatch I grinned. The tea, a very scarce commodity, had been stolen by us a few weeks previously and, until this moment, completely forgotten.

Comforted by Mrs Seawood's tea and thoughtfulness, and no doubt somewhat distracted by her pottering about, the police finished their questioning soon after and left. I immediately asked anxiously where the pork had got to. Without a flicker of change in her voice or expression, Mrs Seawood said: 'You silly boys – you left it in the kitchen uncovered and the flies were getting on it so I covered it up with a nice clean cloth and put it in my room. Shall I make you shepherd's pie or would you like some nice meat dumplings?'

Mrs Seawood's ability as a cook was second only to her great-hearted capacity for loving us desperate young tearaways, and for a week we forgot what it was like to be hungry.

Food, and how to get it, wasn't the only thing that occupied our minds. When we were well fed, our thoughts tended to gravitate to that other pole around which life revolved. Sex. That was another small necessity which the Germans were, unwittingly, kind enough to provide us with. But then maybe they owed us that favour. Girls had never been in short supply until the occupation forces arrived, but now, unless one had a German uniform, it was difficult to find a girl, since a large part of the female population seemed to be doing its best to keep Jerry happy. In many cases it was, of course, the food and cigarettes which influenced their choice of boyfriends, but simple, healthy lust had a lot to do with it as well.

The German military personnel had been warned not to mix too freely with the local girls, but, as everywhere else in wartime, this injunction was largely ignored and a blind eye turned by the officials, so the island women, with their adaptable standards of virtue, made hay while the Jersey sun shone. Hoping to get at least their officers to set a good example by diverting their attention from the forbidden home-grown fruit, the German authorities called in professional assistance.

There were 12 of them: long, shapely legs, fashionable dresses clinging provocatively to well-moulded hips and bottoms. What matter if the pretty faces were a little hard and businesslike! As they walked down the gangplank laughing and chattering, they were like a flock of tropical birds bringing a welcome colour and gaiety to St Helier's drab quay.

The idea was that the French girls would provide the officers with all the light – or heavy – entertainment they required. It was a very good idea. But it didn't work. Competition from the enthusiastic local amateurs was far too keen and well established. The French girls were the first to complain. They found it difficult to get enough work to make a living and without work they got bored. Inevitably the magnet which draws together the socially despised exerted its influence and we noticed that the girls found the virile Panama crowd as attractive as we found them.

The Panama decided to throw a party and the girls came, bringing with them a healthy stock of German wines and spirits. Mrs Seawood proved, in addition to the rest of her talents, to be a splendid hostess, a skill perhaps acquired in the days when she was a memsahib in India, where her late husband was at one time stationed. Absorbing to the full the mood of the occasion, and whatever was going in the way of drink, she bustled about with renewed youth and energy and, towards the end of the evening, took it upon herself to pair people off and direct where each couple should sleep. When beds ran out, she busied herself like some industrious mother hen providing mattresses and blankets.

'I ain't having you boys a-fighting!' she kept saying most firmly, although a quarrel was the last thing we had on our minds at the time. 'Now git you off to bed and keep the peace, bless yer all – even if you don't sleep, yer little devils you!'

Even though we never said as much to each other, Mrs Seawood gave to 'her boys' a warmth and genuine affection which I think we all needed at that time. To the authorities it may have appeared that the Panama was merely a den where the despised 'Jersey Jackals', as we became known, hung out, but to us it was home, and I, perhaps more than the others at one time, was glad it was there. Quite early in the occupation I struck a very gloomy personal patch when my own wife became enamoured of the German uniform and all the benefits it could provide. Before very long she left me to set up as housekeeper to the Germans. We had been married scarcely two years. But wartime has a curiously distorting effect, like one of those mirrors in an amusement arcade, pulling one's sense of perspective into peculiar shapes. Perhaps I would have felt this desertion more sharply in peace time, perhaps not; certainly I would not have had the sense of complete betrayal I experienced when, later, she gave evidence against me before a German tribunal.

But that's running a bit ahead. I took it badly enough when she did leave me, but in those days we were all infected with the euphoria, the carelessness for the future, that hangs in the air like a dust cloud in the early days of war. There is a feverish quality to life, a sense of urgent immediacy that influences everything one does and thinks, that annihilates the customary restraint and caution which usually govern our actions. Live now, cram everything you can into today, because what's to come is more unsure than it ever was.

I wouldn't waste the day I had fretting over a mirage of happy days I might have had with my wife in an uncertain future, nor would I poison it with bitterness and self-pity. I was alive and, with a little judicious thieving from all quarters, still strong and healthy, and I intended to keep it that way.

Chapter 2

THE POACHERS FROM THE OLD PANAMA

The thieving and black-market business can be rewarding, even stimulating, but like any other bread-and-butter job it can get very tedious when you see it stretching into infinity. Good times alternated with bad, full stomachs with a growling emptiness, but overall the prospect of an indefinite stay under the Germans in the uncongenial company of the Jerseymen was decidedly gloomy. And *they* weren't going to leave the island so it rather looked as if we would have to move.

That was the solution: the question was how. We spent long idle hours hanging about in what seemed to be likely places, hoping to pick up useful information, tips on boats, crews, smuggling, but all to no avail. Then one day, while a group of us jackals were basking in the sun outside our usual lair, the Panama, Stan Craig burst in on us with his habitually explosive energy. Pulling off his clothes, he flung them on the ground in a heap and sank down on them with a satisfied grunt. Silence once more settled gently down like dust. Anticlimax. The way Stan had bounded in we thought he might have some news, but he said nothing.

'What's doing, Craigy?' someone murmured after a bit, prompting him hopefully, but Stan was too busy rummaging in his trousers for his pipe. At last he found it and stuck it in his mouth, sucking emptily, for his tobacco ration had already gone up in smoke. Then he was ready to give us his attention and turned back to us, the massive shoulder muscles rippling. Without removing his pipe from his mouth he said carefully: 'There is a chance for us to get off this bleeding island tonight.'

I felt something like a physical shock of excitement run through me, followed immediately by suspicion.

'How do you know it's not some kind of bloody trap fixed up by the Germans or the Jersey coppers?' I demanded.

'You are an over-cautious bastard! Do you imagine for one moment that I'd be daft enough to have anything to do with the idea if Jerseymen were involved?' Stan was indignant. None of us really liked the islanders, having found them to be a hypocritical, German-serving bunch too often to trust them. Not that I blame the islanders for that, only I wish that now, more than 30 years later, they wouldn't make themselves out to have been patriotically whitewashed heroes.

Stan went on to explain that a fellow Communist, an Irishman named Lenahan, had told him that he had a boat and would give us the chance to get away from the island with him. It sounded all right, and with a suppressed sense of excitement we began to make plans for the evening. Three of us – John, Joe Anderson and I – agreed to meet Stan on the cliffs at a disused summerhouse half hidden in gorse bushes.

Well before curfew, John and I started across country towards Bouley Bay. Dark rain clouds were gathering in the evening sky and as we got to the summerhouse the first fat drops splashed down. By the time it was dark the rain was sheeting down. John and I waited until the other two arrived and then we all made our way down the cliff to some point where Lenahan was supposed to meet us. Cursing the rain, we slithered down the sand slope to a spot near the shore where we crouched in the spitefully prickled gorse bushes. I felt the rain trickle uncomfortably down the back of my neck as we waited. I heard Anderson mutter: 'There can only be one puddle on this fucking slope and I've got my arse in it!'

All at once we tensed as a shadowy form loomed up. It was Lenahan, clasping what appeared to be a heavy pistol in one hand. The way he waved it about made me a little anxious but it was too late for doubts. Even so, if I'd known Lenahan was a complete madman I'd have been back up that hillside faster than a rabbit.

'Come on!' he hissed, urging us on with his pistol hand. 'It's all right – follow me!'

He swung off down the cliff and we followed hesitantly, sneaking past the German guard hut to the bay where we now saw a boat bobbing at her moorings. Instructing us to stay ashore and hold onto the mooring ropes, Lenahan rushed out on deck firing the pistol at random and screaming orders and generally going berserk. Immediately the lights went up in the guard hut and two German marines rushed out to see what was happening. Lenahan directed his last four shots in their direction and then the boat surged away from the jetty, leaving the four of us standing there feeling stupid.

The two marines jumped back into the hut and slammed the door shut and the four of us started racing back along the jetty to find cover in the hills. We got to the shadow of the cliffs just as the guards started shooting through the hut windows with rifles. From sea level to the top of Bouley Bay cliffs is a stiff climb, but you do it in a hurry when you're being shot at, the rain-black night a mixed blessing. I realised I'd lost the others and didn't see them again until eventually, one by one, we dropped disconsolately into the Panama.

The following day we saw an item in the newspaper about a body being washed ashore and the wreckage of a boat found after the storm, but no identification was given. To this day I don't know who or what Lenahan was, except crazy.

So we were still stuck on the island. We wanted to be there as much as the Jersey police wanted us to be there but they couldn't get rid of us, however hard they tried. And they really did try, fat stupid Constable Le Jontier even going as far as to try to plant stolen goods among my things at the Panama. Fortunately, I caught him in the act and booted him out with a hefty kick in the seat of his shiny serge trousers; he left his helmet behind in the process of making his hasty exit and it adorned our lavatory cistern as a trophy for a long time afterwards. I enjoyed that little episode. It's not often you can assault the law and get away with it, as I'd found to my cost a few years earlier when six policemen dragged me, struggling savagely, to a Black Maria during a London demonstration against the Spanish Civil

War and I registered my protest against the unfair odds by biting the little finger of the one holding my head. It had been a peaceful demonstration until the mounted police rode in to break it up, but I paid for my part in it with a few days inside.

Even so, my regard for the law, if not its officers, had remained intact until I landed in Jersey, when environment, circumstance and the need to eat made me adapt my views. But maybe it wasn't such a complete turnabout because, thinking about it, I realised that most of the real-life heroes of my Norfolk boyhood had lived outside the law, a fact which never conflicted with my deep respect and love for my law-abiding gamekeeper father. Those old Norfolk poachers were a colourful crowd. One of them was an amiable giant, who for 30 years lived well by tree felling and taking the local gentry's pheasants. They found him eventually with half his head blown away by his own gun; an accident supposedly, but those who knew him well said he knew too much of guns for that to be true. Then there was the red-headed poacher who shot a gamekeeper, not while trying to avoid being caught poaching, but because this keeper, a right rural Don Juan, couldn't keep his hands off the comely backside of the poacher's young wife. Another was, when I knew him, a sprightly keen-sighted lad of 80 from Spowsten. A familiar sight as he rode his tall, old-fashioned cycle over Mousehold Heath, he had a record of having spent nearly 20 years in Norwich Jail for poaching to his credit. Yet another, who rarely worked and always had plenty of money to spend, still made it a rule to ask the magistrates for time to pay his fine. They were never known to refuse, although once or twice he had been caught the following night poaching again to make the money to pay the fine.

For the young country bloods like me and my companions, notorious locals such as these had the same glamour as pop stars have for youngsters today. Snaring a rabbit or knocking a pheasant out of a tree was for us a prestige-builder and came as naturally as eating or sleeping, but nonetheless we all had a high respect for the law. Nearly all of us attended Sunday school or church with devout regularity, although generally at our mothers' insistence. As the time went by, the religious caper failed to make sense to me so I cut it out, but I was always a law-abiding citizen until, as I say, Jersey and the war changed a few things.

Eventually things got to such a pass that even the imperturbable Mrs Seawood began to show some concern at the frequent visits 'her boys' were receiving from the Jersey police and it became clear that, for everyone's peace of mind, we would have to find an additional, alternative headquarters. The ideal, no-questions-asked bolthole turned up in an unexpected quarter.

John and I would usually spend some part of the day scrounging about in small cafés and the sort of haunts frequented by questionable characters who were either dodging the law or about to do something to make it necessary to dodge the law. I don't know what category Francis Caesar Jegou came into, but that was how we met him. For some reason known only to himself, he took to us and finally offered to share with us the dilapidated, two-roomed cottage he called home. Of course we accepted at once and the tumbledown house, with its litter-strewn courtyard in the back streets of St Helier, became the scene of many a midnight loot-laden arrival.

Jegou never actually took part in our raids, but he kept his mouth shut and his ears open for tips which would be to our advantage. We shared our food with him, much as he would share with us whatever he might be able to bring home from his job as a kitchen porter in a German-occupied hotel. To him, as to everyone else on the island at the time, the wages were of little importance: the main object of the job was that it enabled him to purloin odds and ends of food from the German kitchen. On our 'hungry' days we would sit waiting for his return like three characters in some nursery rhyme expecting mother hen to come in with the goodies.

'Bloody hell, I'm hungry! What would I give for something really substantial to eat!' It was a familiar cry from Stan Craig. He sucked morosely on his empty pipe as he pushed his muscular bulk out of Jegou's only armchair.

'Where are you going?' asked John, looking up from a large book he was reading on the history of the Channel Islands – part of the plunder from a raid on an evacuated house.

'I don't bloody well know!' snapped Stan, whose temper was always bad when his pipe and belly were empty. 'I wish that I could walk straight off this pissing island!'

'All right, Stan, all right!' John said soothingly. 'My guts have been rolling since yesterday and by the look on Eric's face I'd say he's feeling a bit peckish.'

I groaned. Peckish was hardly the word for it. At that moment the door opened and Jegou came in. Often uncommunicative to the point of rudeness, he entered without any greeting, threw himself onto his bed and started to read an old magazine he pulled from his pocket. We all looked expectantly at him, but he said nothing.

At last Stan asked tentatively: 'How is the food situation today, Jegou, old sport?'

'There ain't a thing!' came the answer in the singsong Jersey dialect. He paused. 'But if you clowns is really hungry I know where there are plenty of rabbits which would be easy for you to knock off.'

'Where?' the three of us instantly jerked out together.

Jegou, assuming an important voice, told us there was a large house in St Brélades where the owner, a rather grand lady, kept a small rabbit farm. The rabbits were apparently kept in hutches which were dotted all over the lawn in front of the house. Almost as an afterthought he added: 'This lady knows everybody and everything on the island worth knowing and she's loaded' – meaning wealthy, not the other.

Less than an hour later John and I made a reconnoitring trip out to the farm, which we intended to raid that night. Sure enough, looking over the six-foot fence we could see the hutches scattered at random on the unkempt lawn. The breeze was in our direction and my nose twitched at the familiar odour – rabbits!

'Do you think they're in there?' asked the city-born John anxiously.

'They're there all right!' I said confidently.

'But how do you know?' he persisted. 'Those little hutch things may be empty!'

'I can smell them!' It was the most elementary piece of detection to me, who had learned to read the signs of nature quicker than I learnt basic arithmetic and who was snaring rabbits for pocket money long before I was 14 years old.

We retrieved our tandem from its hiding place in the bushes and pedalled briskly back to St Helier. In Jegou's cottage, Stan was still sprawled in the armchair, sucking on his pipe. His face broke into an uneasy smile when we gave him our report. The prospect of having to commit a crime of any kind never appealed to this Marxist stalwart, but his large, strong body needed feeding as much as ours did. We knew that the instinct for self-preservation would compel him to join us, and we were right.

The three of us put our heads together to plan our course of action. We decided first to cycle back to St Brélades; time was getting short and we had to get clear of the town and be at our destination before curfew. Once more John and I mounted the tandem, while Stan followed us decorously on an ancient, sit-up-and-beg type of woman's bicycle belonging to Jegou.

We arrived at St Brélades about 30 minutes before the curfew, empty rucksacks rolled tightly on the carrier of the tandem. Hiding our cycles in an isolated spot, we waited quietly for curfew to fall.

A few minutes after nine we sneaked across the field to the wooden fence surrounding the grounds of the manor, clambered over and dropped silently down on the inside, immediately diving into the bushes for cover, where we crouched until it was completely dark. The sun was gone and there was a chill in the air, but the ground and dead grass on which we huddled was still warm. The shadows of the trees grew longer and the twilight deepened. I heard a slight rustling as John and Stan cautiously changed their positions from time to time to ease their cramped limbs. It seemed an eternity before the big house through the trees was obscured by night.

I knew that from now until those rabbits were dead and in their rucksacks it would be up to me, the country lad, to make sure that things went smoothly. It would have to be me that caught the scared, wildly scampering animals, and for me to despatch them quickly by deftly stretching their necks as my father had taught me. As usual, complete silence and speed were essential. Any suspicion aroused in the house and a telephone message would bring the Jersey police accompanied by the German gendarmerie. We knew full well that the civil police would not discourage the Germans from shooting if the need arose, as in such a small community it would not be difficult for the police to suspect who the marauders were. Those rabbits could have cost us very dear.

At last it was dark enough. I picked my way cautiously through the long grass and weedy flowerbeds. My companions followed as quietly as they could but making what sounded to me such an alarming noise that my heart was nearly in my mouth by the time we reached the edge of the lawn where the hutches stood. There was no sign of life from the big house. The windows, like blank, unwinking eyes, made us hesitate before committing ourselves by stepping into their range because we couldn't know for sure whether they could see us or not. We paused, surveying them apprehensively, then crept cautiously from the cover of the bushes into the open lawn, in full view of the house.

A hurried examination revealed that the hutches were runs covered with wire-netting, about two feet high and six feet long with a door at the top in the middle. I motioned John and Stan to position themselves at each end of a run so that they could herd the rabbits to the middle, where I stood by the open door, grabbed them out and broke their necks. As soon as one was dead I flung it on the ground behind me and reached for the next. The poor creatures tore wildly to and fro, the bucks thumping a warning with their hind legs on the ground. Occasionally a frantic animal would crash into the wooden side of the run and we would pause, glancing anxiously towards the house, but no alarm was raised.

We systematically emptied every run. Then Craig held the rucksacks open while John hastily picked up the rabbits and packed them in. We dragged the bulging sacks across the lawn but when we got to the bushes and had to lift them, we realised to our dismay that they would be far too heavy even for us to get on our backs and cycle back to St Helier with. But after all our work I wasn't going to leave any of them.

'Tip them out onto the ground again and I'll hulk them!' I hissed.

'What the bloody hell is hulking?'

'That is Norfolk for taking their guts out!' I snapped, forgetting that these things were not obvious to everyone. 'Give them to me one at a time.'

'Christ, we'll be here all bleeding night!' groaned Craig. John said nothing and just passed me a rabbit. Producing my pocket knife, I slit it open with the speed of long practice and removed its insides. I worked on steadily, crouched on the ground in the dark, and the stinking pile of intestines beside me grew. The other two squatted beside me, fascinated.

'Slap me down!' whispered Craig in amusement. 'It took my old man nearly all one Saturday afternoon to do one like that, and in the daylight as well!'

The stripped carcasses were much lighter. Once again we stuffed them into the rucksacks and dragged them over to the fence. John and I clambered over and Craig hoisted the still hefty sacks over to us as if they were feather pillows, then he sprang after them like an agile gorilla.

Helping each other hoist the rucksacks on our backs, we staggered off across the fields to the rivulet which led to the cliff top where we had hidden the cycles. The ground at the edge of the rivulet was soft and marshy. We had crossed the first time without any trouble but now the additional weight of the dead rabbits was too much. John must have chosen an extra soft patch to make his crossing. He was a little in front of me and I suddenly saw his indistinct figure growing shorter and heard his urgent but still subdued appeal for help. I called over to Craig and, putting down our burdens, we both scrambled over to John, who by this time was thigh-deep in the sticky mud but still valiantly clutching hold of his precious sack of rabbits. Craig tried to pull the lad's legs free from the mire only to find himself sinking into the same state with the effort. Cold with fear, I turned and raced back towards the house, scaled the garden fence and slithered across to the now lifeless rabbit hutches, grabbing a hutch door that I had seen lying loose on the ground.

Breathing hard, I rushed back to find Stan and John still thrashing about ineffectually in the swamp. I threw the hutch door down near them and Stan, less entrenched than John, managed to scramble onto it. With a firm base to stand on, he now succeeded in hauling John out of the mud, which sucked angrily after his departing legs as though annoyed at being robbed of a victim.

After struggling once more into the straps of our loads, we succeeded in finding our way back to the cycles without further mishap, where we flung ourselves down to wait until curfew lifted. Cold and wet as we were, we fell asleep almost instantly, our heads pillowed on the soft rabbit-filled sacks, and slept soundly until the noise of the traffic on the not-far-distant road awoke us. We stretched our cramped limbs in the early-morning light, mounted our cycles and pedalled our way warily back to St Helier and the safety of Jegou's house. After carefully hiding the rucksacks and contents, we collapsed onto our beds, where, without troubling to take off our wet and muddy clothes, we fell asleep again until the late afternoon.

We kept the rabbit stockpot simmering constantly on Jegou's stove. One afternoon we'd just come in from ferreting out six more rabbits from our hoard to top it up when there was a violent hammering on the courtyard door. The police.

I dived over to Jegou's old HMV wind-up gramophone in the corner, the dimensions of which resembled those of the average gas cooker so that the cavity under the mechanism, which could be removed, was large enough to accommodate several rabbits. By the time the police knocked again, even louder, the HMV dog had a full belly and a satisfied look on its face, a record was blaring out and John was on his way to open the courtyard door to our guests.

Our three blue-uniformed visitors charged past, ignoring John completely, straight across the yard to the cottage door. It opened as they reached it and Stan came out carrying the stockpot in full view, heading purposefully for the lavatory which was in the corner of the yard. In their mad rush to get into the house the police paid no attention to him either. Stan calmly flushed away the rabbit contents of the casserole, rinsed it methodically under the yard tap and followed John back into the house.

Meanwhile, the police, having stated their intention to search the place, immediately started turning it upside down. I thought I'd help them with some more music while they worked and turned the record over, and to the tune of 'Empty Saddles in the Old Corral' they continued their upheaval. Then we noticed with some apprehension that one of them was looking towards the gramophone with a curious expression on his face. I could see what was going through his mind so to distract his attention I suddenly hurled myself across the room at poor Stan, shouting, 'You bastard – you're wearing my red shirt again!'

The suspicious policeman was standing next to Stan. I leapt between them to confront Stan so that my back was to the constable. I brought my arm back violently to clobber Stan and somehow my elbow managed to catch the unfortunate policeman behind me in the pit of the stomach, an accident which not only winded the unfortunate bobby but also knocked him to the floor some distance away. Our little fracas stopped the search completely while the other two policemen stood uncertainly watching our antics as Stan and I rampaged around the room locked together like two mad bulls. The injured bobby meanwhile crawled as fast as he could across the floor to take refuge near John, who was laughing helplessly in his ringside seat in the armchair.

'I've heard about those two – they're fucking lunatics!' I heard him gasp as, still clutching his stomach, he dragged himself upright holding onto a chair near the wall. John took the opportunity to mention that the fight was only just a warming-up and we would probably be at each other's throat for a while yet as the two of us were obviously quite crazy. Perhaps the police might like to come back when Jegou returned from work – he might be able to help them find whatever it was they were looking for . . .

The police left with grateful promptness.

To go with the meat – bread. On our reconnoitring trips we had been casing the German bakehouse but the only possible means of entry was through a tiny window high up in the wall, too small for any of us to fit through. One morning my eye fell on young Bognor as he was being given a fatherly talking-to by John, all of one year his senior, on the ethics of petty pilfering. We had always left Bognor out of our excursions; he was too young, too different from us. But he badly wanted to be one of us so he would steal little things, like milk from doorsteps, to contribute to the food supply, and of late this habit of his had began to alarm us.

'Look, Bognor, old mate,' John was saying, 'don't go nicking odds and sods in this fashion or you will certainly be coming home with a dirty great Jersey copper on your elbow!'

Bognor, whose upper-class sense of fair play made him feel he had to bring in something, was hurt and offended so I hastily stepped in and told him not to do things without consulting us first. But if he really wanted to help there was something only he could do.

'How much do you weigh, Bognor?' I asked suddenly. He was taken aback by the apparent change in tack but told me about eight stone. I turned to John, who had already guessed what was in my mind, and stood there grinning at me.

'What do you think?' I asked him.

John shrugged his shoulders. 'Might as well. If he carries on like this, he's bound to get us lumbered anyway, so he might as well have a real good go.'

That night, under cover of blackout darkness, four of us raided the bakery. We formed a human ladder to young Bognor to reach the small window high up in the side wall.

'Hurry up!' hissed Stan. 'It's bleeding heavy!'

Stan was at the bottom, I was on his shoulders and John was standing on mine. We all cursed Bognor for his clumsy clambering but he redeemed himself by slipping through the window with surprising ease. As soon as he was through, John and I jumped down and we all slipped round to the door which Bognor had already opened from the inside. The appetising fresh-bread smell of the bakehouse wafted out to us through the briefly open door and then we were inside, enveloped in its dark, delicious warmth.

John fumbled about for his candle stub then lit it, shielding it with his hand. Its uncertain flame revealed an old-fashioned baker's cart – brought out of retirement by the petrol shortage – packed full with Germany army commis bread. We all groaned softly with delight and hunger as we gazed at it a moment and then, with the precision of unspoken accord, we took up positions around the handcart and pushed it out into the deserted street. One of us closed the door carefully and we set off.

We were on the short journey home, ears pricked for the sound of German patrols, when a tall figure on a bicycle loomed down the road towards us. The surprise was mutual. He grated to a halt and stopped wordlessly a few yards from us. Craig hunched his shoulders, John's hands tightened on his stick and little Bognor's jaw dropped. For a few moments nothing happened. No one said a word. Then the policeman suddenly leapt back onto his bike and pedalled back furiously in the direction from which he had come. We in our turn trundled off with increased speed, slowing on our way through the poor, working-class district to drop off some loaves of bread where we knew they would be found gratefully by the hungry denizens. The common precious loaf. We had a load and weren't going to miss a few.

We didn't get a chance to enjoy much of it. The Germans came round to Jegou's to see us the following day, discovered the bread, arrested us and kept us in jail for interrogation for three months.

Chapter 3

NAZI JUSTICE

Jersey jail, 1941. The tired daylight dragged itself through ceiling-high unglazed windows and fell exhausted onto the flagstones, barely touching the ponderous door with its unsleeping spy-hole. We might as well have been in the Bastille 200 years ago for all the evidence of the twentieth century there was in this cell. There was an impressively large pipe for hot water running through the cell but it was permanently cold and, if possible, only managed to make us even colder as winter hardened.

Above all there was the pervasive, pungent smell of urine from the chipped and battered pisspots. They stank abominably because the only cleaning equipment supplied was cold water, sand and a stubby, well-worn brush. The prison governor, Mr Briard (from his well-furnished, comfortable office), maintained that the prison budget did not run to the expense of more advanced cleaning methods. Personal cleansing equipment for prisoners suffered a similar fate since the regular portions of soap, a precious commodity in wartime Jersey, never got past the household of Mr Briard and one or two more favoured prison staff.

Because the order had been to arrest all the occupants of Jegou's house, where the stolen bread had been found, the comparatively innocent, tight-mouthed Jegou himself had been thrown into jail with

Stan, John and myself, although we managed to keep Bognor out by swearing he had absolutely nothing to do with it. Jegou accepted the misfortune with his usual philosophical taciturnity. There were even times when the privation of prison life seemed to improve his behaviour, and now and again his dour face would light with an unexpected flash of humour over some trivial incident in our generally cheerless situation.

Many years later it was suggested to us by police investigating Jegou's murder that he could have been an accomplished informer paid by the Jersey and German police. Maybe he was. It was certainly very odd that, despite the overwhelming evidence against us, none of us was ever tried for the bakehouse theft and after being held in prison for three months and interrogated about the incident we were all simply released. I hardly think that that would have happened had it been just John and I who were arrested.

I can't know for certain what Jegou's role was one way or the other, but I do know that one reason why the police investigating his murder were unable to discover anything of his life before 1952 was that all records of police activity and other documents pertaining to transactions between the Jersey state and the Germans had been destroyed by somebody who thought such an action to be necessary. It is possible that officials and people of influence with adjustable scruples made good use of this golden opportunity to safeguard themselves from any future unpleasantness. Around the time of his murder something of a stir was being created in the chicken coop by suggestions, enquiries, to the effect that the part played by several Jersey notables during the war was not as stainless as they would have posterity believe. The records, the inside information, had been destroyed, certainly; but there were still people like Jegou with tenacious memories who perhaps saw an opportunity to capitalise on their wartime recollections – and perhaps paid the inevitable price.

Making an educated guess at Jegou's past history, I would say it went something like this. Jegou had at one time been a sailor, not in the Merchant Navy as he told me, but in the Royal Navy. His surname was actually Murin (this, said the police, was the name of the man found murdered in Maidstone Park). When war broke out, Jegou deserted from the Navy and went back home to Jersey to hide out, cautiously dropping the name Murin and taking, perhaps, his mother's maiden name, Jegou – a common enough name on the island. Once Jersey was occupied by the Germans, Murin/Jegou began to feel safe from arrest by the British but, unfortunately for him, there were still the Germans to deal with: if it were to come to their attention that he was still, strictly speaking, in the service of the Navy he would, at best, be taken prisoner of war or, at worst, shot.

My guess is that he was found out by the Jersey state authorities, who gave him the unenviable choice of either working for them as an informer or being turned over to the Germans. Jegou, of course, would have chosen the former, picking up whatever he could that might be useful to his masters – information on the small-time criminal fraternity, on the affairs of the mainland residents, on any likely black-market leads – there was very little going on that the state officials wouldn't find of interest. In the course of keeping his eyes and ears open, Jegou would undoubtedly have learnt that it wasn't only the small fry who were making what they could from the German occupation; profiteering and collaborating in high places there certainly was, but at the time this knowledge would have been useless to Jegou.

When the war ended, he was paid off and told not to show himself on Jersey again, and he, glad to get out of the whole mess, complied willingly. For several years he kept his head down and lived quietly and simply. Then in the mid-1970s interest in the part played by the Channel Islands during the war revived. An official history was published and a gallery of the German occupation of the islands was opened in the British Imperial War Museum. Viewed through the rose-coloured spectacles of time the overall picture presented of Jersey was of a gallant little island and its staunchly incorruptible citizens heroically resisting the enemy in fact and in principle at every turn. But there were those who knew it wasn't so; some, like a Norwich publisher of my acquaintance, brought their accusations publicly, while maybe there were others, of whom Jegou was one, who saw the chance to make a little private capital by threatening to make what could be some very embarrassing revelations about people in the public eye currently being given official recognition for their patriotic wartime activities. He could have met with some initial success:

police investigations showed that shortly before he died he had been in possession of £15,000, and for a man who lived as he did, and with no visible assets, that is a lot of money.

But for smalltimers like Jegou blackmail is not a long-term insurance against poverty and he must have known it couldn't last. He certainly knew during the last few days of his life that he was in danger, for enquiries showed that he had been behaving like a hunted man, travelling feverishly and apparently aimlessly from one place to another – possibly he was trying to get himself and his money to some place of safety before it was too late. If so, he didn't make it. He was found dead in a public park in Maidstone, Kent, in December 1976, although he was probably killed elsewhere and his body simply dumped on a park bench. The park is one of those constantly open to public view, either from passers-by or from overlooking windows, and the several vicious stab wounds on the body would seem to indicate that whoever killed him was in no hurry to get the job done and get away before he, or they, were spotted.

There was no obvious motive for the murder, such as robbery or a jealous husband, but if, in the course of their investigations, the police did discover the true reason, they never said what it was. My feeling is that they did find out what was behind it and thought it politic to close the investigation and say nothing. Of course, they are not bound to disclose the results of their enquiries and I might not have put too sinister a construction on events had they not come back and told me that the dead man was not Jegou but a man named Murin who was definitely not my former acquaintance. I was astonished because they had already shown me photographs of the dead man, whom I had recognised, and of the tattoo marks on the body, which I had previously described to them. But the photograph which was printed with the newspaper story of the killing was not one of the murdered man but of a complete stranger. And why, if it was not him, did I see with my own eyes at the funeral the police had advised me not to attend, the inscription on the brass coffin plate: Francis Caesar Jegou!

There is no doubt in my mind that the coffin contained the murdered remains of my wartime acquaintance, that there was some official cover-up of his murder and that in all probability the reason for it dates back to German-occupied Jersey. Poor Jegou. I owed him something for those years and I could have wished him a happier ending for the good there was in him.

Christmas 1941 came and went almost unnoticed and unmemorable except for one of those trivial recollections that stay in the mind, that of one of the most obnoxious screws to disgrace a prison sauntering about the yard during exercise tauntingly munching a large bar of chocolate under the noses of us hungry prisoners. But then Fisher was an exceptionally unpleasant man, a nasty little bully who carried callousness to the point of calculated cruelty. Since then I have been in many prisons in my time, but conditions in Gloucester Street Prison were among the worst I have experienced, not merely from a physical point of view – the medieval cells, the meagre and disgusting food – but also because of the attitude of the warders in general. Most of them exhibited an absolute disregard for the human dignity and feelings of the prisoners in their charge that was unique in my experience.

Despite the general discomfort, however, we were surprised to find that, contrary to popular belief, time in prison passes very quickly. Fortunately we all shared the same cell and passed many an hour quarrelling, debating, laughing and joking together. When possible, we would read. The prison library was very limited and the books tattered and well thumbed, but I still have an affectionate memory of some of the classics of English literature from those days. Judging from its dog-eared condition, George Eliot's *Adam Bede* must have had the unlikely honour of being one of the most sought-after works. On one occasion, one of us was put in solitary confinement for three days for some minor infringement of prison regulations, which also meant three days of bread and water and not even a lumpy mattress to sleep on, but on the whole we whiled away the time as pleasantly as circumstances permitted.

There was also the customary prison diversion of trying to communicate with the inmates of the other cells. The so-called hot-water pipe was directly opposite the spy-hole in the door but if one of us stood in front of the Judas-hole another could tap out a message at the bottom of the pipe with a spoon without being seen. The message would be relayed in this way throughout the prison so that we were able to exchange news and information with the rest of our unfortunate brethren. So it was that we learned the whereabouts of the soon-to-be notorious Eddie Chapman of later *Triple Cross* fame. We gathered, via the prison telegraph, that Chapman had in fact completed his sentence for burglary but was still being kept inside so that the prison authorities could hand him over to the mainland police in connection with various safe-breaking offences in England. It didn't seem right to me that a man could be detained indefinitely like that because there was no way he could be delivered to the English police until the war ended and there was no saying when that would be. John and I discussed Eddie's predicament and decided that upon our own release we would try to do something about it.

The morning we left prison we went straight to the headquarters of the island's German Kommandant and made an application to see him. Several days later he granted us an audience and we told him Eddie's story, emphasising that the prison governor, Mr Briard, was apparently seeking some recognition from the British for his action. We appealed to the Kommandant's sense of fair play and asked him to rectify what appeared to be an abuse of authority. The meeting obviously had some effect, for Eddie was released soon afterwards. We met him outside the prison and took him back to the Panama, where we had already arranged with Mrs Seawood, who accepted yet another criminal without turning a hair, for him to move in with our friends.

Even though we were once more at large, our common sense made us realise that living as we did, in constant conflict with the law, we must be the ultimate losers, that the prevailing powers must eventually remove us from the scene to protect their own interests. That is the irreversible rule of the game, no matter where or with whom you play it.

By a fine irony the rule caught up with us as we made preparations to try to cheat it by escaping from the island.

We successfully stole a boat and a young fellow called Green, who owned a lorry and worked for the Germans, brought it down to a hiding place a short distance outside St Helier and only a stone's throw from the beach. Once in possession of the boat we still had the problem of equipping and stocking it. Food, clothing and a reliable compass were acquired by various and devious means but most difficult of all was finding petrol with which to fuel the craft long enough to give us a fair chance of getting clear.

Motor fuel of any kind was extremely scarce, almost non-existent, and we were compelled to take terrible risks to get it. The first method yielded a few gallons but we soon abandoned it as too hazardous. We would sit in the bushes surrounding the college, which was used as a headquarters by the Germans, and wait for the staff cars to arrive and park with meticulous military precision facing the building. This proffered their rear ends to the bushes where we sat waiting, shivering with cold and often very hungry, with a length of rubber tubing to siphon their tanks.

It nearly got us shot one night, for as we were draining the tank of a large Mercedes we were caught in the headlights of another car swinging into the drive. As we dashed away into the shrubbery, the occupant emptied his automatic into the rustling bushes in the hope of hitting one of us. Luckily no one was hurt but, discretion being the better part of valour, we abandoned the attempt that night.

Finally, and not without one or two more narrow escapes, we obtained about 200 litres of fuel in all. The larger part of this was from a single haul in the shape of a barrel of German petrol. Most unfortunately for us, however, it was discovered by the Jersey police while they were investigating some totally unrelated crime. Their superior, Mr Tostivan, duly handed us over to the German police. The Jersey government of that day must have been eternally grateful to them for ridding the island of the nearest thing to some form of resistance that had existed there so far.

It was February 1942, only a few weeks after our earlier release. Once more we found ourselves in Gloucester Street Prison while we awaited trial. After three months, we were brought before a German war tribunal with full military pomp. Judge, prosecutor and even our ineffectual defence counsel were impressively clad in uniforms laden with yards of braid and silver lace. As John wryly remarked, it was indeed an extravagant display of wealth and power to try a couple of young layabouts like us. The outcome of this miniature military pageant was us being sentenced to two years' hard labour in France.

Our effort to get off the island had succeeded, but not in the manner, or the direction, we would have chosen for ourselves.

The realisation that the next two years of our lives had been snatched from us and donated to the cause of hard labour did not trouble either of us very greatly. It was just another challenge, and in any event we had every confidence that we could slip away much sooner than the authorities intended.

What did anger and depress me at the time, though, was the fact that my wife, who had left me some time before to consort with the Germans, had supplied the investigating authorities with information as to my activities and character which proved highly prejudicial to my case. This information, some of it untrue and all of it biased against me and, in part, John, was used by the prosecution and was one of the factors influencing sentence.

I was, I think, as much bewildered as hurt and angry by her malice. I had by now accepted the fact that she had left me and could even understand it to some degree; after all, when we married I had been a successful athlete and showman and life had been a comfortable, fairly glamorous affair. Her somewhat humdrum existence as a typist had suddenly become one of tours and theatres all over England and Europe, where she was recognised and entertained as the wife of Eric 'Panther' Pleasants, well-known wrestler, boxer, weightlifter and strong man extraordinaire. And now what was I but a hunted criminal! I could accept that she might feel some bitterness against me for the reversal in her fortunes and that she would turn to the Germans, who held all the trumps, for those things which she had once sought through me. But I've never understood why she hated me so much as to want to hit me when I was already down. I felt for a long time the pain of that blow delivered intentionally well below the belt.

Gloucester Street Prison, where we were returned after sentence, did nothing to improve my humour but it was several weeks before we were deported to France. Eventually, our escort came to collect us for delivery to Fort Hauteville, a prison in Dijon, to the north of France. They turned out to be two amiable military policemen going home on leave.

On the train journey from Grandeville to Dijon they took care to see that the handcuffs chaining John and me together were reasonably comfortable. The thought of escape was ever present in our minds. Often the warmth of the carriage made our two guards doze off and we would glance up at the luggage rack, where for comfort's sake they had stowed their belts and holsters, complete with guns. We each knew what the other was thinking – trying to calculate the distance from unoccupied France. To have overpowered the guards would not have been difficult. In fact, sometimes, as the guards slept, John would slide his small supple hand out of the handcuffs and wave it in front of my surprised face with an impish grin. But for some odd reason we made no attempt to get away. To this day I don't know why; we had in the past taken greater risks to extricate ourselves from lesser situations. Perhaps momentarily we lacked the energy or incentive and were content to let fate take its course.

Chapter 4

'THE ARSEHOLE OF THE UNIVERSE'

After a three-day journey we arrived at Fort Hauteville, Dijon, a forbidding heap of granite which we learned later had been condemned during the First World War as being too damp for a munitions store. It was a filthy night. Saturated to the skin during our escorted march from the railway station, we stood miserably before the massive arched gateway to the fortress. The summer storm appeared to have completed a circle and was now raging directly above us. Brilliant orange-blue flashes lit up the entire countryside for a few vivid moments, making the ensuing darkness even more dense.

Our guards hammered impatiently on the door to attract attention. They too were soaked and bedraggled and anxious to get rid of us as quickly as possible. A small door built into the timber archway opened and, after a rapid discussion with the figure that emerged clad in floor-length oilskins, they ushered us through the opening and into a small open courtyard. Leaving us standing out in the rain, our escort talked with the prison officials inside the small hut situated in that no-man's land found at the entrance to all prisons. The papers they produced were duly signed and their job of delivery was complete. Through the window we could see them warming and drying themselves and clasping their hands gratefully round mugs of steaming coffee.

John looked at me as I stood beside him clutching all my worldly possessions in a sodden battered Gladstone bag and said weightily: 'I believe that we have actually stumbled upon the arsehole of the universe.'

At that crucial moment of revelation a French prison warder approached, motioning us to follow him. We squelched down a passageway and into a dingy storeroom. Here we were each presented with a tin plate and spoon, a straw-filled palliasse and an evil-smelling, damp, ragged blanket. He beckoned us to follow him again and we weaved in and out of winding passageways, carrying our newly acquired stock of goods, and were eventually confronted with a flight of stone steps. They seemed to lead into the very bowels of the earth. The deeper we descended, the more dank and musty the air became. The naked yellow light bulbs sent weird shadow shapes dancing along the whitewashed walls. Moss and strange mushrooms clung to the stonework.

At the front of the steps was a heavy metal-studded door. The guard slid back the two massive bolts and, opening the door just a little, he indicated that we should go through. No sooner had we manipulated our unwieldy mattresses through the narrow aperture than he swiftly shut the door on us, leaving us listening to his footsteps receding down the passage.

We found ourselves in impenetrable darkness. Using the wall as a guide, we inched our way forward, stumbling as we went over what we identified by touch as occupied straw sacks on the ground. Then abruptly the wall came to an end and made a right-angled turn. Several yards along the new wall there seemed to be enough room to put down our beds. We lay down and, rolling ourselves in our issue blankets fully clothed, fell asleep almost immediately, overcome by nervous exhaustion.

Early next morning we awoke to find our palliasses awash in a pool whose smell quickly identified it as urine. The reason towered immediately above us in the form of a roughly constructed timber platform housing a 40-gallon diesel drum with the lid cut off. Five wooden steps led up to the platform, which was level with the top of the drum, across which lay a short scaffold board for either standing or crouching upon. A rough screen of planks nailed carelessly together provided the only minimal privacy. Clearly this was the lavatory, and equally clearly its capacity was insufficient for the several occupants of the large cell in which we found ourselves.

As I was registering the reason why we had found this particular area of the floor unoccupied the previous night, I became aware of the sound of bolts being drawn and cheerful voices outside in the passage. At the same moment two inmates came splashing past me carrying an eight-foot pole, which they speedily thrust through the two handles welded onto the latrine drum. Then, the pole on their shoulders and the reeking drum between them, they charged at full gallop towards the now open door amid rousing cheers from the men still sprawling on their sacks in various stages of undress. Those in their path hastily snatched up their beds and backed away from the runners and their swaying drum, now disappearing through the doorway with the speed of the possessed. No sooner had they gone out than they seemed instantly to change their minds and return, until I realised that this was another pair of runners now charging into the cell with an identical drum, only this one, it seemed, had our morning coffee in it.

Later we found out that this race was a daily occurrence, with both teams determined to be the first through the door, the shit carriers rushing towards it from inside the cell and the coffee bearers steaming down the passage from the outside. It helped to supply a little light relief in the monotony of the daily routine and made for an exciting diversion at the start of each day. The excitement lay in the fact that neither team could see the other's progress or position. On those fatal mornings when they did collide in the doorway, the contents of each drum slopping across into the other amid tumultuous applause, we chose to forego our coffee ration. The coffee was made from ground acorns and was, when not visibly contaminated, quite delicious. Strange how actually witnessing the event can be the deciding factor: if we saw the crash, our desire for coffee vanished, but if we didn't, we drank it with enjoyment – even though we knew that the coffee drum had previously served two other cells and that the same game had been played at the doorway of each. Of course, we never enquired about the drum's earlier progress because if we did we would probably never have drunk any coffee at all!

The coffee-run apart, life in Hauteville was a pretty dismal affair, especially in the beginning when no one believed we were English and it was rumoured that we were German stool-pigeons. Because of this, our cellmates were unfriendly and suspicious and even physically hostile towards us until two men, each in his completely different way, changed this state of affairs.

The Apache was a tough from the Marseilles waterfront, a tall, sallow streak of whipcord meanness with a reputation as a knife-fighter to match. One day there was a rapid, heated argument between him and another inmate and, not understanding much French, I went over to a boy standing nearby to ask what it was all about. He was an unusually pretty boy – olive-skinned, slim, big dark eyes, and instead of replying he just simpered and modestly lowered his long lashes. The Apache, seeing me talking to the boy, broke off his argument and came over to me to object. I now realised, too late, that the quarrel had been over the boy.

The Apache pushed me by the shoulder and I instantly knocked his hand away. His face grew darkly furious and bending to his nearby palliasse he retrieved something and turned, crouching, circling, the knife switching easily, hypnotically, from one hand to the other. A sudden jab. I dodged it and countered with a lucky punch which caught the Apache on the shoulder. The half-breed staggered back, momentarily unbalanced, but it was enough for me to move in and complete the crumpling-up process with my fists.

I turned away and went back to my palliasse only to find the boy, the cause of the original argument, curled coquettishly there, adoringly surrendering himself to me as the victor's prize! Unfortunately for him, I've never had the slightest sexual interest in males, however girlish they may look or however long I've been without a woman. I guess I just appreciate the genuine article too much.

But the fight brought its own reward because our formerly hostile cellmates were now all interest and respect. They gathered round full of curiosity wanting to know who and what I was – they reckoned that anyone who could beat a fighter like the Apache must be something special. I could see that what puzzled them more than anything was my deceptive appearance, since I was only about 5 ft 4 in. tall, small-boned and slim and, apparently, slightly built – so long as my clothing concealed the disciplined strength of my well-developed muscles.

This deceptive appearance has stood me in good stead all my life. Several years earlier it had landed me a job in the Bowes-Lyon family as bodyguard to the Royal princesses Elizabeth and Margaret. I suppose that, apart from being a good marksman, what made me ideal for a job like that was the fact that I didn't look remotely like the popular idea of a security man. I laugh when I think of the fights I've been in when some bully-boy has picked on me as the 'little guy' only to discover with painful surprise that he's made a bad error of judgement!

Our cellmates' change of attitude eased things for us but the first real friendship we encountered was from an English-speaking Belgian engineer. I'm not sure why Edmund Vandiebroot was inside, or why he took a liking to us; maybe he simply had one of those kind, courageous natures that respond instinctively to the needs of the underdog. Whatever it was, we were grateful for his friendship, for his thoughtfulness in sharing his food parcels with us (we never received any, of course) and particularly for the way he spoke on our behalf to the prison authorities. He must have been a man of some influence because, as a result, we were allowed, during the day, into the youth sector, where we acted as physical training instructors to the younger prisoners, for John was also a keen athlete and had the makings of a promising wrestler.

All this made life much more tolerable but not enough to make us want to stay in prison. We were still determined to escape, and Edmund, who was to be released shortly, promised to help us once he was on the outside. While we were waiting for the promised assistance we decided to try a little self-help to swell our financial resources: we planned to rob Rossi.

Rossi was the prison's arch black-marketeer, as nasty and greedy as the fat lice that crawled in the seams of the blue boiler suit he habitually wore. A Frenchman of Italian origin, his many relatives on the outside fuelled his black-market activities by sending him large and frequent food parcels, the contents of which were crammed into a padlocked laundry basket beside his palliasse. That hamper must have held every conceivable food item available outside, and quite a few that were not. You name it, Rossi could supply it – at a price.

Louse-like, his business thrived on fresh blood. New prisoners were brought in daily for everything from murder and sabotage to illegal crossing of the border into unoccupied France, like the four professional jazz musicians who were thrown in amongst us one day. They were battered, filthy and starving, stunned by the hardships of a journey beginning in hope and ending in prison. It was a story with which we were all familiar but it still moved us. Not so Rossi. His avaricious little mind took in only two things – that they had so far managed to hang onto their watches and gold wedding rings, and that they were very hungry. A starving man doesn't drive a hard bargain. Their food purchases didn't even make a dent in Rossi's food hamper but he was quickly several pieces of jewellery the richer.

There is a sort of natural justice in robbing a man like that. Waiting for our chance, John and I watched his movements. We noticed that before going to bed he removed his boiler suit, withdrew his money surreptitiously from his pocket, counted it and then returned it to the pocket of the now discarded boiler suit with a four-inch safety pin stuck through the pocket to prevent it falling out. Then he would fold up 'the bank' and put the lot under his pillow – the only one in the cell and another of his perks. We also observed that Rossi appeared to suffer from a weak bladder and several times in the night he would get out of bed and climb to the top of the staging to splash about in the diesel drum below. But on his return from each trip he would check his pocket under the pillow; it was, of course, pitch dark in the cell but the little scuffling and patting noises could, knowing Rossi, have only one interpretation.

One night, as he started out on his fifth trip to the drum, John slid out of bed and across to Rossi's, dexterously removed the wad of notes from the bulging pocket and replaced it with ready-cut newspaper and then fixed back the pin. We heard him check it as usual when he returned and he seemed satisfied.

Next morning he was up early as usual and when the coffee-run steamed in he took out his wad to pay the bearers for something as they were prison trusties and naturally he had a few fiddles going with them. It was worth several months inside just to see the expression on Rossi's face as he registered the fact that he was holding in his hand a neatly cut-up edition of *Paris Soir*. Incredulity, amazement, anger chased each other in a succession of colours over his contorted features and finally resolved in a scream of rage from his speechlessly open mouth. He roared and raved and in the ensuing chaos we discovered just how much influence he really had.

There was a frenzied exchange with the coffee guard as a result of which we were all stripped, searched and put out of the cell into the corridor clutching our coffee mugs. Naturally, most of the occupants were totally mystified as to the cause of the uproar and clamoured round the guard to know what was going on. Playing up to the full, I enquired solicitously whether Mr Rossi's mother had just died as he seemed so upset. We were told it was much more serious than that: Mr Rossi had been robbed of all his cash and there must be thieves in our cell. The information was greeted with loud cheers on all sides, for Rossi had few friends.

After about an hour we were allowed back into the cell. An incredible sight greeted us. There was straw absolutely everywhere, for every palliasse had been cut open and emptied, and in one corner the straw was piled almost to the ceiling. Despite the thoroughness of the search, the money had not been recovered. However, the whole cell benefited from the theft because fresh straw had to be stuffed into the hitherto louse-ridden, stinking mattresses. True, nothing could be done about the lice in our clothing; those we continued to pick off one by one, squatting, trousers off, under the naked electric light bulb in 'Hunter's Corner', scouring the seams where the bloated lice would lay their eggs. But clean straw was something.

So was the money. That benefit John and I kept to ourselves, about £80 in francs. After the fracas had died down, we retrieved it from the underside of the cell table, where we had impaled it with a table fork.

Exactly as arranged, two weeks after Edmund's release, we received from him a parcel of food. It's not only in fiction that there's a file baked into the cake, for in the huge lump of farm butter Edmund had hidden a circular bar cutter and in the jam we found a reasonable sum of French money and an address where we could go for help on our arrival in Paris.

Carefully we laid our plans for escape, taking two French boys into our confidence. At first we thought we might need them to help us to get across to Paris but even though we later decided that we could manage without them, it was agreed they would still make the break with us. One of the boys also gave us an address in Paris to which we could go for help if necessary.

Well past midnight on the chosen night the four of us climbed onto the lavatory platform, shivering with cold and excitement. From there we were able to reach the barred window. Slowly, painfully slowly, we started cutting through the bars, stopping, breath held, every time the guard patrolling the wall outside passed beneath us. It seemed to take an eternity and our nerves were stretched taut by the time we had cut through and were ready for the next step. This was to prise out one of the boards screening off the lavatory area. It had to be done soundlessly and every squeak and scrape seemed deafeningly loud, but between us we managed to slide it out and over to the window.

Quietly lifting out the bars, we rested one end of the plank on the window sill and pushed it out until the other end rested on the outside perimeter wall, providing us with a bridge. Then we had to move fast before the guards came round again. One by one we scrambled quickly onto the plank, over the abyss and slid down the wall on the other side. We crouched in a bed of stinging nettles until the last one was over, pulling the plank down with him, and waited there until the guard's footsteps completed the return journey and moved on. As soon as he had passed we sprinted madly from the nettles across open ground to the cover of a clump of trees and threw ourselves down, gasping for breath and trembling in every limb, unable to speak. Gradually we got our breath back and then a hoarse whisper broke the silence with, 'Christ, I've got to have a shit!'

The incongruous comment broke the tension and we giggled and relaxed a bit to gather our wits for the next move. After a few minutes' whispered discussion, the French boys said goodbye to us and disappeared into the night, going their own way. Then John and I struck out in the opposite direction, free to go where we wanted, do as we pleased.

We were free with that total, paradoxical freedom that only the hunted can know.

Chapter 5

PRISONER AT KREUZBURG

We paced up and down the street for a long time, covertly watching the house on the opposite side. Scruffy and unkempt as we were, we attracted little attention in that quarter of Paris. We had not asked the French boy any details about his contact; to us it was just a name and an address of a safe house. Finally, we plunged across the street and through the open doorway. The children playing on the dirty staircase scarcely glanced up as we stepped over them on our way to the second-floor apartment.

We knocked at the door, then knocked again. We waited, looking irresolutely at each other, then tried once more. After a pause, there was a coughing and scraping on the other side of the door. It opened a crack, revealing a dishevelled, grizzled female head.

'Henri?' we queried, not trusting our French any further. The old woman peered at us through her stringy hair. Then she rasped: '*Il est parti!*' and slammed the door shut, leaving us in no doubt that it would not be reopened. There was nothing for it but to try the address Edmund had given us.

Despite our limited knowledge of the language, we found the place without too much trouble. The neighbourhood couldn't have been more different – quiet, bourgeois, respectable. This time we went straight to the door, knocked and were admitted immediately we mentioned Edmund's name.

Our benefactors turned out to be a family of unregistered Jews, one of many such families in Paris living undercover from the Germans. We would have appreciated their warmth and generosity at the best of times; but now, after the months of hostility and deprivation in prison, it seemed to us little short of divine. The things of everyday life that people generally take for granted – sufficient food, cleanliness, the presence of women – were wonderful to us. There was no doubt that this was a matriarchal household but one ruled by the strength of a mother's warmth rather than by female tyranny.

Briefly, my mind went back to my mother, to the small gamekeeper's cottage in the Norfolk countryside of which she was the undoubted mistress. Her strong-willed, undemonstrative character, balanced by my father's more pliant warmth, maintained within that house that sense of security so vital to a child, and my certainty of my parents' love, no matter what I did, was always for me a tangible reality. I had heard nothing of or from them since I left for Jersey and for all they knew I could be dead, and yet I could imagine them stubbornly waiting for the return of their only prodigal son with a belief that nothing could shake.

We could have spent a long time just enjoying the company of this close Jewish family, but John and I did not want to abuse their hospitality by making our continued presence a threat to their safety, so after a few days we decided with regret that we must go. Where to we didn't really know, but Marseilles seemed as good a place as any as it was not at that time occupied by the Germans.

The family supplied us with food coupons and fresh clothing and set us on our way to the station. Even so, we managed to lose our way there and had to be put on the right track by a man who, to our alarm, turned out to be a member of the Sûreté.

Once at the station it wasn't a simple matter of buying a ticket and being safely directed to the right train for Marseilles since, of course, we had no identity papers, and what with the language difficulty in finding the appropriate train to jump, we finally got on the wrong one. Rather to our surprise we wound up not in Marseilles but in St Malo.

St Malo was clenched tightly by the Germans and was definitely not a good place to be in at the time. The building of the Atlantic Wall was in progress and the town was crowded with workers from the German labour units, the Organisation Todt. The only saving factor was that most of these workers were foreigners drafted in by the Germans and, unless we were actually stopped and asked to produce identity papers, we would be relatively inconspicuous. Even so, we would have found it difficult to survive had we not made the acquaintance of a Polish woman who took rather a liking to us. She was a member of one of the female labour units and with the assistance of the rest of its members she managed to smuggle us into their quarters, where we held out for several months after our money was gone.

The 20 or so women in the unit were housed in wretched conditions. After my recent experiences, I was no stranger to such squalor but I felt sorry for the women, torn from their homes by a stupid war and compelled to endure an alien, miserable existence. Rough peasant stock they may have been, but nothing in their home life or upbringing could have prepared them for this. They were kind, warm-hearted creatures who will always have a place in my memory.

However, living in intimate proximity with a host of healthily lusty women does of course have its compensations and John and I naturally made the most of it, to the mutual satisfaction of all concerned, despite the rather awkward sleeping arrangements: because of the real danger of a night raid on the quarters, the two of us always slept side by side. Obviously this had its disadvantages. One morning after a particularly heavy night I sat up yawning wearily.

'Christ, I didn't get much sleep last night!' I growled turning to John, who was already up. 'Did you?'

'Did I hell!' he snapped irritably. 'How could I with your arse going like a fiddler's elbow next to me all night?'

Often there would be heated discussions among the girls themselves over whose turn it was, when and with whom the two of us should bed down. But then, as John remarked in one of his more pensive moods: 'It's better to have too much of these things some of the time than to be without them all of the time,' adding, after a pause, '. . . I think.'

He was right to add the reflective afterthought: it wasn't an unmixed blessing. After a while we realised that the pace was getting too heavy, even for us, and the expectations of this tribe of demanding amazons became one of the factors weighing in favour of our moving on. There were more serious considerations in the balance too. Informers were our biggest fear and the longer we stayed the greater grew the threat of betrayal to the special police of the Organisation Todt or the military police, whose numbers grew daily. We decided to leave, although, as usual, we had no definite destination in mind.

Racking our resourceful brains for inspiration, we hit upon what at first seemed an absolutely crazy plan – to go back to Jersey! If we could get back on the island unobserved, we could, with our detailed knowledge of the terrain, successfully go to ground for an indefinite period, of that we were sure, and it would be the one place no one would think of looking for us. Boats still sailed between St Malo and Jersey and, with the idea of stowing aboard as soon as the first opportunity presented itself, we took to hanging around the docks.

One morning we were sitting in a waterfront café, discussing our plans in low voices. It seemed safe enough to speak English. From our table beside the high counter we could see the whole room and the only other visible occupants were two French workmen at the far end, drinking their ersatz coffee. Suddenly, to our consternation, there was the sound of someone pushing back a chair on the other side of the counter and a man, unseen by us until that moment, stood up and looked down at us.

'Please do not be alarmed, gentlemen, but I could not help overhearing your conversation,' he said quietly in perfect English. He paused, looked across at the two French workmen, then continued. 'I may be able to assist you in some way. Will you please follow me.'

We rose, ducked under the oak counter flap and followed him into a small bar behind the dining room. He instructed the woman in the kitchen to prepare coffee and food for us and then came and sat down beside us. He wanted to know where we had come from and where we were going. We told him of our escape from Hauteville prison in Dijon, but as to our future destination there was very little to tell because up to that point our plans were very vague and left a lot to chance and circumstance. One thing was clear: that we couldn't stay where we were.

Our companion listened, nodding silently from time to time. I suspected that he was probably a member of the Resistance, and now he confirmed it. He could, he said, have identity documents and photographs prepared for us within a week which would satisfy not only the French police but also the Wehrmacht street patrols. But the question of where we should go still remained. He thought for a few moments.

'I do not know if you are aware that there is from time to time shipping leaving the harbour bound for Portugal.' We didn't, but we were instantly interested. 'I believe that through one of my contacts I can arrange to get you stowed away on one of those ships, if you wish it.'

He didn't need to ask twice. We were ecstatic at the prospect. In our minds we were already in Lisbon and completely away from the madness crowding in upon us.

We were given a meal and a room for the night. The following morning our benefactor said he was going to visit friends to get our forged identity papers set up. We were to meet him after lunch so that the photographs could be taken, but meanwhile we thought we would take a walk down to the dock to acquaint ourselves with the area.

'Take care!' he cautioned as we started out on our reconnaissance trip. 'There are many German street patrols about – but I think you can manage to stay safe until noon.' He smiled and we parted company.

As we walked along the harbour I felt a tingle of apprehension that something was about to happen, and at that precise moment it did.

Flying in very low, almost skimming the sea, nine fighter planes conjured themselves out of the horizon. For a brief moment those RAF youngsters must have had one hell of an exciting time, dropping their small anti-personnel bombs and spraying with machine-gun fire everything that moved. Then they disappeared as suddenly as they had appeared, before the anti-aircraft guns had a chance to open up.

We were at the far end of the harbour and right in the thick of it all. Fortunately, we had been standing beside a giant crane mounted on a massive steel base plate which ran on rail tracks. As the planes lifted themselves out of the sea, machine guns blasting as they came, both John and I dived under the crane and frantically crawled into the space beneath the base plate, which surely saved our lives.

As the drone of the aircraft receded into the distance and the anti-aircraft guns began their belated retaliation, we emerged from our hiding place, coughing in the thick dust and smoke. The sooner we were away from the area the safer, but to our dismay we saw that timber barriers had been swung across the exit and that the guards manning it were demanding to see all identity papers. Our only chance was to join the crowd of civilians jostling to get off the pier, where the pressure on the police was greatest, and hope that in the milling confusion we might get through. We joined the queue and suddenly it was our turn. An impatient officer held out his hand brusquely demanding our papers.

John's quick wits met the occasion with a fast flow of persuasive German. I remained silent and watched his brilliant performance. The moment he opened his mouth the happy-go-lucky Cockney was replaced by a typical blond, disarmingly innocent German youth. It was a talent which was to cause me as much amusement and admiration in the months which followed; after a fluent, eloquently phrased speech in faultless German, he would turn to me and say out of the corner of his mouth, 'Blimey, mate, we 'aven't 'arf got a right one 'ere!' or something so equally incongruous in style and manner that I would be hard put not to laugh.

On this occasion I listened as he invented on the spur of the moment a convincing explanation of how at the first sound of the raid by those wretched English planes he and I (whom he introduced as a Dutch worker) were overcome with concern for the safety of a consignment of materials and equipment. Being billeted nearby we had hastily thrown on our coats and hurried along to see if we could help in any way, in our haste forgetting our identity papers.

It seemed that they were almost convinced and on the point of telling us to go about our business and be more careful in future when, as an afterthought, the sergeant remarked that it was curious that *both* of us had forgotten our papers. This swung the decision against us and he said, not unkindly, that he would accompany us to our billets, as they were so near, and we could then produce our documents.

The streets were alive with patrols after the raid and the chance in a million that we were looking for did not present itself, so we kept walking. Ten minutes later, when the sergeant enquired how much further it was, John said we were almost there. Fifteen minutes after that, and with us still in a crowded area, he stopped and said it would have been impossible for us to come this distance so quickly on hearing the raid, and that he intended to arrest us as he did not believe our story. There was nothing we could do but accompany him meekly to the nearest police station.

The story we gave when we were interrogated at the police station was that we had stowed away on a boat from Jersey. And so, after several days in another dirty French jail, they sent us back to Jersey. Two Feldgendarmes collected us at St Helier port, and once again we found ourselves back in Gloucester Street Prison.

Back to Jersey, back to Gloucester Street and the nauseating stink of stale urine. We sat dejectedly gazing up at the open sky beyond the barred window, prisoners once more. We had spent a lot of time wandering beneath that sky, sometimes free, sometimes captive, but we had to admit that most of our travels had been from one jail to another. Most galling of all was the fact that we had travelled full circle to finish up in the very place we had most wanted to escape from.

Christ, but I wished I'd never set foot on that bloody island! I cursed it venomously and I cursed the idiocy of a war which had so utterly blighted my life and that of hundreds of others like me. For the first time I felt a morbid blackness of spirit creep over me. I knew that speculation of the 'if only . . .' kind was stupid and useless, but all the same, as I gazed at that patch of sky through the bars, I couldn't help my mind slipping back to the freedom I'd always known and I saw the sky stretching across to the flat East Anglian horizon of my youth, reflecting deep blue in the rivers where I would poach the squire's fish . . .

It was one of those mornings when you knew you were part of the new day, with the sun pushing its first warming rays through the twirling wisps of mist over the brook flowing beneath the blossoming elders, past the gap between the bramble bushes where I stood drying myself on my shirt after a swim. Pulling on my trousers and buckling the belt, I was hanging the shirt on the bushes to dry when I froze, all senses alert, my nose suddenly catching the warm, sharp smell of a horse: there were cows in the field behind the tall hawthorn hedge but

I had seen no horses. Then came the faint tinkle of metal, of bridle and bit. I spun round suddenly and caught her trying to pull her mount back out of sight from the gap in the hedge.

'Mornin' to yer!' I yelled defiantly, annoyed at her intrusion and yet a little apprehensive, for it was her father's land that I was on, even though I never could understand why the local squire should have the right to own this lovely, solitary little stream with its watercress and trout. Assuming an air of authority to hide the sheepishness she obviously felt at being caught watching me and then trying to hide, she rode boldly through the gap onto the grass where I stood.

'You are Eric Pleasants,' she said, looking down at me. It was a statement, not an enquiry.

'That's my name and I've never made a secret of it,' I answered, deliberately avoiding addressing her as 'miss', as local custom required.

'I suppose you are aware you are trespassing?' she went on haughtily, but I just grinned with all the brashness of my 19 years. It wasn't worth replying to such an obvious statement. She turned in the saddle and slid down from the horse on her stomach, the cream cord jodhpurs stretching tight across her neatly rounded arse. She turned to me, holding the bridle.

'My father says you're a bad lot, always poaching and fighting. He says you've never done an honest day's work.' It was a challenge and I rose to the bait.

'Your old man has never done any work, honest or dishonest, in his whole honey-smeared life!' I retorted. Nettled by her remark, I faced her squarely to counter the next accusation. It didn't come, or if it did I didn't hear it. I was looking straight at her and her eyes were a deep, soft brown and I could see the stream behind me reflected in them . . . I'd never dealt with jodhpurs before and the tightness of them over her calves made it difficult for me to get them down, but she helped, pulling them down anxiously.

Some time later I noticed that the sun had climbed well up into the sky and heaven knows how long the birds had been singing so exquisitely, unnoticed. It was the first of many such summer mornings, of meetings in barns and haystacks, or erotic wrestling bouts in the grassy glades of her father's land. The experience tore through my 19-year-old being like a summer storm. She was scented and smooth with a polish quite new to me. But how long I'd have lasted on this lotus diet I'd never know because one day she stopped coming and I heard she'd been sent to a finishing school in France. Some sharp-eyed, foxy village creep-arse had been whispering in her father's ear and I was left alone to mope and fret until the little factory girls regained their attractiveness; only I had a curious feeling of having betrayed somebody.

One morning I was clearing brushwood when up rode the squire. He ordered me over to him and I told him to piss off so he rode at me, his riding crop raised. I dropped my hedge-hook and caught his arm as it descended, yanking him from his horse. I pinned him to the ground as I crammed handfuls of earth down his neck, then I let him get up while I threw his velvet riding hat into the bushes and yelled at his horse so that it took off at a frightened gallop. He scrambled to his feet and I laughed pitilessly at the ridiculous, dishevelled figure he cut as he hurriedly made off in the same direction as his horse, but with much less dignity. For the first time I saw the feet of clay which supported the squirearchy to which my family and my kind had touched their forelocks for generations. I had pulled down the pathetic façade for myself and seen the fear in his eyes. But such is the strength of tradition that, instead of seeing things as I now saw them, the village folk ostracised me and cold-shouldered my folk, and the two-man local police force hovered constantly around our house like shit flies round a cow-pat. I was learning my first adult lesson in one of the basic facts of life: you may win the odd battle against authority, but you'll never win the war.

Coming back to the reality of the bars across the cell window as I lay on my bunk in Gloucester Street Prison, I had ample time to reflect morosely on the truth of the maxim. At last we learnt that we were to be deported back to the Continent, destination unspecified, and we idled away three or four weeks waiting for the order to take effect.

The day finally arrived, announced by the sudden appearance of the supercilious little screw Fisher in the doorway of our cell one morning. Trying hard to look menacing, he jerked his head back theatrically – to the great peril of the too-large peaked cap which only his ears seemed to prevent from falling over his eyes – and motioned us out of the cell. We went slowly, grinning insolently at the contemptible little man who, pretending not to notice, ushered us self-importantly ahead of him down the stone-flagged corridor until we emerged into the courtyard.

Blinking in the unaccustomed brightness of the sunshine, we saw two men in the uniform of the German Sicherheitsdienst (Security Service) waiting. Obviously our escort. The inevitable papers were produced, signatures flourished and then, the formalities complete, we were handed over to them.

One of the first things we noticed after the hand-over was the change of attitude in the guards. No longer could we sense any personal animosity. They were two German police detailed to escort two English prisoners. This they would do to the last letter. They addressed us politely, made no attempt to bully. But, on the other hand, we knew that if we tried to escape or resist, they would not hesitate to shoot us. They took us to a waiting staff car and we were driven through the warm sunlit streets of St Helier, for us a wonderful contrast to the urine-smelling, chilling interior of the prison.

In far too short a time we arrived on the quayside where the ship was berthed, its load of deportees already aboard. In the several hours that remained before we were due to sail, John and I took stock of our new surroundings. It didn't take us long to discover that all the others had been supplied with a parcel of food by the Jersey government containing tins of fish, milk and other delicacies we no longer thought existed. With our usual audacity and directness, we demanded to see the officer in charge of the convoy.

John's fluent German enabled us to bypass the Jersey officials and speak directly to the captain, who immediately went to work in the most business-like manner, calling in a Jersey official and demanding to know why we had not been issued with rations like everyone else. Hurriedly consulting his list, the confused Jerseyman finally announced with malicious triumph that we had come straight from prison. However, the explanation cut no ice with the captain. Summoning the two guards who had escorted us from prison, he reprimanded them for accepting us without proper rations and then sent them off to rectify their mistake.

It was obvious what had happened. The crews at the prison could not resist the temptation of the food in the parcels and had therefore conveniently forgotten to hand them over to us. We chuckled when we thought of what would happen when the German guards arrived back to collect the 'forgotten' rations.

Late that evening we set sail for France. Watching the Jersey coastline recede in the misty setting sunlight, I felt no regrets. One cannot fight against circumstances all the time; and so, clutching our precious food parcels, we found a comfortable place on the deck out of the wind and stretched ourselves out to relax.

We scarcely spoke to any of the other deportees, amongst whom morale was depressingly low. That was hardly surprising, for no one knew our destination and speculation as to our ultimate end was imaginatively gruesome. Rumours of concentration camps, genocide, extermination by hard labour were all rife. On the other hand, there was also talk of exchanges of Channel Islanders for German nationals from some obscure place, and of 'special arrangements' made by Churchill under which we were being used as pawns in a wartime political intrigue.

The passengers were a motley crowd, 'foreigners' for the most part – that is, Englishmen who had not been on the island long before the war broke out, or Jerseymen of Italian descent who held English passports. Poor Mr Tostivan: that pathetic little Jersey Goebbels of a public prosecutor must have had a difficult time sorting out the people whose records made them eligible for transportation. In some cases he really had to scour his books to provide him with the necessary reason. Minor infringements of regulations by small shopkeepers, doubtful ancestry – but influence and wealth carried a lot of weight towards tipping the balance in favour of exemption.

Once we docked in France, we were split into four groups and each was despatched to a different destination. John and I found ourselves in a group of about 50 on a train bound for an English internment camp in Upper Silesia. Camp Ilag VIIIZ, Kreuzburg, formerly an asylum for the insane.

Chapter 6

IN THE MADHOUSE

There were times during the eight months that I was in Kreuzburg when I wondered whether there had been any real change from its former use as a home for the mentally bewildered. The initial sight of the barbed-wire entanglements, the watchtowers, the patrolling sentries, the institutional buildings, were enough to scatter anyone's wits; actually having to live within that set-up went a long way to completing the process.

Nor did the company in which I found myself do much to dispel my misgivings. Most of the inmates had held British passports but they were the most un-English lot of Englishmen it has been my misfortune to meet. Some had never even seen England and spoke the language only with difficulty; and, anyway, most of them were unlikeable and uninteresting.

The camp leader, however, was an Englishman to the marrow. His negotiations with the German authorities were masterpieces of diplomacy, but I couldn't help noticing that when those dealings involved John and myself there appeared to be less need for these ambassadorial skills, since both sides usually joined forces against us. It was scarcely surprising. Together with a few more young fellows, merchant seamen who had been lodged temporarily in the civilian camp, we played havoc with the discipline and became for the worthy

Mr Duncan and Oberleutnant Schumann, the German Kommandant, one huge headache.

At first we tried to beat the stifling monotony by organising sports, boxing matches and games, but then the corrosive canker of boredom and pettiness that is endemic in camp life set in and began insidiously to eat into us. Prison existence makes one small-minded and things we would have ignored in other circumstances became disproportionately large and important. Personal dislikes developed into hatred, minor annoyances into calculated insults, and we accepted it as the normal order of things that the camp should be divided into rival factions.

The one currently in supremacy when we came in was the homosexual element. I personally have nothing against homosexuals but I didn't see why their proclivities should procure for them advantages over the rest of us. Nor did the rest of the group of merchant seamen of whom John and I became part because of our rebellious and boisterous ways, and we quickly offended camp protocol not only by attacking the established hierarchy but also by undertaking nefarious little projects of our own, such as stealing liberally from the Germans, without reference to anyone else's plans. In short, we generally stirred up a hornets' nest. The earlier somnolent attitude of waiting, waiting safely for the end of the war, which had up to then slumbered over the camp, was utterly destroyed.

We were in and out of the cells, acclaimed as heroes by some, condemned as troublemakers by others. A few charitably wrote us off as mad, and perhaps they were right.

Not that the opinions of our fellow prisoners mattered much to us, for we in our turn took a rather dim view of them. But there were exceptions, like Charlie Grant and Bill Price, each of whom in their own way provided us with something to think about.

Charlie, a hearty 13-stone Canadian racing driver from Montreal, had been caught up in the war by pure chance. He had been at a race meeting at one of Europe's leading circuits, intending to fly to London the next day, but overnight Hitler's army had advanced in its initial headlong blitz across Europe and when Charlie awoke the following morning he found himself pinioned in German-occupied territory with only a small holdall containing a shaving kit and change of clothing.

Within 14 days he was an inmate of the British civilian internee camp at Kreuzburg and one of its assets. His unquenchable sense of humour and clowning practical jokes were probably the finest morale booster any bunch of prisoners could hope for – except their release, of course.

The whole camp enjoyed the benefit of his good humour early one crisp November morning. It happened when we were all lined up as usual, in the yard, for the daily count by the German camp Kommandant, who would pass slowly along the ranks of prisoners accompanied by his subordinates. The party was usually preceded by a solitary Unteroffizier who made sure that everybody was correctly in line and fit to be gazed upon by his Kommandant.

On this particular cold morning, this awesome group was approaching the spot where Charlie Grant stood prominently in the front row in blue driving jacket with scarlet-embroidered maple leaf and, on his head, a woolly pompom hat. The Unteroffizier seized the hat with horror and flung it to the ground. The rule was hats off on parade, but Charlie clearly didn't approve of the rule on frosty mornings so he stepped out, retrieved his hat, put it back on his head at a jaunty angle and smartly stepped back into line.

The enraged officer turned the colour of Charlie's maple leaf and bawled him out soundly in German. Of this Charlie understood not one word, but in the pregnant silence that followed the officer's outburst, Charlie's voice boomed across the parade ground loud and clear. Pulling his pompom hat tightly round below his ears and holding it with both hands, he shouted back: 'And you, sir, can kiss my right royal Canadian arsehole!'

By this time the Kommandant had reached the spot and enquired as to the cause of the disturbance. Charlie, realising that he had won only a temporary victory, gave as his explanation the fact that sudden changes in temperature gave him pains in the head. Knowing his robust constitution and rude good health, we all grinned quietly, but the Kommandant seemed to swallow it.

'Very well!' he snapped, jumping at the chance to air his English in public. 'Your hat you may keep on if its absence your health endangers!'

Thereafter, even in the hot weather when Charlie, like everybody else, generally went bareheaded, he always dutifully pulled the blue wool hat firmly onto his head for parades, determined not to relinquish one vestige of the first tangible victory for the Allied forces.

Bill Price was as different from Charlie Grant as it was possible for two men to be, yet in his own way as likeable and memorable. Gentle and quiet, he had no special friends, but it would have been difficult to find anyone with anything against him, even though he was a Negro (as we called black people then) and colour prejudice was one of those pettinesses that flourished in camp mentality. His nimble fingers were always busy making or converting something – sandals from old pieces of leather, beautiful belts from scraps of string – his ingenuity was both practical and artistic.

He wasn't alone in this form of occupational therapy because many of us found that keeping ourselves busy by making things helped relieve the boredom and keep our minds off useless speculations on the future. But Bill threw himself into his handiwork with that air of determined concentration that is sometimes born of near despair, as though he were making a desperate effort of will to ward off the hopelessness that would otherwise overwhelm him.

One had to be fairly perceptive to notice this underlying current because he never complained or indulged in self-pity. On the contrary, he was very pleasant company. He could talk interestingly about lots of things and it was always with some surprise that I listened to the broad Scottish accent, initially so incongruous with his dark skin. He himself had no chip on his shoulder about the fact that he was a Negro. 'Only real men are this colour, pasty!' he quipped good humouredly one day when, finding him sunbathing, I complained that despite my best efforts I never managed to achieve a tan even approaching his.

It was only when the conversation came round to the war, as it inevitably did, and its prospects and duration, that one saw behind the façade and a look of deep melancholy filled his eyes. I myself would be affected by a corresponding sense of gloom after such conversations, but whereas I could, and did, dispel these moods by getting involved in some mad escapade to irritate authority, Bill's unaggressive good nature would not allow him even the relief of transgression.

A few days after the light-hearted exchange when I had found Bill sunbathing, John and I were busy making a bow and arrows with which we intended to shoot messages over the high wall that divided us from the Polish girls working in the laundry, when we were interrupted by a young Belgian running breathlessly up to us. Grabbing us urgently by the shoulders, he gasped: 'Hi, you two better come have a look. I think something no good has happened in the hospital!'

We knew instantly that something was very wrong and not stopping to ask questions we raced after him across the compound to the hospital block. We burst through the door and tore up the stairs to the single bathroom, which we found locked. The Belgian lad pointed to the fanlight over the door. I put my back to the door, my clasped hands low in front of me to enable John to step up onto my shoulders so that he could see through the fanlight into the bathroom.

'Bloody hell!' he muttered tensely and, springing down at once, began to attack the door with a series of vicious kicks. Together we made short work of the door, but we were already too late.

Stepping over the splintered woodwork into the bathroom, we saw Bill's muscular black body lying stretched out in the bath, just visible through the reddening darkness of the water. It was still warm. The last threads of blood oozed slowly from the slashed wrists. Bill's head, with its wet, black curly hair, rested comfortably on the back of the bath, the sightless eyes staring up at the ceiling.

We left the room; I felt slightly sick. We did not trouble to report the matter – somebody else would do that soon enough. Shocked and depressed, we returned in silence to our room and threw ourselves down on our beds.

As I lay there, my emotions became concentrated into an intense hatred and contempt for all forms of authority instrumental in creating conditions which caused human beings to treat their lives and the lives of others with such complete indifference, which drove men like Bill Price to lock themselves away alone with their yearnings and a razor.

This incident, so close, so unnecessary, epitomised for me the stupid pointlessness of this war, all war. Fragments of childhood memory submerged by time and experience jagged themselves into my mind: a young woman's horror of the shells and gas and mud of the trenches seen through the embittered and now blind eyes of her husband – she was one of my first schoolteachers; a visit to a war veterans' hospital; the small metal badge in the lapel of my father's jacket glinting in the sun as he limped painfully about his gamekeeper's rounds. With the illogical half-sightedness common to most people, he was proud of the badge, which denoted that he was a wounded ex-serviceman, even while he spoke against war and cursed the inconvenience of the wound. Like so many others, he felt he ought to be proud of having fought for king and country, although they meant nothing to him personally and even though it had ruined his life and health and strength.

Maybe he would have done things differently if he had had his time again, maybe, subconsciously, that's what he was trying to do through me.

'Be strong, boy!' he would say to me. 'You've got to be strong!' The urgency of his voice made a deep impression on me and in times to come that image of my father, with his air of quiet strength, became for me a kind of touchstone to which I frequently turned for reassurance. Even so, I don't think he realised the full implication of his own sound advice. Unless you are strong in body and mind and spirit you will be stamped on, dragged around and ground down until your life isn't your own, you will be nothing more than victim, like the unfortunate Bill Prices of this world.

The instinct that had so far guided me deepened and strengthened: war was wrong, to participate as a combatant was to perpetuate and condone that wrong. I had no option but to continue to do things my way.

The weeks passed in monotonous succession and, try as we might to vary it, there was a sameness that blighted our existence. We fought and quarrelled, studied, read, dreamed, endlessly told and retold our experiences of times past, relapsed into abysmal depression and grew elated at trivial incidents. The roundabout always followed the same circle, however many of its horses one mounted. But at the pinnacle one preoccupation stood alone: escape.

It wasn't that I had anywhere to run to. For me it was, logically considered, an unreasonable thing to do. After all, I had no duty to escape and nowhere to go if I did. England would scarcely welcome me back without clapping me either into uniform or prison. Materially I had nothing to gain, for I would be exchanging the relative safety and comfort of the internment camp for the danger and deprivation of an escapee's life. Yet these things weighed not at all in the balance of my considerations. I simply wanted to get out of that excruciatingly monotonous round, its pettiness, and its nit-picking, interfering authority.

Eight of us finally hatched a plot. The preparations alone, which began just before Christmas, improved my outlook because it meant doing something with a positive end in view. The exit route was to be through the ceiling of the top-floor gymnasium and out onto the flat roof, from where we would lower ourselves to the ground four storeys below.

We saw a lot more of the top-floor inmates than usual while the necessary hole was being carefully cut. They probably knew what we were about, even though we didn't take them into our confidence. They seemed rather a weird bunch to me: six merchant seamen from Liverpool, a homosexual padre to cater for the spiritual needs, a fat, jovial Cockney coffee-stall holder from the East End of London and, at the other extreme, a collection of British passport holders who spoke no English at all.

Where to find enough rope to get us down was a puzzle at first until someone had the bright idea of using fire hose. On each landing was a glass-faced wall cabinet with a coil of hose; the distance from the roof to the ground was measured and the requisite number of hose lengths calculated, cut and hidden in the roof area. Denim overalls were rubbed with a sort of beeswax to render them waterproof against the heavy snow, so that when the wearer's body heat melted it, it would not penetrate the fabric. Boots too were treated in a similar manner.

We started hoarding rations, packing them carefully in tins, and stole provisions whenever the opportunity occurred. I stole a hundredweight of cheese from the German kitchen when the cook's back was turned for a few minutes and then had the infuriating luck to be almost safely back to my room with it when I collided with the German corporal on duty inside the camp.

I was sentenced to a month in the cells but the others continued preparations without me. When they were ready, John smuggled through a message to me, together with a hacksaw blade secreted in the binding of a book. Unfortunately, the blade was discovered by some vigilant screw but I managed to get a message out telling them what had happened and to find someone to take my place and not wait for me. I wished them good luck and settled down to finish my month in the cells, feeling horribly despondent and lonely.

They made their break on Christmas Eve, when roll call was extended to midnight, giving them more time to get away. By that time everyone in the dormitory knew of their escape and tried to cover for them. We would normally parade on the landing, lined up in threes, and the Kommandant and guards would come up the stairs and start counting. There were two entrances from the landing into the dormitory, one immediately at the top of the stairs and the other at the end of the passage. When the guards reached about halfway along the line of mustered men, a bunch who had already been counted raced through the door at the top of the stairs, along the length of the dormitory, out the end door and mingled back in with those who had not yet been counted. Result: two men too many. Christmas Eve, home-brewed hooch and everyone's anxiety to help accounted for the confusion. There was a recount. This time there were three too many.

The Kommandant was furious – he had better things planned for Christmas Eve than spending the rest of it counting half-drunk prisoners. Now it was the name and number system instead of the block head-count, and the result of this foolproof method revealed the fact that eight men were missing and out went the patrols.

However, it was only a month later that I saw John again. He had eventually been recaptured, along with the others, but had been held in the Gestapo prison at Oppeln for some weeks before being brought back. He returned to Ilag VIIIZ looking pale and much thinner since I had last seen him. After much gleeful backslapping, I took him off to enjoy his first real meal in weeks, which I had managed to scrounge from the Red Cross parcels of our associates.

But there were others in Kreuzburg who were not so pleased to see us both at large in the camp again, least of all camp leader Mr Duncan. We disrupted the order and routine of camp life and some of our activities had in the past led to some restrictions being tightened and privileges withdrawn. And so a delegation of British prisoners, led by an embarrassed Mr Duncan, who hated making decisions – the poor man wasn't to know that he would be compensated for his tribulations with an OBE at the end of the war – approached the German camp Kommandant with a request that we be transferred. Everybody seemed to think that that would be a remarkably good idea and one which would ensure the return of the desired tranquillity to their wartime existence.

Their request was granted.

Chapter 7

IN DARKEST GERMANY

A few days later John and I were called to the Kommandant's office and informed that we were to be transferred to a merchant seamen's camp near Bremen. They had, said the Kommandant, taken into account our friendship with the merchant seamen and thought we would surely prefer to be among them in their own camp, even though we were only civilians. Tongue in cheek, we thanked him.

That was how we came to be classed as merchant seamen. It wasn't something we chose out of vanity, as one author rather pretentiously claims. However, we did in fact welcome the transfer: at least it was a change and that, combined with the novelty of the train journey to Bremen, put us in a frame of mind that was positively cheerful by the time we reached our destination. Not even the first sight of Marlag Milag Nord, with its formidable barbed-wire compound, scanning watchtowers and heavily armed sentries could dampen our spirits, unless it was that we were by this time simply hardened by experience.

The camp was exclusively for merchant seamen and at first we did like being there, so far as one can like such things. At least the inmates behaved like men and not like the bunch of old women we had left in Kreuzburg, whose passing we mourned not at all.

We found ourselves among seamen of every nationality –

Canadians, Aussies, Negroes, Irish, Americans, Chinese – you name it, the camp had it. They were still on pay. More days, more dollars, they would chant. The general attitude was: 'It doesn't matter how long this fucking war lasts, there's enough to eat and still a bit of ass – lots of guys are much worse off.' Nevertheless, despite their apparent carelessness, suicide was not infrequent, and the hospital housed more than one mentally disturbed patient.

The reason, as always, was boredom, that terrible sameness of camp life that finally preys upon even the most well-balanced, cheerful individuals. Realising this, they tried, each in his own way, to do what they could to beat the monotony. Some studied and quite a few first mate and master's certificates were achieved via Red Cross correspondence courses. Even John later took up Spanish and shorthand, poring over his books after lights-out in his 'home study unit'. This comprised a tea chest with a bulb wired to the inside and a blanket nailed over the opening. The contraption stood on a table while he sat on a chair in front of it, head and shoulders inside with his books and the blanket draped down his back to block any light from the hawk-eyed night guards. Not surprisingly, he got himself nicknamed 'The Photographer' as from the outside it did look rather like a giant, old-fashioned camera.

Sports and boxing matches were already well organised. At one of these events a coloured boy claiming to be Kid Silver boxed an exhibition bout. I knew that there was at that time a boxer of that name who had been a contender for the middleweight championship of Europe but, watching him in action, I doubted he could be one and the same. I challenged him in the next tournament.

As there were many who believed in *his* claim, while nobody there except John had seen *me* in action, betting odds were heavily in his favour and my chances were rated very slight. John naturally backed me with everything he had and got fantastic odds from the camp bookies.

We celebrated in style on his winnings . . . I knocked 'Kid Silver' out cold in the third round and John collected a substantial sum in camp marks.

Although it was a few years since I had given up boxing professionally, I had, even though I say it myself, been a good professional and it still showed. Not that I had given up boxing entirely: I had kept up sparring practice in the gym, fought the occasional friendly bout, but I had been careful to avoid situations that would have meant exposing myself to risk of real injury. It sounds laughable, and if anyone had told me as a youngster that I would be hanging up the gloves just when I had everything going for me I would have laughed them to scorn in sheer disbelief. At the age of about 15, which was when I made my first public appearance, there was no other thought on my horizon but that I would be a boxer, and a good one, and for the next few years I never wavered in that drive.

And then one morning I woke up seeing double. It didn't go away so, finally, my old man dragged me down to the doctor's. The quack scratched his head, peered into my eyes again with his little light, asked me whether I'd fallen off my bicycle and hit my head. I was as mystified as he was; I hadn't been doing anything out of the ordinary – there wasn't much time for much else when I'd done my day's training, especially if I had a contest in the evening. The old doctor instantly pricked up his ears and looked at me keenly.

'Ah!' he said, as if that expressed everything. 'If you want to save your eyesight – and your brain – my boy, you'll give that up at once!'

I was dumbfounded. For a moment I felt as though the world had collapsed around my ears. I went away and tried to shut his advice out of my mind. But it made me look about me rather more observantly. I began to be aware of the one-time boxers I saw in every gym, hanging around at every contest; now I saw not only the cauliflower ears and broken noses – I noticed too the very large number who walked on their heels, whose speech was slurred, who seemed slow of understanding. Brain damage, the doctor had said. I got to thinking. I began to notice just how much punishment a boxer's head does take. Even if it is protected in training, there is still the frequent jarring that does the damage. It seems ironic, but the gloves introduced to reduce injury to the contestants actually promote the most serious damage of all.

In the days of bare-fist pugilism there probably was more blood in the ring, but this was most likely to be from surface cuts to the body. There was very little punching to the head because the hardness of the skull was more likely to injure the knuckles of the man throwing the punch than the head of his opponent, and the most telling blows were therefore to the comparatively softer body. The introduction of gloves, however, changed the picture dramatically and the head, housing the most sensitive and vital mechanism in a human being, became a major and very vulnerable target. Comparatively speaking, there are few deaths caused by brain injury in boxing, but the long-term effects of the constant battering, though less spectacular, are just as destructive, devastating and terrible.

I didn't find all that out overnight, of course, and it was some time before I realised the dangers were a sufficiently urgent reality to make me give up the dream of a lifetime. It came hard, but by then I had started wrestling, to which I took like the proverbial duck to water, and gradually this began to replace the part boxing had played in my life. I had kept in training as a wrestler right up to the time I had been imprisoned and that, together with my almost fanatical devotion to physical culture of any description, which I continued as far as possible in the camps, undoubtedly played a very large part in my survival for the next 11 years. And if, incidentally, it earned me a little material benefit in the shape of camp marks and respect in a world which recognised only physical strength, I couldn't complain.

Boxing had its following but baseball, under the strong American/Canadian influence, was practically the national sport of the camp. On league final day everyone turned out to watch, the excitement as crisp as the fresh limewash markings, the bookies doing a brisk trade in cigarette and chocolate bets as the start of the match became imminent.

The game had been in progress for about half an hour when a giant Canadian struck the ball and landed it between the two sets of perimeter wire fences. The inner safety wire was only three feet high but the main, outer wire, a distance of about ten feet from it, was of course at least six times that height. Although it was easy enough to step over the inner wire, we were forbidden to do so. The guards patrolling between the two fences and those in the all-seeing watchtowers made sure the command was obeyed, and transgression was not a good idea unless you were contemplating suicide. In order to retrieve the ball, therefore, permission would have to be asked of the guards in both watchtowers, and as they were a considerable distance apart the side in would have run away with the game by the time the ball was back in play.

Fortunately, the German censor was as much caught up in the game as the rest of us. Although a German national, he had spent most of his life in America and baseball was the sport nearest his heart.

'Don't worry, fellas,' he shouted, 'I'll get the ball!' and he set off to the perimeter at a fast trot. Naturally this would get the game going quicker since, being in German uniform, one would have thought he would not have to ask permission at the watchtowers. He jumped over the low wire but as he bent to pick up the ball there was a rapid burst of machine-gun fire from one of the towers. It may have been just a warning round but he was out of there like a rocket.

The gunfire brought the Kommandant out of his office demanding to know what was happening, and his disciplinary measures have always been a source of amusement to me.

All three of them, the watchtower guards and the censor, were sentenced to 21 days in the cells together. The censor for not reporting his intention to both guards before crossing the safety wire; the guard who opened fire – for shooting at a German uniform; and the other guard, who had obviously recognised his comrade and did not fire – for neglect of duty! Bewildering justice indeed!

The only other time I saw anyone cross the safety wire without permission and without being shot was a drink-crazy seaman who, not content with getting over the first fence, clambered up the outer barbed-wire fence also. There was a warning burst from the watchtower sentry – which earned a round of applause from all of us watching on the ground – but he went right to the top and then climbed carefully down on the outside. Once out, he walked round to the main entrance and thumped on the guardroom door, loudly demanding to be let in again because he could think of nowhere in the whole of bloody Germany as good as his prison camp!

The whole affair was treated as a joke by both Germans and prisoners alike, and perhaps by this stage in the war (it was about April 1944) many of the German soldiers thought it unnecessary, or unwise, to execute their duties too rigorously.

Cloistered away in a spectral and irrelevant foreign legion far from the fighting front, I had only the foggiest notion of the progress of the war and the disastrous outcome of Germany's strategic campaigns to date – the defeat of Rommel's Afrika Korps in the south, the crushing victory of the Soviet Red Army at Stalingrad in the east, the defeat of the U-boat Navy in the Battle of the Atlantic in the west, and the impending Allied invasion of France, heralding the opening of the Western Front and the advance on Berlin by huge enemy armies from the west as well as the east. What I was aware of was the Allies' almost unchallenged supremacy in the skies over my head and the remorseless and unending destruction of the Fatherland by British and American bombers by day as well as by night.

A lot of the seamen spent three parts of the time being absolutely, hopelessly drunk – it was, I suppose, escape of a kind. Brewing and distilling were big business in the camp and most of the concoctions were fierce and raw. Not the raisin wine, which was delicious, but that was rare as it depended on Red Cross parcels containing the necessary fruit. Hooch was mainly potatoes and sugar fermented with yeast and water. At the end of the rapid fermentation process the muck was distilled in old pressure-cooker-type utensils and then dripped out of a copper tube. The brewers' standard test for potency was to catch a few drips in a teaspoon from time to time, and if this ignited when a flame was held near it then it was strong enough; if it didn't, a fresh potful was indicated.

This hooch, which could literally send you blind if you drank enough, was an explosive potion. I have seen spirit gum, boot polish, metal polish and various other weird additives being stirred into the already lethal tipple, which you had to hold your nose to get down sometimes, but there were some prisoners who lived for nothing but to drink it until they were nearly insane.

Saturday night was booze night. The British camp doctor, himself a prisoner, didn't bother to go to bed on Saturday nights. By late afternoon those who so intended were already on their way to becoming drunken raving maniacs, past all reason and caring. One young seaman in our hut, suffering from 'metal polish fatigue', unthinkingly switched on his light one night just as the perimeter lights were doused for the Allied bombers droning into a raid on

Bremen. The guard patrolling the outer wire, screaming obscenities into the night, was either not heard or not heeded, so he raised his rifle and fired at the offending light through the hut window. Inside the hut the young seaman, lying on his bunk smoking, suddenly found to his dismay that his cigarette was mysteriously carried away, and with it half his hand.

It was an unfortunate and isolated case because, generally, the light rules were well observed. But a few weeks after this incident, as Bremen was again being hammered by the night raiders, someone came into our hut and switched on the light. Totally undeterred by the volley of abuse and other more tangible missiles, he stood with both hands over the switch, roaring like a bull moose and prepared to defend it with his life. However, remembering the seaman's hand, I climbed out of my bunk to turn it off myself. The drunk surveyed the scene, swaying, red-eyed, and at the last moment put out the light.

Instantly the hut was in darkness. I, with my back to the window, could see nothing, but the drunk, facing me, could see me clearly silhouetted against the window by the searchlights scanning the sky outside. I didn't see him snatch the heavy iron teapot from the stove beside him and John's warning shout came too late to prevent it descending heavily on my head and down I went. As the seaman raised the pot to strike again, John made a flying tackle from yards away, miraculously managing to bring him down, while an Aussie joined in, grabbed the pot and flung it into a far corner.

The drunk was by now fighting crazy. The Aussie had him by one leg – being kicked by the other – while John hung onto one arm and struggled with the other for a firm grip on his hair. Together they finally managed to lift him and flung him with full force against the hut wall. He slithered down the wall, crumpled onto the floor and stayed there.

By this time I had tottered to my feet. Blood pouring down my face and neck from a wide gash on my head soaked into my shirt and dripped onto the floor. John and the Aussie got a greatcoat around me with some difficulty – I was still a bit confused and kept reeling about, squaring up to them – and supported me between them as we set off for the doctor's hut. The planes were on their homeward flight and as we got outside the all clear sounded and the perimeter lights came on again. The doctor saw us limping across the yard and opened his door as we reached it.

'Why you people can't get pissed without half killing each other, Christ only knows!' he grumbled. They sat me down on a stool, above which hung a powerful electric light bulb, gave me a shot of hooch for medicinal purposes and kept a firm grip on me on either side as the doctor, with the speed of long practice, deftly cut away the hair from around the gash and inserted eight stitches.

I insisted on walking back to the hut unaided and though still rather unsteady I was managing quite well by the time we reached it. I was going to give that dirty bastard something to remember me by and it had to be now.

Inside the hut the light was on and the inebriated stevedore was sprawled out on his bunk snoring. I went over and shook him awake roughly. He lumbered up and I set to work on him with my fists. It wasn't very long before he had had enough and crawled back onto his bunk out of the way to safety and I went back to mine feeling satisfied.

Before many weeks had passed John and I had run through every form of entertainment that even this cosmopolitan collection could provide. Boxing, wrestling, sports of all kinds, getting drunk on poisonous liquor – it all palled. Nothing has any objective when you are living in confinement and won't resign yourself to it.

Yet somehow we were never reduced to the last resort of the hopelessly frustrated – violence for its own sake. It was common enough, a symptom of the sense of impotent helplessness that gnawed visibly at the minds of men who in other circumstances were ordinarily decent, quiet human beings. Frequently, this violence took the form of pitched battles between the white Americans and their coloured countrymen, armed with baseball bats, broken bottles and knives. After my victory over 'Kid Silver', it was tacitly assumed that I would be part of the white American faction, and my refusal to take sides made life rather unpleasant for me at times, but I saw no reason to join in a dispute which was nothing to do with me.

The days began to drag. John and I became restless, contemplating new ways of escape. We even joined several volunteer working parties to explore this as a possible means, although escaping from working parties was always disapproved of by camp leaders. And then a completely new diversion presented itself.

One day, in about the middle of May 1944, a curious fellow visited the camp. His arrival had been preceded by the circulation of a leaflet within the camp. It read as follows:

> Fellow countrymen! We of the British Free Corps are fighting for you!
>
> We are fighting with the best of Europe's youth to preserve our European civilisation and our common cultural heritage from the menace of Jewish Communism. Make no mistake about it! Europe includes England. Should Soviet Russia ever overcome Germany and other European countries fighting with her, nothing on this earth would save the continent from Communism, and our own country would inevitably succumb. We are British. We love England and all it stands for. Most of us have fought on the battlefields of France, of Libya, Greece, in Italy and many of our comrades in arms are lying there – sacrificed in this war of Jewish revenge. We felt then we were being lied to and betrayed.
>
> Now we know it for certain.
>
> This conflict between England and Germany is racial suicide. We must unite and take up arms against the common enemy. We ask you to come into our ranks and fight shoulder to shoulder with us for Europe and for England.

The contents of the leaflet, which was published by an organisation called the British Free Corps (of which we had never heard), aroused very little interest. Somebody, motivated more by a confused sense of loyalty than knowledge of human nature, hung bundles of them in the latrine. The gesture was no doubt well intentioned, but there is in fact no better place for the undisturbed contemplation of any tract. Despite this, however, the propaganda fell on stony ground. A large percentage of the prisoners were only too glad to have landed safely in the comparative comfort and safety of a camp and they weren't going to risk death or injury by venturing forth, particularly at this late stage of the war.

For myself, although I was inclined to agree about the threat of the thing Communism had turned into, and did feel that it was crazy for England and Germany to be at war, I was completely put off by the fighting shoulder to shoulder bit at the end, with its implications that one should be prepared to sacrifice one's life.

Life to me is for living, a thing to strive for, because you are a long time dead and in that condition you have little influence on affairs.

I don't think I was alone in that conviction but, unlike most people, I saw no reason to dress it up as some kind of glorious, socially acceptable ideology. However, even though the contents of a package might be the same, if it hasn't got the familiar label on it, people are going to be very suspicious of it.

If the leaflet was received with predictable apathy, the reception given to its evangelist was equally predictably hostile.

Our visitor was a tall, thin, unhealthy-looking young man of about 22 years of age and obviously very nervous – as well he might be. He was dressed in the uniform of the German SS with an incongruous-looking English Union Jack emblem on the field grey sleeve of his jacket. Closer inspection revealed the words 'British Free Corps' (Britisches Freikorps) on an armband at the cuff. He would have made a poor impression anywhere, but in that German uniform he was nothing but a pathetic clown. He oozed insincerity from every pore.

From his rather disjointed, incoherent talk we gathered that he was looking for recruits among the British prisoners of war to join a unit of the German army to fight against Russia and Communists.

He was promptly rushed out of the camp. His life was threatened by the tough section of British seamen who condemned him out of hand and gladly welcomed the opportunity to act aggressively to some single common object. It was better than fighting among themselves and it made a change.

John and I were as unfavourably impressed as the rest of the inmates by this fidgeting, stammering young man, but such of his talk as we had managed to hear above the vociferous heckling had started us thinking. Lying on our bunks that night, we talked reflectively into the small hours, our quiet conversation punctuated by the snores and murmurs of our sleeping companions.

The message which came clearly across to us was that *here was a chance to get out of prison camp.* We had been exploring avenues of escape and now we had been presented with the most promising one so far. What made it different from any other escape route was the prohibition against collaborating with the enemy in wartime.

It wasn't any *moral* consideration of right and wrong that made us pause because, as far as we were concerned, the question simply didn't arise. For one thing, as we had deliberately refused to take a partisan interest in this war, we did not recognise an 'enemy' side as such. For another, we had no intention of collaborating with anyone: even if we did join the Corps, no one could force us to fight on their behalf. But bitter experience of the official mind made us realise that it conceived of the actions of men only in regulation black and white and we had to weigh up whether we would be jumping out of the prison frying pan into the Allied fire.

It was by now clear that it was only a matter of time before Germany fell and the Allies moved in. We could of course simply have stayed put and waited to be released, but it had never been our way to sit around when there was an active alternative. We fully realised that the present alternative could be deemed a treasonable act punishable perhaps even by the death penalty but – such was our naive belief in the intelligence of mankind! – we did not see how anyone knowing our background could seriously regard us as collaborators. Looking at our past record, how could they? Two vagrant non-combatants, finally imprisoned by the Germans for theft, transported by them as undesirables, escaping from their prisons, undermining their authority and being pushed from one camp to another because we were a headache to any authority. If we were now, in theory, to break the English law against collaborating by joining the Corps, surely no Englishman in his right mind could believe we had been seized with a sudden desire to give practical assistance to the Germans, especially now, at this late stage of the war, when they were clearly on the losing side and we had nothing to gain.

So we talked and reasoned between ourselves. We weighed up the possible disadvantages against the immediate, very real advantage of getting out of the camp and the attendant possibility of getting away from the war altogether (which was all we had ever wanted), and came to the conclusion that the proverbial bird in the hand was worth two in the bush. The decision to join the band of renegades was accompanied by a feeling of having irrevocably burned our boats, but then our whole trail across Europe was littered with the ashes of boats we had burned.

As I write this, more than 30 years have passed. Unlike others in the British Free Corps, I feel no guilt or regret. Whatever I did, I did my way: right or wrong, I made my decision and I stand by it still. Naturally, most people then, and perhaps some now, will write off my actions as traitorous without stopping to define the word or consider its implications. But I feel that my way of thinking and behaving is more comprehensible today than it was 30 years ago. Not because of the benefit of hindsight, but because social attitudes have changed so greatly. It is not a question of patriotism being unfashionable now, of duty being outdated, but of thinking beyond these parochial confines.

The world is a smaller place today, nationality is less well defined than it used to be. The threat now is not to a specific community but to civilisation as a whole, not to any particular land but to our entire earth. By quarrelling among ourselves we jeopardise this civilisation, this earth. Somehow I don't think people today would rally with the same prompt, unquestioning enthusiasm to a mass call to arms, not because they are made of poorer stuff than their fathers, but because they are more aware of the possible consequence of their actions and because they are the inheritors of that social revolution that had its seed in the war.

By the end of the war the beliefs and convictions of a great many people had been completely turned about. The training and traditions in which their patriotism was rooted had been badly shaken. In place of the unquestioning obedience and blind loyalty arose the doubt: why – what's it all for? Once that question was admitted, once the thinking and analysing began, nothing could ever be the same again. You could turn your back on the doubts, refuse to pursue them, but still the easy, comfortable divisions into right and wrong, good and bad, were gone. You could either resign yourself with a sense of morbid, despondent unease, or you could start again and construct for yourself a set of values which were empirical rather than traditional or theoretical. The first basic premise was that your life was your own, you were responsible for yourself and no one had the right to manipulate or use you for their own ends.

I had no intention of letting myself be used by the Free Corps or anybody else. On the contrary, I myself intended to use it much as I would any other escape route.

And so on a day warm with sunshine and prickling with that maddening sense of spring in the air, John and I left Marlag Milag Nord. Our prisoner-of-war outfits had been changed for a garb resembling that of an English seaman. I suppose it was a weak attempt at subterfuge on somebody's part, but to this day the reason for it escapes me, as we made no effort to hide our actions. The German soldier escorting us was uniformed but unarmed and friendly. As soon as he discovered that we understood his language he kept up a lively conversation.

He was amazed when he learned what we intended. '*Was Eben jetzt!*' ('What! Just now indeed!') he exclaimed, surprise overcoming caution, for the remark could have cost him dear, implying, as it did, doubts as to his country's victory despite the propaganda to which he was daily subjected. He was right, though. It was a crazy thing for any Englishman to do at that point in the war.

The guard accompanied us on the train journey from Bremen to Berlin, where he delivered us to a Waffen SS head office in Fehrbelliner Strasse. His duty done, he said goodbye with a friendly handshake and left us alone to face the next chapter of our lives.

Chapter 8

THE BRITISH SS

At the time we joined it, the British Free Corps was little more than a year old, by which time the puny bastard organisation, brainchild of a renegade Englishman, had been adopted by Hitler himself and given a new name.

Its founder, John Amery, had little to do with its development and shaping and yet, strangely, the organisation which he had created seemed to reflect his personal characteristics. It was as unruly and wayward a son as he was. Born into an eminently respectable family – his father was a barrister, Member of Parliament and wartime Cabinet Minister under Churchill – he flouted the conventions of the society in which he was bred with a flagrance which delighted the gossip columnists; he ran up huge debts, went bankrupt and left England for the rather more exciting world of the Spanish Civil War and Franco's Fascists. Still in Europe at the time of the Second World War, he offered his services to the Germans to make propaganda broadcasts to the English. He did in fact make several such broadcasts, the basic theme of which was the same: his belief in the threat of Communism and the need for England and Germany to join forces to combat the danger.

It seems to have been a sincerely held belief and one which motivated his other proposal, which was to raise a corps of British volunteers, recruited from the prison camps, to fight on the Eastern (Russian) Front. It was not an original idea, as many similar forces had been composed from other national groups, and the Germans gave this newcomer their blessing. But, despite their support, the infant British Legion of St George, as Amery called it, was almost stillborn, for the first recruiting drives were a dismal failure and Amery quickly lost heart and interest.

The Germans, however, must have believed it worth saving, for they now adopted the all but abandoned foundling, Hitler himself ordering the preparation of plans for such a force which, he decreed, should be taken under the wing of the SS.

Recruiting was slow, but, eventually, a nucleus was formed, future policies drafted, a uniform approved and with it a new name: the British Free Corps. This change of name was in itself indicative of the breach with Amery, who had practically disappeared from the scene. And yet his organisation was to turn out as prodigal, ineffectual and ill-fated as John Amery himself.

As a fighting unit it never got off the ground, and even if it had it was so small and undisciplined, never numbering more than 35 (see editors' notes) at full strength, that it would have made not the slightest difference on the formidable Eastern Front or anywhere else. To this day I don't know whether it actually got to the front or not. If it did, I certainly wasn't with it: I hadn't the slightest intention of fighting on any front and got out while the going was good.

Broadly speaking, members of the Corps fell into three categories. First, the ardent National Socialists, indoctrinated with Nazi zeal and, no doubt, some self-interest; then, those who joined to get out of prison camps; and finally, the opportunists, individuals prepared to use any vehicle to get where they wanted. John and I came into this last group, but we never managed to achieve the success of one of our fellow opportunists, a quiet Australian who was so unobtrusive that I don't think I even found out what his name was. As a prisoner of war he had made friends with a German girl while a member of a party working on her father's estate. The family were importers of timber from Norway and Sweden, her father holding sufficient military rank and authority to enable him to continue his timber shipping traffic between Scandinavia and Germany throughout the war. When the opportunity presented itself, the Australian jumped at the chance of getting out of the prison camp by joining the British Free Corps, where he was relatively free. After a few weeks within the Corps, he simply disappeared as quietly as he had come and it was eventually filtered through that he, together with his German girlfriend and her entire family, had secretly boarded one of their timber vessels and made their escape to Scandinavia.

That was just the sort of break I was looking for, but, unfortunately for me, it never came up. However, as I sat in the waiting room at Fehrbelliner Strasse on that first day, my principal concern was nothing more momentous than wondering when I was going to get something to eat, after that I would think about the next step.

At last someone came to collect us, the first stage being the inevitable medical examination and the usual abrupt 'Take off your clothes, please!' Our deeply suntanned bodies contrasted oddly with the clinical sterility of the examination centre, where the starched medical manner creased into grunts and nods of approval at our fine physical condition.

We made an even more favourable impression on the homosexual masseur who came next. Fortunately, no one else was around to witness our rejection of his advances, otherwise our career in the BFC could have ceased almost as soon as it began.

More questions, formalities, details, then everyone seemed to lose interest in us again and we were left in another waiting room still wondering when we were going to get some food. It did occur to me, however, that so far we had not been asked to sign any document pledging allegiance to the German cause. In fact, I never did put my name to anything – neither my own nor the one I assumed (Erich Doran) on joining the BFC. Apparently it was customary for members to enrol under a pseudonym, but whether this was to give them a new sense of identity, to protect them in some way, or merely part of the fantasy, I've never been quite sure.

If the object was concealment, then some of them, like Unterscharführer (Sergeant) Peter Butcher, didn't make a very inspired effort. As we were sitting there in the waiting room, a pimply adolescent in the immaculate uniform of an SS sergeant swaggered up and greeted us with the distant friendliness of supercilious authority.

He asked a few aloof questions, including whether we knew Berlin. When we said no, he tried to hide his delight at the chance this gave him to strut. We must, he said condescendingly, accustom ourselves with the world of freedom as quickly as possible. Naturally he felt it his duty to educate us and offered to show us around. We accepted humbly.

We quickly found out that our boy sergeant took the route calculated to attract most recognition of his silver-laced uniform. After the usual landmarks – or those still standing after the Allied bombing – he took us along Kurfürstendamm and Unter den Linden, past the Reich Chancellery with an armed sentry in each of its many doorways. At the sight of the approaching uniform each sentry sprang instantly to attention with a military clang, which Butcher acknowledged each time with the Hitler salute extended with studied disdain. Falling in with the game, John and I gave an excellent performance of being suitably impressed by the childish exhibition of playing at soldiers.

By the time the conducted tour was over, we were rather tired of humouring him, but we still had to bear his company for several hours more as he was to accompany us on the final leg of the journey, from Berlin to Hildesheim. However, the uniform secured us comfortable seats on the train and, much to Butcher's disgust, we showed our appreciation by falling asleep in the middle of one of his monologues.

Hildesheim was probably the most unlikely town for the headquarters of a renegade organisation. It could have come straight out of one of the fairy tales of the Brothers Grimm: little winding streets and crooked sugar-white houses. A quaint place if ever I saw one. After that it came as no surprise to find that the headquarters was located in a former monastery.

Haus Germania, as the monastery was now called, was supposedly in course of conversion to a centre of European culture. It was so crammed with members of the Waffen SS that the relatively few members of the BFC, who had been assigned part of the old monastery, were scarcely noticeable.

In fact, I began to wonder whether they existed at all because as soon as we arrived Butcher disappeared upstairs – to the 'Upper

Sanctum', as we later learnt to call it – and no one else seemed to want to claim us. At last a rather pale and unhappy-looking young man, who introduced himself as Mr Rose (alias Owens), the quartermaster, grudgingly took us in hand. He turned out to be as uncommunicative as Butcher was talkative and we quickly gave up trying to make conversation because he just mumbled his answers inaudibly to the piece of string he kept nervously twisting into knots.

It was a relief when he passed us on to a Corps member with the outstanding original cover name of Tommy Atkins, a complete contrast with his loud mouth and raucous laugh. Slouching along in front of us, Tommy Atkins led the way to the dormitory, a lofty sunlit room with 18 beds, each with its own locker beside it. John and I took over two beds near a large window, prodding the soft mattresses, fingering with wonder the luxury of the clean, blue-and-white-striped sheets. We threw ourselves down, silently enjoying the feel of the mattresses for a few minutes.

Gazing through the open window overlooking the courtyard and garden of the old abbey, I wondered what the monks would have thought of it now. It still seemed so peaceful, the sun shining through the golden laburnum trees of the ancient cloister garden, their blossoms scenting the breeze drifting through the window. We continued to lie there without speaking until, all at once, in unspoken accord, we got up and walked through the cloisters into the garden.

Sitting on a low, crumbling flint wall in the shade of a magnificent copper beech, we talked quietly, comparing our present situation with our much less pleasant past circumstances. The tranquillity of the old garden did not blunt our alertness or raise in us any false illusion of security. Things could turn out to be very awkward indeed, but for the moment we were as well placed as we could hope to be: live for the present and let tomorrow take care of itself.

It took me about a week to get the measure of the Corps and the sort of people with whom I was dealing. I did not trouble to find out the real identities of most of them, partly because it did not interest me a great deal and partly because we all had an instinctive mutual mistrust of each other, which was, I suppose, to be expected in the circumstances. Each man played out a role, a pose, starting with the new name and identity he was compelled to assume on joining. It was often difficult for an observer to discover the borderline between reality and fantasy, and I am sure that even the actors themselves confused the two and were incapable of distinguishing between mundane fact and wishful thinking. But with some, such as Butcher, the play-acting was obvious for all to see and it was apparent that they were aping characters and personalities they greatly admired and lived out a pure fantasy.

Promotion in the BFC was unknown, but there was a ranking military hierarchy of sorts. As long as the Corps members were not too obvious a nuisance, the SS seemed content to keep a sort of watching brief in the person of one of their Hauptsturmführer, known to us as Captain Roepke, who must have had one of the most highly polished leather belts and pistol holders in Germany; the quartermaster, Rose, took an inordinate pride in cleaning and shining the Captain's equipment, performing this small voluntary task with such zeal that it caused him real pain if anyone else touched it, in case they left finger marks on the gleaming black leather.

Theoretically in charge of the Corps, which I rapidly came to regard as a comedy troupe, was a small elite body variously called 'The Big Six' or 'The Big Five'. For myself, I would put 'Those Up Top' (as we knew them, since they inhabited the upper regions of Haus Germania) at four and two halves, and that's a generous estimate.

The most prominent figure was certainly our Berlin boy soldier Peter Butcher. He was the result of a union between an English father and an over-protective German mother, which produced an odd mixture of childish arrogance and premature disregard for the well-being of his associates. A rash, incautious exhibitionist, he nevertheless managed to cover considerable cowardice and cunning with a thin veneer of good breeding. One of his principal concerns was to create an impression of being interesting and erudite, and generally he managed to give the impression of being at the same time the strutting Nazi, the oriental mystic and intellectual dispenser of destinies. More German than the Germans themselves, he nevertheless basked in the curiosity aroused by his being an Englishman in wartime Germany. He had already spread the tale of his having had to flee England because he had killed a Jew in a street fight, but personally I gave that very little credence.

I was more prepared to believe in his erudition, for clever and intelligent he undoubtedly was. But during one of his infrequent moods of friendly condescension while he was with John and me, I noticed that he repeatedly took a small slip of paper from his pocket and read from it softly to himself. In answer to my eventual look of enquiry, he told us it was a Latin quotation which he was learning by heart because, 'It's easy to lead a conversation into the required direction where such a quotation can be used to impress your listeners with the extent of your learning.' He was quite serious.

The incident certainly dispelled my inclination to admire his scholarship, and it seemed to me that that line of thought inspired most of his behaviour.

Tug Montgomery, too, lived half in a world full of weird dreams, one in which he was a celebrated general, vested with extensive powers. His choice of cover name was no accident; asked by German acquaintances if he was related to the great British general of that time, he gave no definite answer but preened himself visibly, subtly creating in his audience's mind the thought that he could well be. In fact, I was frequently asked by Germans how it was that such a distinguished person came to be in the Free Corps!

His rank in the BFC was actually that of sergeant, and a typically bawling, swearing sergeant who hid behind his rank. Although military parades were virtually non-existent in the Corps, there were occasions when he managed to muster enough of us to march through Hildesheim with him strutting at the head of the column, encouraging us to sing in imitation of a German marching song. In our case it was usually some well-known bawdy English barrack room ballad, or the BFC's own signature tune or marching song, the words of which Montgomery himself composed. To the tune of 'Bless 'em All!', we aired it vigorously through the streets of Hildesheim:

> It's onward to Moscow we go,
> Up to our cobblers in snow,
> Digging slip trenches through six feet of ice,
> Living on sauerkraut and tortured by lice;

Oh, we'll never get rid of them all,
As over our bodies they crawl,
They don't give the shits to the Red Russian blitz,
As they do to the British Free Corps.

I always felt somewhat embarrassed by these childish public demonstrations and took part reluctantly only when they were completely unavoidable, but Montgomery was in his egocentric element. He was a man who loved being reminded of how clever and marvellous he was, how attractive to women. After himself, his principal interest in life was the pursuit of women. No doubt he saw himself as some writers with more imagination than truth have described him, as a handsome man with rakish charm. In fact he was just over middle height, a tubby figure with pale-blue staring eyes and a small petulant mouth.

This chubby, pot-bellied Puck was more irresponsible than most of us, but in the presence of women his behaviour became positively ridiculous. Everything he did was in an effort to attract their attention. He would often sit on the steps of Haus Germania bawling out obscene English songs in his raucous voice, accompanying himself on a Red Cross guitar, his pale-blue eyes staring from window to window overlooking the courtyard to see if any of the girl secretaries were watching. His favourite song was the filthiest version of 'My Girl Salome' – perhaps it was a good thing he didn't sing it in German.

He eventually contracted gonorrhoea from a Danish SS girl. (She was not a Gestapo agent, as one misinformed author would have it; there must have been literally thousands of similarly infected girls in Germany at the time, the inevitable flotsam of war.) Montgomery, despite advice, tried to treat himself, obviously without success, and then characteristically declared that his failure to effect a cure was intentional as it enabled him to infect other people and he was endeavouring to contaminate as many as possible so that he could hinder the German war effort. As he said, combining business with pleasure. I honestly think that he believed at least in part in what he said because it helped console the nagging feelings of guilt which he, like many of the Free Corps, felt hidden in the remote depths of his mind. However, when pressure was eventually brought to bear on the

Free Corps to play an active part and they were sent to the front line to fight the Russians, Tug immediately entered hospital for treatment.

If any one of Those Up Top were regarded by the majority of the Corps with favour and without too much suspicion then it was the jovial, easy-going Courlander. A lean, energetic type who spent hardly any time with the Corps – being nearly always on a journey somewhere in Germany recruiting, or on the pretext of doing so – he kept busy doing nothing better than the rest of us. He interfered with nobody and was always polite and friendly. If girls were handy, he enjoyed their company and took advantage of any favours they might provide but, unlike Montgomery, he never exerted himself to obtain them.

Courlander's weakness was of a different order: he was a compulsive weaver of fabulous tales. It wasn't that he had some great ambition to become a brigadier of a strong British force fighting for Germany, but merely that he couldn't resist the opportunity to let loose his vivid imagination whenever he had an audience. He could, and did, fabricate stories of the strength and influence of the BFC and the support behind it, which no doubt made him the ideal recruiting officer. In his fertile mind the 30 or so slippery, conniving young opportunists and zealots who made up the Corps grew to formidable proportions, but I don't think he was ever foolish enough to be taken in by his own fantasy. When slightly drunk or simply in a fit of exuberance, he would sometimes confess to his tall tales, bragging about them and laughing at those who were credulous enough to swallow them.

'Teeny Weeny' Woods would hardly have qualified for Big Five status by virtue of his size, but his intelligence and cunning were equal to that of Butcher. He hated Butcher with the vicious jealousy tinged with grudging respect of a person who has to watch his own desires and ambitions being achieved by somebody else. A slightly effeminate man, he had none of his rival's ostentatious assurance and lacked any gift for making friends and influencing people.

To these four pseudo-leaders – Butcher, Montgomery, Courlander and Woods – whose attempts to gain authority were continually frustrated by their undisciplined, wayward troupe, I would add only Milton and Handrupe as a half-unit each.

Milton was one of those young men one is more inclined to pity than blame. Indecisive, nervous, hesitant, I was always astonished that this unaggressive fellow should have found the guts to take a step as hazardous as joining the BFC. But he had, and in his own quiet fashion he was intent on enjoying the euphoric life the Corps provided. Nothing he did or said was original. He lived in the shadow of greatness cast by the more imposing members of Those Up Top. For a short, glorious period in his mediocre life he found himself a member of a small exclusive elite, hobnobbing with quiet, intelligent Woods, arrogant Butcher and entertaining Courlander, and he was always amazed by his own achievement.

It was Milton who attempted to recruit John and myself back in Marlag Milag Nord. I say 'attempted' because he was in no way personally responsible for us joining. If we had never seen Milton I am certain we would have learnt about the Corps from some other source and the result would have been the same. Certainly there was nothing remotely inspiring about Milton himself.

Handrupe's recruiting efforts must have been as unspectacular as Milton's. A small, frail, unassuming man, he was careful to avoid opposition or trouble, his most notable characteristics being his fastidious cleanliness and the care with which he wore the SS uniform. He did not seek company and passed his time in making a wonderful show of being busy while not actually doing anything, thus bringing no undue attention to himself.

The Big Five might have become six if Buck Rogers, a Canadian recruit, had been less headstrong and individualistic. In the short time he was with the Corps, he did take over some of the few instruction duties and act in place of Butcher on occasion, but I hadn't been there very long before he left, unable to reconcile his views and his way of doing things with Those Up Top.

I rather liked Rogers and Courlander, but I had very little time for the others. However, once I had worked out the daily routine, I found I didn't need to see much of them or my fellow members and, compared with the rigours of my earlier existence, life in the Corps was fairly pleasant and normal.

The day started with a breakfast parade at 8 a.m. and at least 50 per cent of us managed to attend this – the other half were either scrambling over the wall at the back of the barracks or had simply refused to turn up, having found more desirable company elsewhere. Later on they would plead accident or illness as their excuse and almost invariably get away with it.

Tug Montgomery usually called the parade to attention for inspection by Rogers or Butcher. During the inspection, Montgomery would strut about in the background, preening himself like a fat peacock for the benefit of any female SS staff that might be watching from the windows overlooking the courtyard. The parade over, we would be marched to the dining room for a good breakfast and to collect the daily ration of sausage and bread or substitute cheese.

If the BFC ever had any real purpose, it was certainly not apparent at the time I joined. Consequently, once we returned to billets after breakfast, the leaders didn't really know what to do with us and were hard put to find something to keep us occupied. Obviously, it was desirable that we should have some instruction on National Socialism and on political ideology in general, and Hauptsturmführer Roepke set some store by this. Lectures were set up by Butcher, Rogers and Handrupe, but nobody was interested. I think the only one I went to was given by Handrupe, but no one even made a pretence of listening to him and he was left with rows of empty chairs to talk to. There was a feeble attempt at physical culture but it was so half-hearted as to be useless, and John and I got in our own private training with one or two of the others with the aid of some simple equipment we managed to get hold of and kept in a garden shed in a quiet part of the grounds.

I think John and I must have held the record for not attending any lecture or organised activity: as far as I recall, we were present at about six parades in the whole time we were with the Free Corps. Indeed, if anybody had succeeded in performing the nearly impossible task of getting John out of bed in time for morning parade, he could have congratulated himself. No one below the rank of German Hauptsturmführer would have dared to insist, for the Corps members quickly learnt to respect our 'fistic' abilities and were not anxious to alienate us.

We didn't even bother to attend pay parades to collect the few marks paid to us because most of our financial needs were supplied by our black-market projects, the trade being mostly in chocolate and cigarettes and one or two luxury items which we received as Corps members or from Red Cross parcels – fortunately for me, I have never smoked.

It has always amazed me that the disciplined, efficient Waffen SS put up with us in their midst: a handful of enemy countrymen who flouted the rules and regulations, laughed openly at their militarism, mimicked and mocked them by throwing up our hands in the Nazi salute with exaggerated enthusiasm and yelling 'Heil Hitler!' louder and more ostentatiously than necessary. We stole their rations and their women, we were insolent and abusive, obstructive and unmanageable. How it was possible for intelligent, experienced German officials and army officers to believe they could ever make a useful force out of a crazy collection like us is incomprehensible. There were so few of us, absolutely at their disposal, and yet they let us get away with behaviour unheard of in their own ranks. I rather felt that if any people could be naive enough to be taken in by such a bunch of psychopaths, eccentrics and egotists, they deserved to lose the war – or any other project they embarked on.

Writers purportedly documenting the BFC have made much of the sexual exploits of its members, and the general portrait which emerges is of some unnatural creature prowling the streets of wartime Germany with a bundle of propaganda leaflets in one hand and his penis in the other, sowing the Nazi doctrine and his wild oats, dragging down the knickers of every available female.

Of course there *were* available females and of course we took the opportunities offered, but our activities were scarcely anything out of the ordinary. These things happen everywhere at all times in normal circumstances, let alone in wartime, when it is a truism that the constant threat of death and disaster naturally engenders the procreative instincts. The women of battered Germany were no exception, and nor were the BFC members, who, as mad or as bad as they may have been in other respects, were in this respect only behaving normally. There were the compulsive womanisers like Montgomery, but that was a tendency peculiar to him and not to the BFC as a whole. Then, too, maybe we had rather more opportunity and freedom than the average soldier – or the average man, come to that – and an abundance of willing females. Given all that, it would have been unnatural if we hadn't taken full advantage of the situation!

But not all these encounters were casual or totally calculated to satisfy a temporary lust, for many of us had women whom we kept very close to our hearts. Sex apart, there is a need for female company, for their companionship, their tenderness and gentle affection, more perhaps in time of war than at any other, and it is my view that too many writers (in response to audience demand perhaps) tend to emphasise the purely sensational and ignore the deeper but less spectacular relationships which undoubtedly grew up.

Female companionship has always been of the greatest importance to me. In the harsh crudeness of my life at that time it was a haven of warmth and sweetness, one of the very few flowers on the dung heap. I cherished that flower and to the end of my days I will cherish the memory of the woman who became my touchstone, my point of reference when everything around us was crumbling chaotically, who brought love and peace into a world crazed with violence. Rare orchids grow in strange haunts, but even so the headquarters of a crackpot organisation was probably the last place I would have dreamt of being fortunate enough to come across one. But I was, and that on my first evening in Hildesheim.

As John and I sat under the copper beech on that first evening, discussing our present circumstances, our rather serious train of thought was interrupted by the quick, light tap-tap of female footsteps approaching down the stone-flagged corridor. We both pricked up our ears and focused our attention expectantly on the door to the cloisters. It opened and a girl, neatly dressed in SS uniform, appeared. Perhaps that first picture of her is the one that stays most clearly in my mind: the slight figure dwarfed by the huge archway, the evening sun just catching her short mid-blonde hair. She wasn't beautiful but the rather round face was open and attractively pleasant.

Neither John nor I made any comment and we continued with our conversation, but I had glanced quickly at the sun to establish the time and the next evening I was back there at five o'clock in case she passed that way again. Things happened as I hoped. Again the brisk footsteps; again the small upright figure framed in the archway. This time I greeted her in German and she smiled and stopped to exchange a few words. I noticed the direct gaze of her hazel eyes, the pleasant cadence of her voice, the ready smile with its hint of mischief. I found out that her name was Anneliese Nitzschner and that she was secretary to the Kommandant of Haus Germania himself.

As the friendship between his superior's secretary and me grew, Hauptsturmführer Roepke was heard to remark: 'What in heaven's name can an intelligent German SS girl like Fraülein Nitzschner find so interesting in the muscular Englishman?' It probably did seem an unlikely association to him, but then I don't suppose it occurred to him that a man can have both brains and brawn and that the bond which grew up between Anneliese and myself was based not only on mutual physical attraction but also on mutual strength of character and spirit.

'My dear little enemy', as I affectionately nicknamed her, compensated for her lack of inches with a gigantic soul and enormous courage. Right from the start she took tremendous risks for my sake, never demanding or expecting any more than that we should enjoy each other's company. Her friendship and unremitting love stand out for me like a beacon on a dark night, unquenched by the hardship and misery that were to come.

And I, for my part, would live through all that again rather than forego the experience of having known her.

Chapter 9

HITLER'S BASTARD

By the time I had been in the Corps a few weeks I had it summed up: a bastard gleam in Hitler's eye that would never get as far as the delivery room, if only for lack of time. It was so obvious that the end of the war was in sight that John and I decided to shelve any immediate plans for escape, just waiting to see what each day might bring, and meanwhile we made the best of the situation. All in all, we didn't do too badly.

Right from the beginning, as usual, we took the precaution of asserting ourselves very firmly, knowing from experience that those who didn't were simply trampled upon. This time, however, we did the job a little too thoroughly and wound up as the Corps' law enforcement squad. It all started with a trifling argument in the dormitory one night, again over a refusal to listen to a polite request to turn out the light.

Among the girls smuggled into the barracks one night was a plump, willing little blonde called Gerda, who had two admirers in the Corps. Gerda was already in bed with one of them when the second one came in, disconsolate at having found no replacement talent at the local café and then downright disagreeable when he turned on the light and discovered, among the frilly undies, pink bottoms and breasts revealed by the naked glare, the lovely Gerda stretched out beside his rival.

There wasn't much he could do about it and he retired to his lonely bed muttering something about people having perpetual orgies when others wanted to sleep – and without turning the light out. He ignored the urgent cries for darkness so someone, wanting to continue his interrupted session in private, nipped out of bed and turned it off, but before he was back under the covers the light went on again. This time I turned it off, adding a rider to the effect that if it didn't stay that way he was going to have cause to remember the occasion every time he saw an electric switch in the future.

'If you want to entertain those bloody whores go some place else – I want to sleep!' came the sour reply and once more the room was illuminated.

Under normal circumstances that would be fair comment, but here things were different and this was one of those occasions when positive action was called for. As I climbed out of bed again, a hush fell over the room. If it is possible to look menacing when one is stark naked and picking one's way through a foam of bras and knickers, then I suppose I did. I flicked off the light, knowing it would come on again immediately and as it did so I smashed my right hand into the side of the poor fellow's jaw. He crumpled slowly down the wall into an unmoving heap on the floor. Silence.

Gerda sat upright in naked horror. '*Himmel! Der Junge ist tot!*' she exclaimed, going pale all over, but a little while later he was heard to scramble to his feet and totter unsteadily to his bed, so obviously he wasn't dead.

Little or no comment was made about the incident, but it had the desired effect of achieving a grudging respect among our comrades. It was a trivial enough affair, but it impressed Tug Montgomery, who saw in us allies worth having. He tried to cultivate our goodwill, even invited us to put our beds in his room – we graciously declined – and eventually suggested we be appointed the BFC's military police, an honorary position which carried neither rank nor salary. The idea was so in keeping with the rest of the farce that it appealed to our sense of the ridiculous and, of course, we were quick to see that it could mean more freedom for us, so we accepted.

For the short time that John and I were in office we must have been the most popular law enforcers that existed in any military organisation. Butcher was the only one who made any criticism, but to Hauptsturmführer Roepke it was quite immaterial who was doing what in his troublesome little unit. The men, of course, knew we wouldn't do anything to upset their private concerns as long as they did nothing to inconvenience our plans. All except Walters, one of the few Corps members who seemed to have absolutely no redeeming features to his character. Most of them may have been fanatical, ruthless, inconsiderate, bad tempered, but they could sometimes be entertaining and interesting to talk to: Walters wasn't even intelligent.

One of his less endearing habits was to sit in the local café in Hildesheim cleaning his nails with a nine-inch-long SS dagger, leering menacingly at passers-by, his close-set little eyes darting restlessly about like two eager, blood-hungry ferrets. It seemed to keep him happy and no one else would have minded if one day he hadn't gone too far and stolen a Walther automatic pistol from the holster of an SS man in the restaurant. Not content with that, the brainless ape brought it back and flashed it around the billets.

Montgomery got worried about the German police investigating the affair – and exposing some of the BFC members' less creditable activities – and consulted his police officers.

We shrugged our shoulders – what was it to do with us, what were we supposed to do? He nearly exploded with indignation.

'You're the bloody police – arrest him! Two fine sodding coppers you are!' Adding, as he suddenly remembered his dignity: 'And that's an order!'

So, not wanting the German police nosing around any more than Montgomery did, we went looking for Walters and tracked him down at the Café Korso, a well-known rendezvous for soldiers and the local girls. Stopping outside, we peered through the window before we went in and then looked at each other, grinning rather self-consciously, because we had never done that kind of thing before.

'I don't like being a bleeding copper!' John muttered, as if we had any choice. 'Oh, well – come on, let's get the bleeding thing done with!' He grabbed the door handle decisively and we strode in.

Walters was sitting well back in the room, trying to make his intentions understood by a tall blonde waitress, his gestures leaving little to anyone's imagination. The lecherous leer twisted into a sullen snarl as we loomed up over him, spoiling his play.

'What do you couple of bastards want?' he growled, correctly interpreting the expression on our faces.

We told him. He didn't like it and began to get loudly argumentative.

'Keep quiet!' I hissed. 'You're going to do as we want. It's up to you – but if you don't, I'll wipe the bloody floor of this café with you!'

Walters hesitated, blinked uncertainly and then obviously thought better of taking us on. 'All right!' he muttered ungraciously, shovelling himself noisily out of his chair. He lurched out of the room with us helpfully propping him up on either side. Once back at Haus Germania a jubilant Tug Montgomery placed him under house arrest. The stolen pistol still hadn't been found but Montgomery, swelling with importance, expected it to be recovered at any time.

After a couple of days Walters' fate was decided and he was transferred to a special camp – his life wouldn't have been worth a brass button if he were sent back to an ordinary PoW camp. Now that it was all over I felt rather sorry for him and John and I would take him extra food, cigarettes and sweets while he was in the local jail awaiting transportation. Walters felt rather sorry for himself, too, and would pour his heart out to us, telling us how guns had already landed him in jail before the war. Eventually, he got so morose he even told John where he had hidden the SS Walther automatic, adding piously that we must return it to its rightful owner for him.

John told me about this conversation the following day, adding that he had in fact already returned the pistol to its rightful owner. I was impressed but curious.

'Who is the owner, then?' I asked.

John pointed firmly to himself. 'Me!' he replied. 'By the law of the spoils of war it is now my property. I'm sure it'll be more useful to us than anybody else, even if only to make a few marks on the black market.'

Naturally we didn't tell Montgomery about the gun, but the episode as a whole gained us his increasing confidence. For my part, however, I still didn't feel inclined to trust him but his influence did prove invaluable, if only because Montgomery had the authority needed to obtain the all-important papers which allowed military personnel to travel by train. John and I made full use of this, visiting Berlin almost every weekend, ostensibly on 'official business' but once that was over we were left more or less to our own devices, John generally disappearing off to see Lena, whom he had met on one of his first visits to the city and fallen madly in love with. Lena worked in Berlin for the Reisebüro, the department responsible for the issue of all travel warrants, and was, like John, bilingual in German and English, having been brought up partly in London. The attraction between her and John was instant and mutual, and once he went off with her to her flat in a Berlin suburb that was the last I saw of him until it was time to return to Hildesheim.

Berlin was certainly a change after quiet Hildesheim, where an enemy plane was seldom seen, and the noise and devastation of the capital hit one like a physical shock. It was impossible to get from one side of the city to the other without having to take cover from an air raid at least once, but the citizens themselves were so used to it that they seemed more irritated at the interruption than frightened. As they crowded into the shelters waiting for the all clear to sound, they scarcely seemed worried about the earthquaking crashes all around them, only impatient to get on with whatever business it was they had had to abandon. There were exceptions, of course. On one occasion, when the rest of the occupants of an air raid shelter had piled out immediately following the all clear, John and I were detained by a near-hysterical man who rushed up and grabbed us, gabbling something incoherently which we finally interpreted as the fact that the shock of the raid had brought his pregnant wife into labour and he hadn't the faintest idea what to do about it.

At first it didn't seem to me that there was much we could do about it either – where do you find a midwife or doctor for the asking after an air raid! – but the poor fellow was obviously so distraught that I couldn't just leave him. I'd seen many an animal born – puppies, lambs, rabbits – human beings couldn't be so very different.

'My good fellow!' I cried with a heartiness and assurance I didn't feel. 'You are extremely fortunate, for I just happen to be a doctor of medicine and this' – I introduced John, who bowed gravely – 'is my colleague, a professor specialising in the study of women!'

'Oh, thank God – but, please, learned doctors – my wife, my wife!' the wretched man stammered beseechingly, almost dragging us to the far end of the shelter, where his wife was lying, moaning loudly.

Very fortunately for us, the baby was in a hurry to be born and seemed to know the routine better than any of us, starting to introduce himself to the world even as I tested the edge of my pocket knife and cleaned it. About the only thing I knew about the delivery of human babies was that they, like animals, had an umbilical cord which had to be severed, but as women didn't generally bite through it as did their four-legged counterparts, some sharp instrument was called for and my pocket knife was all I had. It served the purpose admirably and, after I had tied the cord in a knot, I gave the infant the obligatory smack to welcome it to the outside word, to which it responded in kind with a yell of protest.

Cleaning up the child and its mother as best we could, we wrapped it in one of her garments and then called out to the trembling father, who stood fearfully at a distance.

'Our congratulations, sir – your wife has just presented you with a fine son!'

The man's anxious face broke into a radiant smile as he came and took the child hesitantly in his arms. The look of pure wonder on his face as he gazed at that crumpled morsel of humanity touched me, as did the gesture of simple love and thankfulness as he took his wife's limp hand and kissed it, almost as though he were sealing a bond between the three of them.

'We shall never be able to repay what you have done for us today. I thank you from the bottom of my heart!' he said turning to us, his eyes shining with fervent gratitude.

I waved away his thanks airily. 'We are glad to have been able to help you. Just let your wife rest a little now; she's fine, of course, but it won't do any harm to call in at a hospital as soon as you can,' I added, more for my own peace of mind than his. Leaving the little nativity scene, John and I walked out into the death and devastation left by the air raid.

How mad can we all become! In peacetime you hang a man for one murder: in war, the more he kills the more medals you hang on his tunic.

I was right not to trust Montgomery. On some of our trips to Berlin he entrusted us with messages for Major Vivian Stranders, a funny little man working in an office in Fehrbelliner Strasse which controlled the BFC, from which we subsequently realised that Montgomery kept Stranders well informed of everything happening in the Corps with a view to making his own passage easier if and when the need arose.

Stranders was an unusual and interesting character, a shrewd businessman and a spy for both England and Germany in the past. He was an Englishman with a somewhat chequered background, as he had settled in Germany and been granted German citizenship soon after he joined the National Socialist Party. He had been appointed a major in the Waffen SS and put in charge of the office dealing with British prisoners-of-war affairs and, later on, was attached to the England Committee to liaise between it and the BFC.

Some authors have attempted to glamorise him as a tall, typical British-officer type. He was not. In fact, he was small, overbearing and theatrical. He couldn't do much about his physical stature, which earned him the nickname of 'the Gnome' among us, but the pompous exterior covered an adventurous spirit and tremendously cunning nature.

As far as we were concerned, the most dreaded thing about the Gnome was his well-known tea ceremony, an over-dramatised ritual of would-be elegance to which selected people were invited to take tea with him in the English manner – his way of impressing the Germans by being more English than the English. John and I and another BFC member, an ex-RAF gunner named Lofty Nixon, were on one occasion compelled to suffer a whole evening of this, unable to make our escape until 10.30 p.m. Safely out in the street at last, Lofty blew out his cheeks, mopped his forehead and spoke for all of us: 'And not one solitary drink of bloody Schnapps the whole sodding night!'

On one occasion, when we visited Stranders at his office in June 1944, he offered to give us a lift back to our lodgings in Berlin. It was his way of showing us how privileged he was: he had just been provided with a car by the SS, whereas he had until quite recently had to make his way on foot or by public transport. On the way he had to make a call at Grünewald, the wireless broadcasting house and headquarters of the German propaganda organisation. It was here that we made the acquaintance of the founder of the BFC, John Amery, and of the owner of one of the most famous voices of the Second World War, William Joyce, popularly known in England as Lord Haw Haw.

Stranders was clearly a frequent visitor at Grünewald, for the sentry saluted smartly and allowed us to pass with scarcely a glance at his identity card. Once inside, we descended countless steps to a room where some kind of party appeared to be in progress, although we later gathered that such social events were usual daily occurrences. The desperate gaiety, the defiant bravado that hung with the smell of alcohol and cigarette smoke in that crowded room repulsed me. Stranders hurriedly introduced us to various people before he disappeared about his own business, telling us to stay on and enjoy ourselves. We shook hands here and there, the names hardly registering except for the two that we knew so well.

I stood before a small man in a shabby blue serge suit and heard Major Stranders say: 'William Joyce'. I took a small, weak, clammy hand in mine. It left a cold patch in my palm for minutes afterwards. The sad, pale face was scarred from cheek to chin down one side. The man seemed to me a corpse, a walking, talking corpse.

His voice, which I had heard so often over the radio, had created in my imagination a figure totally different from the inoffensive little creature standing here before me in Grünewald. He reminded me of the owner of a dirty bookshop, continually washing his hands with invisible soap and water, putting up a futile struggle to make an impression of importance with the person to whom he was talking. I couldn't get the idea out of my head that the voice had gained its strength by sucking the vitality from its owner and creator, sapping him, draining him, and that it would eventually destroy him – which, of course, is exactly what it did.

It seemed to me ironic that of all the doomed people in that painfully lively gathering the least imposing and attractive should be the two most notorious: William Joyce and John Amery. The latter was sitting on a sofa between two young women, trying hard to keep them interested with his chatter. He didn't appear to have much else going in his favour and one of the women quickly transferred her attention to John, whose suntanned good looks contrasted glowingly with the washed-out bureaucrat sitting next to her. I myself scarcely exchanged many words with Amery, for my attention was pleasantly distracted by Margaret Joyce.

Mrs Joyce was a far more attractive and lively proposition than her husband. As I sat uncomfortably on the edge of a chair, feeling somewhat out of place in that gathering, I felt someone touch my shoulder and ask why I wasn't drinking. I looked up into a very pleasant, smiling face but before I could reply that I simply didn't feel like drinking, she had handed me a glass and seated herself beside me, crossing her silk-stockinged legs. I observed that they were long and very shapely. She asked a few trivial questions, made some small talk, but I could see she was about as interested in social chat as I was. When there is every likelihood that you're going to be blown off the face of the earth the next day, or in the next hour, you don't waste your time making polite conversation to an attractive woman – there are better ways to spend it with her.

We turned off the radio before the evening's propaganda broadcast, before that voice filled the bedroom and dragged us back into its war.

William Joyce was hanged for treason not many months later, sentenced by an English court of law, even though he was not a British national. In my mind I can see the strong, tauntingly aristocratic voice, Lord Haw Haw, standing grinning beside the hangman, looking down the drop at the small dangling corpse of William Joyce, satisfied at last in achieving its aim. That voice will live on; it will find another host to feed upon and bring it further fame. It will be heard again, for it spoke many a true word; those who sit in moral judgement, righteously pronouncing upon the actions and motivations of their fellows about which they can have no personal knowledge, would do well to recall that sarcastic voice commenting: 'If treason is successful, then who dares to call it treason?'

The concessions, the regular trips to Berlin, made the policeman's lot a relatively happy one, but the job rather lost its charm when it came to routine duties back in Hildesheim, particularly when Those Up Top decided, now that they had three policemen, that discipline must be tightened.

The appointment of the third, McCarthy, came after ours and he took the job much more seriously than we did, being somewhat militaristic and ambitious for power in the Corps. McCarthy was an odd mixture. He had been a soldier in the British Army up to the time of his capture and by all accounts a good, courageous one, and yet now he seemed to be obsessed with the idea of being a mercenary, willing to fight for anything or anybody as long as the price was right. He talked a lot about having taken part in the Spanish Civil War, but there were parts of his story which didn't ring true. His slight physique and sharp, pointed features contrasted with the tough character of the 'professional soldier' which he dearly loved to play. He was always so keen to demonstrate to us how such a soldier should behave that I was quite surprised, puzzled even, by his lack of personal aggression and reluctance to take part in any real conflict.

However, the role he assumed made him a natural choice as a law enforcer and John and I accepted him as a colleague with as good a grace as possible. Before long the three of us were allotted a small side room as a dormitory with the intention of keeping us apart from the rest of the Corps members. No doubt this was one of Montgomery's ideas, designed to get us to act more seriously and responsibly and to make us consider ourselves a class above the others. If so, his plan failed utterly as far as John and I were concerned, and one of our lapses nearly ended our career as officers of the law.

It was becoming more common for members to be confined to barracks as a disciplinary measure for relatively trivial offences and one evening John and I found ourselves, bored beyond description, guarding a detainee. Everyone else had gone to town, so we decided to join the prisoner in his room. For a while we tried to read or chat, but time hung heavily. Thoughts of Anneliese in her cosy little flat just around the corner chased through my mind. John shifted restlessly. The prisoner was the only one who seemed resigned to the situation.

Suddenly, John got up. 'Fuck this for a game of soldiers – let's go to Hildesheim!'

'Great idea! But what do we do with this fellow?' I indicated the prisoner stretched peacefully on his bunk humming 'Show Me the Way to Go Home'.

'Take the poor sod with us!' John replied, as if nothing could be more obvious, and turning to the 'poor sod', asked him if he wanted to come.

'Just as you like, cockies – I'm only the prisoner!' he said, grinning cheerfully.

'Stop playing the prat!' John threatened him. 'You just promise us not to piss off so that you're here for tomorrow and we'll all go out somewhere better than this.'

The prisoner duly gave his word and we made arrangements to meet at 10 p.m. at the Ravenstock Inn, so that we could all return together, and then went our separate ways.

Where the other two went I've no idea, but I hope they spent the time as pleasantly as I did. Several hours later I was dragged back to harsh reality by an urgent knocking on the door of Anneliese's flat. There stood the prisoner, grinning as cheerfully as ever and saying it was nearly midnight and high time for us to get back to barracks. John was nowhere to be seen so we decided not to wait, not knowing where to look for him.

Scuttling through the darkened streets of Hildesheim I laughed softly: if any of the inhabitants had seen the two fleeing figures in SS trooper uniform they wouldn't have thought for one moment that they were two Englishmen: a prisoner and his escort! At times like this I couldn't help realising how ridiculously comic the whole BFC set-up was.

Lights-out would have sounded long since and all good young soldiers of the Third Reich were, or should have been, asleep. We two misfits stood looking at the wall surrounding the barracks wondering which was the quietest way to break our way back into their world.

I helped the prisoner climb on top of the wall, then he pulled me up beside him. We dropped to the ground on the inside and found ourselves in the Kommandant's garden. I knew the route, having used it for several night sorties, so I led the way along a series of garden paths leading to the parade ground. Keeping in the shadow of a long hut, we doubled quickly and stealthily across the drill ground when, suddenly, we were startled out of our wits by a movement behind us.

A figure was creeping after us. We froze. The figure stopped dead. The three of us stood like statues watching each other, hardly breathing. Then, to my intense relief, a hoarse whisper rasped across the parade ground: 'Hi – Eric!' It was John, just making his own way back.

The three of us crouched together and debated the best method of completing the last leg of the journey across the large yard in front of the armoury, where an armed guard was on patrol. But before we could make any decision two guards suddenly materialised, fixed bayonets pointed at our stomachs. One of them fumbled for his whistle to raise the alarm but as he put it to his lips John's quick wits and friendly German patter persuaded him to pause.

The guards listened, but it wasn't until a large quantity of English cigarettes was mentioned that they were inclined to make any deal. I was despatched to get the cigarettes while John and the prisoner stayed as hostages. I dashed across to the shrubbery, through the window into the dormitory and groped past the snoring occupants to the passage leading to the quartermaster's stores, where Rose, the quartermaster, slept.

I grabbed his sleeping shoulder and shook him hard. He awoke with a start, fear contorting his pale shrinking face.

'What do you want?' he quavered, his voice high and scared.

'Shut up – it's me, Doran,' I said fiercely, afraid he was going to scream and wake the place.

He was so relieved to find that it was someone he knew that he instantly lost his temper and became authoritative.

'What the fucking hell do you think you're playing at at this time of night?' he demanded angrily.

There was no time for lengthy explanations. I seized him roughly by the front of his shirt and shook him vigorously.

'We've just been copped sneaking in by a couple of Jerry guards and I want 200 smokes to pay them off,' I snapped.

Rose realised I was in no mood to play games, so he swung his long thin legs to the floor and groped for his trousers, grumbling to himself. He fished a key from under his pillow and led the way to the stores, but even in these circumstances he wouldn't let me in, so I had to stay outside to save any further argument. He was back almost immediately with two cartons of cigarettes, which he handed to me, saying something about the conditions of the deal. Scarcely listening, I snatched the cartons from him and raced back the way I had come to where I had left John and the guards.

When I slithered up to them, it was obvious that John had done a good job as public relations man, as they were all sitting on the grass chatting amicably. The guards took the cartons with profuse thanks and disappeared into the darkness, leaving us to complete our journey unhindered.

'We could win this bloody war on our own if we had enough cigarettes!' John giggled as we dived into bed a few minutes later. Pulling the blankets over our heads to stifle our laughter, we slept soundly for the rest of the night.

The whole incident would have passed, like countless others, without further trouble had not the prisoner's absence unfortunately been noticed by Teeny Weeny Woods. The diminutive tyrant in Woods couldn't let it slip without using it as an opportunity to whip some discipline into our unruly ranks. He duly made a report to Montgomery, who, making a great show of concern, promised an investigation and the punishment of the miscreants.

Montgomery had, of course, already guessed more or less what had happened, but, running with the hare and hunting with the hounds as usual, he told us privately that this was more than he could control as Woods was bound to take the tale to Hauptsturmführer Roepke or perhaps even higher. John and I had come to count too much on the perks of being policemen to let the job slip so easily: the only course we could see was to stop Woods spreading the story any further. We set out to look for him.

By chance the incident coincided with the visit to Haus Germania (July 1944) of Otto Skorzeny, whose daring exploit in plucking Mussolini from the formidable mountain prison Gran Sasso in September 1943 was justly famous. Skorzeny was a man whose extraordinary courage impressed even his British counterparts and at his subsequent trial at Nuremberg it was the testimony given on his behalf by Wing Commander Yeo Thomas, GC, MC (author of *The White Rabbit*) which was instrumental in his acquittal.

No wonder, then, that Haus Germania was anxious to do its heroic guest full honour. In the glitter of full spit and polish and high brass dashing about, John and I trailed around pursuing our quarry until it dawned on us that the Big Five would surely be attending the celebrations. In the main hall banners draped the walls, long tables were set resplendently and clean young soldiers of the pioneer battalion were beginning to file in with their best parade-ground style. But no Woods.

In fact we eventually ran him to ground in the lavatories just before he went into the hall. John closed and jammed the door. The poor little fellow was terrified but we just made it plain to him that nothing would happen to him unless he started turning the disciplinary thumbscrews on us.

It was a silly thing to do. Woods went straight for protection and the whole story just poured into the ears of the German authorities who nominally had control of the Corps. There were questions, investigations, discussions. No doubt other reports had reached them in the past but this must have been among the last straws, making them realise at last that we were nothing but a useless, explosively undisciplined bunch of reprobates which was quickly turning into a hot, if rotten, potato in their tender and overworked hands.

They couldn't simply disband us or cause us to vanish quietly since the unit had Hitler's personal sanction, so they must find us something to do before we ran amok. It was time the BFC saw active service.

I had learnt, long before it became public knowledge, that the unit was destined for the Russian front. Anneliese, as personal secretary to the Kommandant, told me of letters she had typed and documents she had seen which suggested that the BFC should be trained and prepared for service in Russia without further delay.

The news came as an unpleasant shock to the Corps members. The Russian front was not, by a long way, synonymous with survival, and survival was the main thought in everybody's mind. We had all lived too much to risk willingly the one possession that is priceless to any normal person – life itself. No one gave any open sign of being alarmed, but from now on the threat dominated our existence. We grew edgy, tempers frayed and we bickered and quarrelled among ourselves over trifles. Some threw themselves with desperate energy into the final pursuit of pleasures they might not know again, others grew morose and preoccupied.

Whatever happened, it was clear that the pattern of the BFC's existence must change, and each man made his private plans. Even those who, incredibly, had convinced the Germans of the integrity of their boyish delight in playing at soldiers turned about face or hedged their bets when it came to the real thing. Butcher, for example, compiled a list of the true names of the BFC members and tried to get it passed on to British Intelligence. John and I, who had never had any patriotic or militaristic leanings, certainly had no intention of exchanging lethal shots with unknown Russians, but we decided to wait and see what would happen before we made any move.

Meanwhile, in an attempt to get away from the pettiness and squabbling of an increasingly confined barrack life, we harassed Montgomery into obtaining travel warrants for us for recruiting trips. These were journeys made by existing Corps members to various British and Allied prisoner-of-war and internment camps in an attempt to attract new members. The dismal track record was only too clear from the fact that there were scarcely ever more than 30 or so members in the Corps. Of course, neither of us had the slightest wish to convert anyone but it was one legitimate way of getting a change of scene. As it turned out, because of my increasing attachment to Anneliese and unwillingness to leave her, I didn't use my warrant, but John, understanding the situation, took off for Bremen on his own, bound for our old camp Marlag Milag Nord. His 'recruiting effort' was spent in chatting to the mates with whom he had broken out of camp and, needless to say, he had a total lack of success to report when he returned.

John did, however, pick up one useful tip, which was that on a recruiting trip it was a good idea to keep the uniform out of sight because it only alienated people. So on the next such excursion, which we made together to Laufen in Bavaria, we persuaded the security officer in charge that we would be more successful if we actually spent a couple of days in the camp posing as new inmates. The security officer thought it an excellent plan, mostly because he had been informed of a secret radio set somewhere in the camp which the prisoners had built out of bits and pieces and he was sure we would be able to find it for him.

Laufen hadn't been chosen by us at random but because we had heard on the grapevine that an old friend of ours was interned there – none other than Stan Craig from our Jersey days.

Stan was in great shape and highly delighted to see us. He hadn't changed in the two and a half years since we had seen him last and nor, it seemed, had his clothes – still the same sandals, fawn-coloured cords and the red T-shirt that we had had a mock battle over in Jegou's house to stop the police finding our stolen rabbit hoard. He greeted us warmly and almost instantly followed up with: 'Quick, the six o'clock news is going to start in a few minutes!'

Having served our 'time' in the camp – most of it reminiscing with Stan over bottles of the usual explosive camp hooch and listening to news broadcasts on the illegal wireless set – we reported back to the security officer. We assured him that there was no radio, or if there was then it was kept most cunningly hidden from our eagle-eyed search. He seemed disappointed but nevertheless accepted our word and drove us to the station to catch the train to Hildesheim.

Standing on the platform waiting for the train, I watched the hands of the station clock tick into a straight line. The six o'clock news was just starting.

Not long after we got back, the war hit Hildesheim, literally. So far, the little town had kept the unmarked freshness of an illustration in a little-read storybook until one Saturday morning five minutes' work by the Allied air force mutilated and defaced it.

By now we were used to aircraft droning overhead en route for the larger towns and we scarcely noticed them, but on this particular morning, as we were packing up our gear after a quiet bit of physical training in the garden, we became aware of something different in the engine noise of the approaching aircraft. Looking up, we saw one group of planes at fairly high altitude and another, much lower, heading straight towards us.

As we watched, the first plane unloaded a stick of bombs that screamed over and exploded within a mile of us, but superimposed on the screaming was a whizzing sound growing louder by the second which I had never heard before. We dived for cover behind a nearby rockery as a queer object, something like a milk churn, landed a few yards away, embedding itself in the path, where it gurgled and spluttered but fortunately failed to detonate. We stared at it in amazement for a few seconds then speedily took ourselves off to the shelter.

When we emerged, we learned that the short raid had scored a direct hit on the sugar factory. Wayward and unprincipled the BFC may have been, but on hearing the news the members mustered instantly and voluntarily and worked without stopping for several hours fighting the fire that now raged at the scene, dragging dead and dying from the debris. Several barracks nearby, used by foreign workers employed at the factory, had also been hit and casualties were high.

Hildesheim was never quite the same again after that. Like a human face, it grew grey and ravaged overnight, sensing the approach of the end.

Chapter 10

'THE WORST EIGHT
WEEKS OF MY WAR'

The end of the good life at Haus Germania came sooner than I had expected. A series of petty incidents, insubordination, indiscipline, gathered like cobwebs. The two occurrences which landed us in Bandegau punishment camp were minor in themselves, but combined with all that had gone before I suppose they were just too much and someone, exasperated beyond endurance, must have felt it was time we were taught a lesson.

The BFC uniform was a basic grey SS standard outfit embellished with silver thread on a black background. The insignia were two collar dogs, one black and the other with three British lions couchant. On the arm, just below the right shoulder, was the SS eagle and, about two inches beneath, the Britannia shield in red, white and blue. On the left arm, maybe five inches from the cuff, was a black band about an inch wide with 'Britisches Freikorps' embroidered in Gothic lettering with silver thread.

When one of the lads appeared in the barracks one day with a brown substance on his brightly coloured Union Jack arm insignia, one of the humorists commented: 'It looks like the Eagle shat on your Britannia!' This of course raised a laugh and in the half-serious discussion that followed we decided that the uniform had been designed without enough care and thought, since the Union Jack should have been above the Eagle to prevent this unforeseen eventuality. Razor blade, needle and cotton were produced and the error rectified without delay and soon it was impossible for the Eagle, now firmly positioned below the Union Jack, to repeat his offence.

For my part it didn't bother me politically, nationally or personally what the Eagle got up to, any more than I would have minded if he had been pounced on and swallowed by the three British lions. But some idiot took it seriously enough to report the incident, there was an official enquiry and we were found guilty of defacing the German uniform. Before we were actually punished, however, we had managed to add gross insubordination to our list of crimes and the disgrace was complete.

The same group of us were lying out in the sun on a late summer afternoon, eight tough, ruthless young men stretched practically naked in the cloistered monastery garden of Haus Germania. We had successfully dodged the fatigue duty again and couldn't think of a more beneficial or pleasant way to while away the time till evening. We lay there, eyes closed, conversation slow and languid.

Suddenly the peace was shattered. A group of Germans bristled onto the scene; their leader – bull-necked, stocky – wore the uniform of a high-ranking and much-decorated officer. Clearly he couldn't believe the sight which lay before his eyes. His lips moved but no sound came, and the fact that we failed to leap to our feet in confusion and apology didn't help him to recover his speech.

At last he burst forth in a furious bellow: '*Stehen Sie auf, Lumpen!*'

Still not one of us moved and the rest of his entourage goggled in amazement, obviously expecting a divine thunderbolt to strike us for this act of military profanity. But worse was to follow this dumb insolence. Lofty Nixon casually rolled over onto his side and glared back at the group of military might. Then he roared back in equally thunderous tones: 'Please keep quiet or fuck off!'

That did it. There was an immediate order for the arrest of all eight of us. But, as the old saying has it, who will bell the cat? – after all, we were the police and we were certainly not going to arrest ourselves. The Big Five wouldn't do it either because they knew we were the toughest core, and armed to boot. So we waited to see what would happen. Next day four Sicherheitsdienst (Security Service) arrived and did the job with professional thoroughness. We knew from experience that when they appeared it meant business and we weren't disappointed when we arrived at our destination after a two-day mystery trip in their company.

On a lonely, windswept expanse of heathland somewhere in Bandegau stood the SS cottage in the country. A small tumbledown farmhouse miles from anywhere, plenty of solitude and fresh air. To make us prisoners feel at home, the thoughtful SS had erected a high, wide barbed-wire fence and installed three simple-minded, erratically tempered guards. We arrived late at night so our formal introduction to them was made first thing next morning with a typical Bandegau greeting: 'Get up, you lot of pox-ridden motherless bastards!'

It must have been about 5 a.m. and a shabby little man stood in the doorway yelling obscenities at us in German. Lofty Nixon returned the sentiment on behalf of us all.

'What the bleeding hell bit you, you noisy little kraut?' He swung his long legs out of his bunk and stood up, neck bent to avoid the low ceiling, glaring down at the decrepit figure in its ill-fitting German uniform now shambling into the room. Our new jailer fortunately didn't seem to understand English but he suspected that the reply wasn't respectful and screamed a bit more to hasten the rest of us to our feet. If it hadn't been so early in the morning I could have appreciated the funny side of things: a sunken-chested, wrinkle-faced little man with a falsetto voice and watery eyes trying to menace eight burly young men. The ridiculous picture he presented was completed by the way his limp, greasy forage cap balanced on his two enormous, paper-thin red ears.

We immediately christened him 'Lugs' and always addressed him thus even when, to give it an air of politeness, we added 'Herr' in front of it. So it was 'Herr Lugs' this, 'Herr Lugs' that . This form of address undoubtedly gave both him and us a lot of satisfaction.

But Herr Lugs had the gun, and the way he held it was no laughing matter.

So began eight of the worst weeks of my war. Eight lost men without claim to the protection of any nation or convention, completely isolated, our lives entirely in the hands of three unstable guards who could liquidate us at any time and never have to answer for it.

There was a guard commander, whose appearances were as rare and fleeting as a comet, but we had good cause to be aware of his existence. His punishment devices were unimaginative but effective – deprivation of sleep, hard labour under hard conditions and a meagre diet. These can crush a man as surely as any sophisticated form of cruelty.

The hardest to bear was the lack of sleep. Upon the orders of the guard commander we were awakened most nights every hour on the hour, from the time the lights went out at 9 p.m. to the time we got up at 5 a.m. The night guard would bawl at us and if we weren't instantly on our feet standing smartly to attention at the foot of our bunks it was extremely painful. Ronald Barker (also known as 'Voysey') found that out when he failed to get up fast enough on one occasion: he was kicked and beaten with the rifle butt until he had enough bruises to remind him not to do it again.

One of the guards was, however, slightly more lenient and even though he would shout us all awake he didn't always insist on our standing to, and his watches were, needless to say, awaited with relief.

At dawn the now familiar and dreaded '*Aufstehen!*' dragged us into another working day. Grey-faced, haggard and shivering from cold and lack of sleep, we stumbled out to the railway track that ran past the prison. It appeared to be a now defunct branch line and with the years the twisting roots of the desolate and ancient elms that grew beside it had buckled tracks and sleepers. It was our job to remove these roots and the damaged sections of rail. The work was back-breaking and pointless. The ground and all that grew in it was frozen iron-hard by the autumn frosts, tenaciously resisting axe, pick and spade, succumbing only to our stubborn insistence as we hacked our way along in the face of the eternal east wind and driving sleet.

Before many weeks had passed we had reached the limit of our endurance. As far as we knew, we were to be incarcerated there indefinitely and the prospect of chopping our way through the bitter winter at the mercy of our crazy jailers was intolerable. In desperation we reasoned that if one of us could get away it might be possible to alert the neutral Red Cross, guardian of the rights of all wartime prisoners, to our plight. But the problem of how and when to get even one man out was more difficult in Bandegau than in any of our other camps. Escape from the group working on the railway line was ruled out because it was under constant surveillance by a guard, usually the gun-happy Pole we called 'Trigger' because of his unnerving affection for his rifle and readiness to use it. So the break would have to be made from inside the fence.

This was the familiar double barbed-wire affair. Without any equipment or tools, we could neither climb it nor cut it: our only possible exit would have to be under it. As this hadn't been erected as a purpose-built, permanent prison but, rather, put together in a hurry as a punishment camp, we reasoned that it was unlikely that the fencing would have been too deeply earthed. We were right.

As camp cook, it was my job to strip and chop the fuel necessary to cook the evening meal, and this I did on a block just by the perimeter wire. It was constantly patrolled on the outside, but once the guards had passed I scraped surreptitiously but busily at the loose earth at the base of the fence with my heel. Sure enough, I found that the wire hardly went below the surface and that it would be possible for me to loosen a dip which, though shallow, would enable a man to wriggle through.

Once we were sure of the exit we made our escape plan. It was simple enough. One man would squeeze under the wire, get away and try to contact the International Red Cross authorities somehow. It wasn't much of a plan and no one was overwhelmed by it, but it was the best we could do. At first there were no volunteers because the chances of the escapee surviving, let alone succeeding, were decidedly slender, so we decided to draw lots.

The straws were cut and ready and the eight of us crouched together, nervously waiting to see who would pull the short straw. But in the tension of the moment an argument developed and some of the men refused to take part in the draw, retiring to their bunks to sulk. The straws lay scattered on the floor and it seemed that even our one hope had fallen through already. There was a sullen silence.

'I'll go!' a voice volunteered quietly. It was Rowlands. 'I suppose

I'll be shot before I even get near the bloody wire but still . . .' That was Rowlands all over – cynical, pessimistic and courageous. He looked at me and grinned broadly, shrugging his shoulders as though he guessed my thoughts. Then he came across and we began to discuss the details of the break because it would be up to me to find the best place for the exit and then choose the right moment to get him out.

On the appointed day, Rowlands reported sick and was allowed to remain in camp. He pulled the blankets over his head and huddled into a heap of groaning misery. After a bit, the guard stopped checking on him beyond sticking his head in at the door occasionally and satisfying himself that the hump was still in the bed. Meanwhile, by the perimeter fence, I chopped and stripped fuel assiduously with now and then a furtive scrape of my heel to reassure myself that the dip I had painstakingly hollowed out over several days was still there. Trigger the Pole, on perimeter duty, sat down on the other side of the wire to chat, his hand ceaselessly caressing the rifle slung around his neck. I was glad that the old oak stump, which I used as a chopping block, and the growing pile of fuel obscured the ground round my feet from his view. I humoured him with some bad German conversation; actually my German was much better than his but he liked to feel he was one up on us and, simple soul that he was, laughed like a child when I deliberately phrased a remark to sound ridiculous. A dangerous, trigger-happy child who would have shot me instantly had he known what my feet and mind were busy working on.

Eventually, he passed along. I chose my moment, got Rowlands out of the hut, under the wire, watched him sprinting madly across the gravel stretch – no shots, no alarm – he reached the belt of shrubs and disappeared from view. I raced back into the hut, made up a dummy in his bed and was back nonchalantly chopping fuel by the time Trigger sauntered round again. The whole operation had taken scarcely a few minutes but it had seemed like years to me and my heart was hammering painfully.

We had deliberately chosen a time when we knew the most lenient of the guards would be on night duty – somewhere under that untidy tunic beat a reasonable heart – and Rowlands, or his dummy rather, was not required to jump to attention that night. It was not until the day guard came on at 5 a.m. and stripped back the blankets that the

GASTLINGS.
SOUTHILL.
Biggleswade.
Beds.

Sept: 14th. 1938.

The Hon Mrs Michael Bowes Lyon, is very pleased to strongly recommend Eric Pleasants, as a coach and instructor for children. He is excellent at teaching boxing, & has great teaching ability. Children are all devoted to him, & he is a very nice way with them. I am delighted to answer any further questions on his behalf. He taught my son boxing, and is splendid at giving children confidence, if they are nervous.

Elizabeth Bowes Lyon -

TOP LEFT: Eric practises his strongman act in the 1930s.

TOP MIDDLE: Another picture of Eric practising for his strongman act in the 1930s.

TOP RIGHT: Eric's first professional boxing appearance in 1934.

LEFT: A typical Eric 'pose' from the 1930s.

BELOW: A souvenir of Eric's boxing days in the 1930s.

Panther Tit-Bit of the Evening

PLEASANTS

Norwich. Popular ex-amateur. Means to win

TROOPER
BILL ENGLISH

Aldershot. A hurricane battler who fights to win

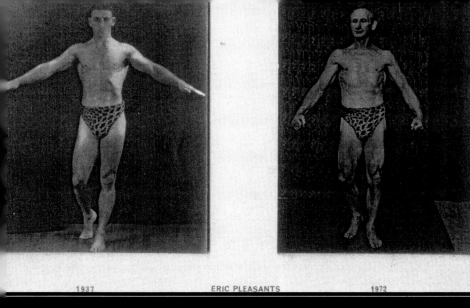

1937   ERIC PLEASANTS   1972

TOP: Thirty-five years separate these two photographs!

ABOVE LEFT: A photograph of Eric in Waffen-SS uniform from his SS personal file.
Probably taken in 1944.

ABOVE RIGHT: Anneliese Pleasants-Dorran (née Nitzschner), wife of Eric Pleasants,

An den

Reichsführer-SS

Rasse- und Siedlungshauptamt

Berlin, den 5. 12. 1944

Ich bitte um Uebersendung der Vordrucke zu einem Verlobungs- und Heiratsgesuch.

1.) Pleasants-Dorran, Reginald Eric   FPNr. 11 388
(Zu- und Vorname)   SS-Hauptamt   (Wohnort)   (Straße und Hausnummer)
                         Amtsgruppe D
SS-Freiw.   --   BFC.   17.5.1911   Saxlingham (Irland)
(SS-Dienstgrad)   (SS-Nummer)   (SS-Einheit)   (Geburtsdatum)   (Geburtsort)

a) Allgemeine SS   nein   Kreis:
b) SS-Wachmann, hauptamtlich, SS-VT., SS-TV.   nein
c) Ordensburgschüler auf der Ordensburg   nein
(Zutreffendes unterstreichen)

2.) SS-Obersturmführer Kühlich   SS-Hauptamt, Amtsgruppe D
                                       Berlin-Wilmersdorf, Westfälische
(Name und genaue Anschrift des Vorgesetzten (Sturmführers) Str. 1 - 5

3.) Nitzschner   Annelies   Berlin-Wilmersdorf,
                                              Rüdesheimer Platz 11
(Geburtsname)   (Vorname)   (Wohnort, Straße, Hausnummer)
                     (vollst. Rufname)
                                              Langenhennersdorf
        --   Rdtsch.   22.9.1913   dorf
(Name als Verehelichte,   (Staatsangehörigkeit)   (geb. am)   (Geburtsort)
Verwitwete, Geschiedene,
Adoptierte)   Kreis: Dresden
(Zutreffendes
unterstreichen)

Familienstand der zukünftigen Ehefrau: ledig, verwitwet, geschieden

4.) a) SS-Obersturmführer   Berlin,
       Luckhardt, SS-Hauptamt, Amtsgr. D, D II/2   Saarlandstr. 36

                                              Rüdesheimer
    b) Dipl.-Ing. W. Schröppel, Bln.-Wilmersdorf, Platz 11
(Name und genaue Postanschrift von 2 Bürgen für die zukünftige Ehefrau, die weder mit
Ihnen noch mit Ihrer zukünftigen Ehefrau verwandt sein dürfen.)

5.) Ich bin bereits verheiratet nein / ja seit: _____

    Ich war bereits verheiratet (bin verwitwet, geschieden) nein
    (Zutreffendes unterstreichen)

6.) Ich gehöre nachstehender Konfession an: __--__

    Meine zukünftige Ehefrau gehört nachstehender Konfession an: ggl.

    Ich beabsichtige kirchliche Trauung, nein / ja, nach nachstehender Konfession:

    Kirchliche Trauung ist erfolgt ... nein / ja, nach nachstehender Konfession:

Wenden!

M 2 C/0755

7.) Ich habe mit dem RuS bereits einmal in Verbindung gestanden, nein / ~~ja~~

in nachstehender Angelegenheit: — —

unter folgendem Aktenzeichen: — —

8.) Nachstehend aufgeführte Blutsverwandte von mir bzw. meiner zukünftigen Ehefrau sind ${\cdot}$-Angehörige / mit ${\cdot}$-Angehörigen verlobt bzw. verheiratet:

— —

_____

_____

_____

(Genaue Angaben über Zu- und Vornamen, Anschrift, ${\cdot}$-Einheit, Verwandtschaftsgrad, bei weiblichen Anverwandten außerdem mit welchem ${\cdot}$-Angehörigen verlobt oder verheiratet, dessen Vor- und Zuname, Anschrift, ${\cdot}$-Einheit)

R. Pleasants-Dorran
(Unterschrift des Antragstellers)

SS-Freiw.   /FPNr. 11 388
(${\cdot}$-Dienstgrad und Einheit)

9.) Anträge von Angehörigen der ${\cdot}$-VT., ${\cdot}$-TV., Wach- und Grenzeinheiten und hauptamtlichen ${\cdot}$-Angehörigen können nur bearbeitet werden, wenn nachstehende Vorlagegenehmigung ausgefüllt und vom zuständigen Führer unterschrieben wurde:

SS-Hauptamt,
Amtsgruppe D
BFC.   -FPNr. 11 388-   Berlin   , den 15.1.45
(Einheit)

Vorlagegenehmigung

Ich bin damit einverstanden, daß der ${\cdot}$-Angehörige, SS-Freiw.

Reginald Eric Pleasants-Dorran

(${\cdot}$-Dienstgrad und Name des Antragstellers)

ein Verlobungs- und Heiratsgesuch beim Rasse- und Siedlungshauptamt-${\cdot}$

vorlegt.

W. Rühlich.
(Unterschrift)

SS-~~Haupt~~sturmführer
(${\cdot}$-Dienstgrad)

An SS document from Eric's marriage application showing his change of name to Pleasants-Dorran and suggesting that his birthplace — Saxlingham — was actually in neutral Ireland rather than Norfolk

BRITISH CONSULATE-GENERAL
BERLIN
BAOR 2

TEL.: 86-6212

29th May, 1951.

Ref: XXII/389

Dear Madam,

I am in receipt of your letter, dated 22nd May, 1951,
regarding your son, Eric Reginald Pleasants.

I regret that, in spite of our letters to the Authorities
in the Soviet occupied Zone of Germany, we have not been able
to obtain a reply. Frl. NITZSCHER, who called at this Consulate-
General a few weeks ago, reported that she had seen your son on
28th August, 1948. She stated he had been sentenced to twenty-
five years' imprisonment on charges of being in possession of
arms, anti-Soviet propaganda and illegally crossing the frontier.

I have reported the matter to the Foreign Office in London
and shall communicate with you again when I hear from them.

Yours faithfully,

W. Frame

Acting British Consul-General

Mrs. A. Pleasants,
"Drintoi",
Salhouse Road,
New Rackheath,
Norwich,
Norfolk.

THF/OZ

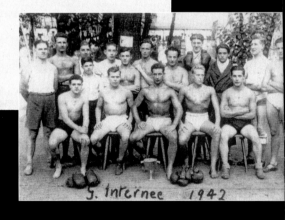

ABOVE: Eric's mother made many attempts to get in touch with her son. This is the result of one of them.

ABOVE: Internees of Ilag VIIIZ at Kreuzburg. Eric (centre) is sitting behind the cup he had just won in a wrestling competition. Eric acted as the sports organiser for the internees.

LEFT: A photograph of a watercolour painting of Eric made whilst he was in Russian captivity. The original painting was smuggled out of Russia but is now missing.

TOP: Bill Piddington and Eric Pleasants on their return to England, photograph taken at Harwich, 10 July 1954. Piddington later wrote a book about his experiences in Germany and Russia entitled *Russian Frenzy.*

RIGHT: Eric carved this village sign for the Women's Institute in Ketteringham, Norfolk, in the late 1970s.

RIGHT: In the 1970s Eric acted as an instructor in several martial arts. Here he shows off his Kendo attire and equipment.

BELOW: Eric's reunion with Lithuanian Kestutis Jokubynas in Norfolk in October 1982. They had toiled together in Russian slave labour camps 30 years earlier.

disappearance was discovered. With a cry of disbelief, the fellow stumbled out of the room and dashed off to get his superior officers.

I was drying my bare torso with the grey communal towel – it had no drying effect but for some reason we all went through the motions – when the three guards and their commander burst into the room. Lugs came straight up to me and shrieked, '*Wo ist Rowlands?*' No doubt they figured that as I was the only one in camp during the day I must know something about his escape, and he must have gone during the day as we were all securely bolted in at night. I stared blankly back at the furious little man and shrugged my shoulders.

With a great flourish, Lugs removed the clip from his rifle and stood it against the wall. Drawing his blunt 1914–18 German-issue bayonet, he crushed it against my bare chest, shrieking out the same question in a high-pitched falsetto. '*Wo ist Rowlands? Wo ist Rowlands?*' The question pierced into me each time the bayonet jabbed forward into my chest.

I clenched my hands behind my back as much for the pain as to stop myself hitting Lugs. I took one step towards him; he fell back one pace. I heard the bolt slide back on Trigger's rifle. I knew he would shoot me at once if I made any move to strike Lugs. Again the bayonet jarred against my chest, again I took another step forward as he withdrew. With each dull, sickening blow, I took another step towards him, my eyes never leaving his face.

To enable him to keep striking at such close range, Lugs had each time to take a corresponding step backwards. Eventually he reached the wall and could retreat no further and I saw the fear in his face as he stood with his back pressed to the wall, unable to strike, the bayonet useless in his hand and his rabbit eyes mesmerised by mine as I stood implacably before him, the bloodied victor. At last I stepped aside and he scuttled out of the room. The others followed him, silent and perplexed.

When I thought about it later, I could see the funny side and I almost felt sorry for Lugs, a pathetic little man with his forage cap askew and his glasses hanging from one ear, scared out of his wits by my unaccountable, inexorable advance upon him. And then I fingered the wounds inflicted by his bayonet and my inclination to pity him lessened, for they took a long time to heal.

Their attempt to bully any information out of me having failed, our guards left us alone to await the 'big man from the village'. When he did arrive, the Major was not in a good mood after journeying his blubber-type physique over 20 miles of rough ground in a pony and trap. Quietly and in reasonably good English he asked us where Rowlands was. We said nothing. In the same bland tone he went on: 'You will be taken out of here one by one and brought before me again. I will ask each of you the same question again. If you do not answer me, you will be taken out and shot. That is all.'

He gave us 15 minutes to consider his ultimatum and then, turning on his heel, he left the room, followed by his contingent.

Complete silence reigned. None of us had anything to say. My reason crawled away into the dark tunnel of intuition – it couldn't happen to me! My mind was possessed by an unthinking conviction that I hadn't come all this way to die stupidly in some godforsaken hole. He must be bluffing.

But was he? How did I *know* it was a threat, not a promise? I couldn't be certain. I became afraid. There was a coldness in my stomach spreading slowly into my limbs. The opening door jerked into my brain and even as the guard marched John out, my mind began to clear and I started thinking rationally. They couldn't shoot us, they didn't have the authority . . .

A single shot.

'Christ almighty!' someone whispered low.

It couldn't be true. It must be a trick. We would be useless to them dead, they would never get the information they wanted. But how could I know for sure? The door opened, another man went out. I began to listen hard. A few minutes, another shot. Why only one shot? It usually took more than that to finish the job thoroughly, to stop the twisting and writhing. Unless it was at close quarters. But it didn't sound as though it was. This shot rang. It didn't have the abrupt muffled finality of a bullet at close range. I kept listening, my ears as sensitive as antennae.

It was my turn. The cold fear was with me as I walked across the yard to the guard hut. I was the last. For all I knew the others were dead, if I did tell there would be no one to point the finger at me. But there was nothing I could tell, even if I had wanted to: the stupid thing was that none of us actually did know where Rowlands had gone. I didn't want to die but I had no intention of giving away any information, even if I had any to give.

'Where is Rowlands? By what route has he escaped and where has he gone?' The Major sounded weary, the question well worn. I struggled to control the involuntary hiccup that caught my throat as I tried to reply. I breathed in carefully.

'I don't know any more than you do.'

The smooth impassivity of the man's face crumpled into rage. I scarcely heard the angry outburst. We had won! I knew we had won – it *was* a bluff and we had called it! My initial smile of relief broadened into an insolent grin.

But I was still shaken and the others, when I was bundled in to join them a few minutes later, looked pretty much the way I felt. They told me how, each time one of them refused to answer, the guard on a signal from the Major had raised his rifle and fired into the wall of the yard opposite the open window of the interrogation office. The guards gave us a bad time of it after that, as though to work out their spite at being thwarted by us, but anything was better than being dead.

Four days later, Rowlands was brought back, a lot the worse for wear. He had made it to the outskirts of Berlin before he was cornered in a railway siding. There wasn't much we could do now except resign ourselves to an unpleasant and precarious existence for the rest of the war, which surely couldn't drag on much longer. And then one morning the guard commander came in, read four names off a list and told the men concerned to prepare for transportation.

A liquidation camp. It must be. What else could they do with us now? When the four were gone, the rest of us waited, four doomed miserable rats waiting for their extermination. When it did come, we gathered into pitifully small bundles our few possessions and sat gloomily in the train carrying us to our unknown but final destination, staring out of the windows seeing only yesterday. I saw myself running to catch another train as it pulled out of an English station, swinging myself onto a moving carriage with the lithe easiness of a youthful athlete, carefree and eager as I left Loughborough College to show my father the diploma I had just been awarded as a newly qualified teacher of physical education. The boyish Eric Pleasants had the world open and all his marvellous life ahead of him, but for Erich Doran it was the end of the line.

Briefly, I tried to recall why I had taken the name Doran when joining the BFC – I wouldn't have bothered to take a pseudonym at all had it not been pressed on us. The name had come to me at random; it meant about as much to me as my life did now to the almighty powers, I reflected bitterly as I gazed half-seeing out of the window. The countryside flashed past but gradually I became aware of the odd landmark here and there impressing itself upon my vision. They were landmarks which I recognised as having seen before. It happened more and more often and I began to take an interest. I'd seen that before – and that and that. Suddenly it dawned on me: we were on the road to Berlin!

Glancing across at John, I saw the same glint of recognition and hope in his face, and then it died.

'They take you to the Waffen SS first and then you're transported on to the appropriate camp,' he said glumly.

Sure enough, we were taken to Fehrbelliner Strasse and left in a waiting room as dismal as ourselves. After a while, who should burst in but Tug Montgomery, grinning cheerfully, slapping us on the shoulders, very hail fellow well met. It finally registered that he was in fact welcoming us back into the BFC and after the initial relief I lost my temper and swore at him – conniving bastard, he did his bit towards putting us in Bandegau, so what the hell was it all in aid of?

'Just forget it, forget it!' he said airily, waving the subject away as though it was nothing, which I suppose it was to him. Then, characteristically, he added: 'Christ – you want to see this new female I've got!' Good old Tug. His interests hadn't changed even if everything else had.

While we were in Bandegau the unit had been moved out of Hildesheim to the SS Wildemann Kaserne, Dresden. It was sobering news. Wildemann was a straight-up, no-nonsense military training establishment and clearly the BFC was being knocked into fighting shape to serve on the Russian front. The threat of active service was now uncomfortably certain.

I didn't like the sound of that. I'd never intended to fight anyone else's war and I wasn't going to change my mind now. Clearly, it was time to part company with the BFC but the next step needed careful thinking out, particularly because it wasn't only ourselves John and I now had to think about. Anneliese and Lena were now not only an inseparable part of our lives but also indispensable to any escape plan. Through their work – Lena in the travel documents bureau and Anneliese in the Waffen SS secretariat – they were well informed of whatever went on and best placed to get any documentation we might need. It seemed, for the moment, that our best bet would be to rely on their advice and judgement on when and where to make a move and to wait for them to come up with all the papers.

Having decided that, John disappeared to see Lena and I to see Anneliese. It was going to be an emotional reunion. Montgomery had given us a couple of days in Berlin, which, after Bandegau, we badly needed before joining the rest of the unit in the Wildemann.

Chapter 11

'MY DEAR LITTLE ENEMY'

SS Wildemann Kaserne in Dresden epitomised a way of life I have always condemned and found repugnant: regimentation, mass identity, unquestioning obedience and submission to authority. Row upon row of wooden army huts caterpillared across the endless expanse of parade grounds, shooting ranges and obstacle courses. Everywhere uniformed men, distinguishable only by little insignia, stripes, hats, hastened busily and importantly, saluting each other with the automatic precision born of long practice and diligent training. On each drill ground the presiding deity of a non-commissioned officer bawled, each doing his best – and succeeding – to subdue the men under him into the same uniform, craven submission which they themselves adopted in the presence of their superiors.

After two blissful days with Anneliese in Berlin, where she now worked, I reported with John to Tug Montgomery. Here in the Wildemann he was very much the formal and official German NCO. Falling in with his game, we stood smartly to attention while he rapped out his peremptory lecture: we must put our foolish and irresponsible behaviour behind us and henceforth batten down to serious training as soldiers in preparation for our imminent service on the Russian front.

John and I exchanged sidelong glances. We knew Tug too well to be deceived by this bit of play-acting and when we saw him later in a more informal moment we told him so. He agreed quite candidly. His immediate concern was to spend as much time as possible with his new girlfriend in Berlin and he had already applied for travel permits using the old excuse that he intended to go on a recruiting trip. Then, casually, as though he was doing us a favour, he said he could arrange for us to accompany him. We thanked him with suitable gratitude for his kindness, even though we strongly suspected he really wanted us along as a sort of personal bodyguard. Tug was well acquainted with our fighting abilities and no doubt felt we would be a useful insurance against the probability of trouble, which was becoming very real now that law and order were rapidly breaking down.

The beginning of the end had already set in in Berlin, as I myself had seen on my brief stay there. Communications were erratic, the trickle of refugees into the city increased daily and the large number of foreign labourers saw this as their chance for escape or revolt. The police, both civil and military, had their hands more than full.

We had to wait about a week for the travel permits and necessary documentation to process through the bureaucratic machine and meanwhile we had to try to adjust to the military routine, a feat which I found the rest of the BFC members seemed already to have accomplished. Despite the slack discipline and relative freedom of Hildesheim, they had knuckled under and accepted this new regime with surprising lack of open resistance. Whatever they may have felt privately, they drilled, trained and paraded indistinguishably from the rest of the soldiers, and if they had any thought of escape before it came to transportation to Russia, they kept it to themselves, just as I did.

But, unlike the rest of them, I could not bring myself to play the military game, even though it was quickly apparent that in some things, like taking down and reassembling a machine gun, I had rather more natural aptitude than the others. I was also an extremely good shot, but I didn't go out of my way to demonstrate that fact more than once.

'Who taught you to shoot?' the incredulous sergeant asked, looking at the marks on my target. I just grinned, not bothering to explain that as a gamekeeper's son I had been able to handle a gun quite competently by the age of 14.

John and I soon found a legitimate way to avoid these rather irksome training exercises and stay out of trouble. We spent as much time as possible in the well-equipped gymnasium, where my ability as a boxer was quickly noticed by one of the officers, himself a heavyweight. He clearly thought I would be a useful asset to the sports team and through his influence I managed to spend more time training in the gym than on the drill ground.

With John holding the stopwatch, I sparred and skipped with the young German soldiers who trained in the gym. Here there was no war, no discrimination between one race and another. We could have been members of an enthusiastic sports club anywhere in the world in peacetime. It made no difference that I was of the enemy race: to them, I was simply a good middleweight boxer with a style new to them, and that was all that counted.

One evening, before Tug's travel permits had come through, the heavyweight Obersturmbannführer burst eagerly into the changing room with the news that arrangements had been approved for a boxing team from the Wildemann to visit Prague to compete against a team of SS soldiers from the occupation army there. Would I represent the middleweight division?

I jumped at the chance, permission for John to accompany me also being given. The opportunity to get away from the oppressive barrack life, if only for a couple of days, was not to be missed. And the irony of it appealed to me too: I was almost certainly the only Englishman to have the singular distinction of representing the German SS in a sporting tournament!

I was still grinning about it as we returned to quarters, where a message for me to report to the guardroom office instantly wiped the smile off my face. Any summons of this kind was always cause for some apprehension, but it changed more to curiosity when I found there had been a telephone call for me and a number had been left for me to ring back. As I dialled the number, I tried without success to think who the caller might have been. I waited. The receiver at the other end was finally lifted and the voice which answered filled me with relief and joy – Anneliese! And in Dresden!

Knowing that I was in camp in Dresden, she had taken her holiday leave intending to stay at her parents' home, which was not far from the city. She was now on her way there and wondered if it was possible for me to meet her. Was it possible – there was no question of it not being possible! Just tell me where and when and I would be there.

I dashed from the office and ran down the roadway, forgetting John was with me until I heard him running behind shouting: 'What the hell's wrong, you crazy sod?'

I pulled up short and gasped out the wonderful news. 'Oh, is that all?' he said, sounding relieved. 'I thought either they had asked you to do some work or the police were after you!'

I aimed a playful punch at him and rushed off to find Montgomery to get permission to leave camp.

I met Anneliese at a café in town.

Anneliese, my beloved enemy, *meine kleine liebe Feinde*, my dear little enemy, as I had affectionately nicknamed her. It was enough to be with her, to sit holding her hand across the table, to look at her and trace the outline of that determined little face with my fingertips. She seemed to carry with her a calm tranquillity that stilled me, that made everything of secondary importance to her presence.

I completely forgot the earlier excitement of the boxing engagement until she asked if I could arrange to spend a few days with her at her parents' home at Wilmsdorf. I would have tried to get out of the visit to Prague rather than forego the chance of being with her, but, characteristically, she insisted that I keep the engagement.

'You carry that appointment out,' she said firmly, 'and when you return let me know immediately that you are safe and sound and I will then make arrangements for you to visit my home.'

It was very late when we reluctantly parted company that evening and I had to get back into barracks by an unofficial route. Lying in my bunk, I thought over Anneliese's words: '*When* you return let me know immediately that you are safe and sound.' She had stressed the word 'when'.

Up to this point Anneliese and I had not really discussed our joint future or made any plans together. It was something on which we both felt an instinctive reticence and, additionally, her grounding as a Nazi

German made her appreciate the fact that if John and I did have any plans to try and absent ourselves from the BFC while we were in Czechoslovakia, then we were wise to keep strict silence about it. Her use of the word 'when' rather than 'if' was probably her way of saying that she would like me to return.

The truth was that neither John nor I had any definite idea of absconding while we were in Prague. We knew that the unrest in Czechoslovakia had increased in proportion to the falling fortunes of Germany but that did not necessarily make it a refugee's paradise, and in the circumstances we could do very little except play it by ear once we got there.

The next day the entire team embarked on the Prague train under the leadership of the Obersturmbannführer, himself the heavyweight contender. No individual travel permits were issued and the team travelled under a block permit made out for 'special duties' to be carried out in Prague.

The Obersturmbannführer was obviously familiar with the city and once there we had no difficulty in finding our way to Radio Festsaal, where the contest was to be held. The place was packed with soldiers of the occupation army, the strong lights discreetly picking out the brass and braid in the ringside seats where the high-ranking officers sat with their women, sleek in black-market stockings and make-up.

It was a long time since I had stood under those lights and felt the heat and excitement and the momentary tremor of nervousness as I climbed from the darkness into the ring. My stockily built opponent and I appraised each other briefly at the weigh-in. Maybe I imagined the flicker of apprehension in his eyes as he took stock of my muscular body – complete with Bandegau scars – but he certainly fought on the retreat all the way. The three-round bout was a tame affair. I didn't think it would be diplomatic to draw too much attention to myself, so I contented myself with repeatedly thrusting out my left hand and occasionally crossing a tentative right-hander to the body in a very orthodox style.

Predictably, it ended in a draw. We shook hands, turned to the crowd and raised our right arms in the Hitler salute before he left the ring. We walked side by side to the dressing room, laughing and patting each other good-naturedly on the back. Here, too, there was no animosity and the subject of war arose only in relation to the difficulties of boxing and training under those conditions.

The boxers invited us to join them in rounding off the night with *'Schnapps und Bier'* but we declined; being foreigners, we said, we would like to make a cultural tour of Prague while we had the chance. Together, John and I left the Radio Festsaal for the streets of Prague after dark.

We had no definite idea of what we were looking for once we got out into the street. Any thoughts we might have had of getting away vanished when we realised that no individual travel permits were to be issued and that such papers as there were would be kept by the Obersturmbannführer; so we couldn't get out of the city legitimately and the chance of doing so illegitimately seemed slight, since the occupational army had it closely covered. Nor could we stay on in the city itself. Even if we managed to get rid of our uniforms we would be picked up in no time at all since we didn't know the place well enough to hide in it, we had no papers and neither of us spoke a word of Czech.

A December night in the middle of a war is scarcely the best time to see the cultural sights. However, before we had ambled very far, a pleasing prospect presented itself in the form of two likely-looking girls. We sloped over and started chatting them up and, considering the language barrier, we weren't doing too badly when we were loudly and rudely interrupted by two passing SS officers.

They strode across the street demanding what the hell we meant by talking to the locals, except they didn't put it as politely as that. We gathered from their tirade that fraternising with the natives was strictly forbidden and that we were to be reported for the offence. The girls, meanwhile, had taken the hint and run off and, seeing my evening unnecessarily ruined by this ill-mannered loudmouth, I lost my temper and turned on him.

'Now look what you've done, you bloody idiot – I'll break your fucking neck!' I snarled – in English, unfortunately, which caused the SS man to drop back a few surprised paces and fumble for his gun. As it came up out of the holster my well-aimed right caught him on the point of the jaw. He must have been unconscious before he hit the ground. The Walther automatic slid across the cobbles and while I was pocketing it John put the second SS man out to join his companion in peaceful slumber.

It was a bit late now but our Obersturmbannführer's last cautionary words to us echoed in my brain: 'Mind you stay out of any trouble because you haven't got any papers and it'll go badly for you if you're picked up.'

If the two SS men came round while we were still on the scene there would be real trouble. We took off at once and got back to the Radio Festsaal building as fast as we could, slowing up as we reached it and sauntering in nonchalantly, surreptitiously checking to see that the slight bulge of the Walther in my tunic didn't look conspicuous. Our train was due out at midnight and we sat there uncomfortably for a few hours, watching the time crawl round, trying to look as though we were enjoying ourselves and keeping an apprehensive eye on the door.

When at last it was time to leave for the station, we had to prevent ourselves jumping up too eagerly, and even then the train seemed to stand panting at the platform for an age before it finally slid slowly out. Not until it gathered speed did we relax slowly, reasonably sure now that we were safe from arrest. I casually folded my arms across my chest, feeling the hard metal lump pressing against me as I dozed off.

A few days after this, John was informed that his secondment to the Berlin headquarters of the Waffen SS Kurt Eggers regiment of war correspondents had been approved. For him, it meant the end of his 'service' with the BFC and, therefore, of his sojourn in the Kaserne.

It also meant the end of the eventful and successful partnership between John and myself. He had decided to make for Italy with Lena as soon as she could make the necessary arrangements, while I preferred to stay on and take my chances in Germany.

When John left the Wildemann Kaserne for his posting to Berlin, we made no plans to meet again and as far as we knew we would probably never see each other again. However, we simply accepted that it was the end of our tandem ride and in the laconic, casual way characteristic of our friendship we parted company.

By the end of 1944 there was very little to be cheerful about. Himmler's optimistic New Year's Eve broadcast raised at best a cynical smile: 'The year 1945 will bring the great German victory, and thus peace, decisively nearer.' I doubt anyone, least of all Himmler himself, believed there could now be a miraculous reversal in Germany's rapidly disintegrating fortunes. Despite the best efforts of the military authorities to conceal the fact, and of the police to maintain law and order, the deterioration was patently obvious.

Inevitably, the unrest was reflected in the Wildemann Kaserne, in particular among those members of the BFC on whom soldiering lay like a very thin veneer. Conversely, there were those for whom this presented the ideal opportunity to indulge in their thwarted military fantasies. Men like Kingsley, who claimed to be a 'professional' soldier to whom the BFC was just another job. In fact, he was little more than a rather domineering bully who rejoiced in the opportunity to throw his weight about to the full when he was appointed acting NCO during Montgomery's absence on a prolonged recruiting trip in January 1945.

Montgomery was, in fact, cautiously trying to edge his way out of the Corps. The pressure and anxiety were beginning to tell on him as well as on the rest of us. On one occasion, to the considerable surprise and alarm of those of us present, he was suddenly seized by an epileptic fit and writhed on the floor foaming at the mouth. I had not known up to this point that he was an epileptic and it seemed to me now to explain several of his idiosyncrasies. Not long after this, when it was clear that there was to be no escape from service on the Russian front, Tug decided to enter hospital to have his venereal diseases treated after all.

Kingsley's leadership did little to calm the increasing sense of unrest and anxiety within the Corps. The propaganda machine could not suppress the news of the inexorable Russian advance along the eastern front – and this was the army into whose path we were to be thrown and mown down like wheat before some vast reaping machine. Deserters all, the members' fate seemed equally unhappy whether they stayed or fled, and not surprisingly several decided to get out while there still seemed to be a chance. Among them was Kingsley, whose soldiering apparently went little more than skin deep when he felt cornered.

Completely isolated since John's departure for Berlin and the Kurt Eggers, I for my part withdrew into myself, protecting my solitude by physical violence at the least sign of encroachment. I fractured Phillpotts' jaw over some trivial incident on one occasion; poor Phillpotts, I didn't have anything against him personally and had even come to like him during the eight weeks we had spent together in Bandegau. After this, the Corps members accorded me a grudging if hostile respect and learnt to leave me alone. That was all I wanted really, for I felt that if I allowed myself to become embroiled in the lunatic personalities and events which surrounded me, I would become part of them, my judgement and vision distorted, until I lost my sense of personal identity and sanity.

In that turbulent existence, which turned even the most common and basic concepts upside down, there was little left by which to measure reason and ideas. Anneliese became for me the only pole star of reality to which I turned and returned for all the essentials of a sane existence: friendship, affection, good sense and clear-sightedness.

Our commitment to each other, established a long time ago but never really discussed, now became the base upon which we considered our present and future position. Tentatively at first, then with increasing certainty, we considered and laid our plans. It went without saying that I should absent myself permanently from the BFC at the earliest opportunity, but the first problem was where to go after that. The possibility of hiding in Anneliese's home in Wilmsdorf was ruled out. We did not wish to involve her parents, who, in any event, although friendly and polite to me, were far too solidly middle class to countenance a flagrant breach of social rule by hiding a deserter. Sorry though I had been to part company with John, I had no wish to accompany him to Italy because I judged the possibility of disappearing quietly into the background would be even more remote there than here in Germany. Here at least we knew the country and I knew the language well enough to pass for a native.

On balance, Anneliese and I decided to remain in Germany and, initially, to return to Berlin, where she had many connections and I was no stranger. For the time being she would continue to work with the SS, as this provided a useful source of information and documentation, and then, when the time seemed appropriate, we could disappear into the city, indistinguishable from the disoriented thousands now thronging it.

We also decided to get married. I was, of course, already married under English law, as Anneliese well knew, but in the present situation quibbling over bigamy was the least of our problems. Nor did I consider myself bound by any moral obligation to my existing wife, since had I been in England I would probably have contemplated divorce proceedings long since, she not only having left me to act as 'housekeeper' to the German officers in Jersey but also having produced a daughter to whom she gave a German name and who most certainly was not mine.

It made not the slightest difference to either Anneliese or myself personally whether we got married or not, but documentary evidence to that effect could be of vital importance in the current state of uncertainty. We would need it if we were to settle unmolested in Germany as we hoped, and if we were swept into some refugee camp it would help to keep us together. It was, in fact, Anneliese who suggested it, as an arrangement of pure convenience, and I could see that her reasoning, as always, was sound. We agreed that she should put in the application as special permission was needed for an SS girl to marry a foreigner and Himmler himself would have to sanction it.

In February 1945 I illegally obtained an official pass to go and visit my dying grandmother. It was my mourning card for the British Free Corps, for I did not intend to return.

As I pocketed the pass I smiled, thinking about the ailing grandmothers who had been at death's door in many a country for years, and I wished them a long and active life. On this occasion she resided at Anneliese's home in Wilmsdorf, where we were to spend a few days, ostensibly on leave, before returning to Berlin.

In some ways I would be sorry to leave Dresden with its peace and order for the battered chaos of Berlin. Quiet and intact, the lovely old city seemed to stand in a time and world apart from the war, essentially unscarred by the twentieth-century violence. Here there were no munitions factories, no war-supporting industries, its one large works produced nothing more lethal than cigarettes. Dresden, with its solid sandstone buildings and stolid citizenry, seemed an enduring monument to the centuries of care, labour and creative talent which had gone into its establishment.

Walking through its streets for what I thought would be the last time and thinking about Anneliese as I made my way to the station, I forgot about the war, the constant threat of being killed, the complications of the present existence and completely unpredictable future. Only when I reached the railway station was there a forceful and bitter reminder that the war, with all its human suffering, was very much in progress. Huddled groups of refugees, stunned and grief-stricken women, children clutching their mothers, a few men – so few! – burdened with household goods bundled in tablecloths and blankets. They crowded on the platforms waiting for trains, any trains, waiting for fate to push them further on in their flight from the dreaded advancing Russian troops.

The pathetic scene oppressed my earlier cheerfulness and I was glad to get to Wilmsdorf and Anneliese three hours later. Her family welcomed me cordially, as they always did, but as ever I felt a slight constraint in their conservatively well-mannered company. It wasn't until Anneliese sneaked into my room that night when the rest of the family were in bed that I felt able to relax; holding her in my arms, pressing her firm, lovely body against mine, we needed no words to express fully our delight in being with each other again.

Later as we lay beside each other we talked and planned. Just to survive the end of the war would, we felt, be enough for now: to think beyond that was impossible. Our first concern was to keep out of the hands of the military police and the Gestapo – the Russians we would deal with when they arrived.

These few days stand in my memory like an idyllic and eternal spring. Although it was only February, and cold, we both experienced a glorious sense of another year starting, of an imminent spring bringing sunshine and warmth, flowers and birdsong. During the day we would clamber about the sandstone hills or wander, our arms about each other, through the pine forests of the Sachsischen Schweiz, the German Switzerland. By night nothing existed but the two of us, and our completeness in each other.

In those few days we lived with the immediacy and vividness known only to those who through sordid and bitter experience have learnt to appreciate life's precious fullness and sweetness. And brevity.

Late on the evening of 13 February we were standing on the porch of the house looking out into the darkness when we heard the drone of a wave of bombers. A few minutes later flame sprang into the sky. Dresden had been hit. It was the first air raid on the city and it was carried out with a calculated and deadly accuracy and ferocity that made any later attacks unnecessary.

In less than half an hour the city was well alight, visible like some terrible beacon for miles around.

Throughout the night we stood and watched as a second and then a third wave of British and American bombers completed the devastation with high explosives. Even where we stood, 20 miles away, great charred flakes floated down on us like hideous black snow.

There is nothing I can say about the destruction of Dresden that has not already been said, nothing which will condemn this terrible and evil deed more than the deed itself and the 150,000 human beings it killed in the most devastating air raid of the war.

I can only relate the sight that met my eyes when Anneliese and I took the train to Dresden en route for Berlin a few days later. It was unrecognisable as a city, let alone as Dresden, so complete was the ruin. A thick pall of smoke hung over it, pierced occasionally by flames from the still unextinguished fires. The stench of charred flesh festered nauseatingly in the air, cloying in my nostrils.

Immediately upon our arrival at the temporary station, Anneliese and I were press-ganged into salvage work, dragging the dead and dying from beneath the heaps of rubble. The bodies were so numerous that they had to be stacked in heaps and the flame-throwers were turned upon them until they burnt to ashes. In some places whole streets were blocked off and bricked up and the bodies left to rot until the salvage teams got round to them to carry out their gruesome task. Although I, like the rest of the salvage workers, constantly tied a mask over my nose and mouth, it seemed to me that I would never rid my nostrils of that indescribable odour of burning flesh and hair, of decomposing bodies and congealing blood.

The rescue teams worked relentlessly, scarcely pausing to rest or sleep – if there was sleep to be had with the imprint of such monumental human devastation seared into one's brain. There was no time to stop and think or reflect, which was just as well because we would have ceased to function like clockwork automata if we had allowed a full realisation to sink in. But there was a moment when the heartrending, despairing lunacy of it all edged in through a chink in my armour. It was a small enough incident in itself, trivial in comparison with the rest, but somehow it caught me off guard. Clambering over the heaps of rubble, I found a little shoe, a baby's. It seemed so small and defenceless lying among the harsh bricks, I picked it up. And then I realised the baby's foot was still in it.

More piteous than the dead were the mutilated bodies of the living and the frenzy of their pain, and there were nowhere near enough medical supplies and assistance to ease them. Some, apparently unscathed, wandered aimlessly about in a vacant bewilderment from which they would never recover, their minds and their lives blasted to nothingness.

There was only one possible military target in Dresden, the SS Wildemann Kaserne. Ironically, it was the only part of the city which was not hit.

For five days Anneliese and I worked amid the carnage and debris and stink of death and suffering until I saw the shadow of hallucinated exhaustion in her shocked and sleepless eyes. She was fatigued beyond her strength and if I didn't get her away she would soon be a candidate for a hospital herself.

We stole away from Dresden, picking our way out, the smell of its cremation clinging to us like a nightmare, and eventually we managed to complete our interrupted journey to Berlin.

If I had ever questioned the rightness of my belief in the essential immorality of war, of my refusal to undertake someone else's killing to order, Dresden would have removed every trace of doubt. If more people had objected at the right time, there would have been no Dresden, no Belsen, no Hiroshima. Governments declare war, but the people fight it.

Back to Berlin and the relative sanctuary of Anneliese's flat, the building still standing incongruously whole among its broken neighbours. Since she had had to accompany her boss, the Kommandant at Hildesheim, whether he worked from there or from Berlin, Anneliese had had this flat ever since I had known her. It was really very makeshift, I suppose, just a small room with a bed and washbasin and an even smaller kitchen, but in all my time in the BFC it had become a haven of tenderness, a refuge from the sordid world outside.

At first I hid indoors all day while Anneliese went to work as usual at Fehrbelliner Strasse, but then, emboldened by her reports of the chaos that reigned at headquarters, I judged I would be reasonably safe from arrest if I went out. Communications between Dresden and Berlin were virtually non-existent and it was doubtful, after the bombing of Dresden, whether I could be listed as a deserter beyond all doubt, and it is possible therefore that my desertion was never officially reported.

In fact I noticed, with considerable amusement, that a so-called 'historic' account of the BFC includes me as an active and combatant member right up to the time the Corps eventually got near the Russian front! However, the fate of the Corps after I deserted early in February 1945 is something of which I have no personal knowledge, and I had no interest in its future. For me it had been a vehicle, and once it had served its purpose, I simply stepped off.

I was concerned only with keeping Anneliese and myself alive and out of the hands of the Gestapo and the police. I soon realised that they had their time more than fully occupied by the hordes of unruly refugees and imported labour gangs, and that scarcity of food could very soon be our biggest survival problem. Deciding to take a risk, I donned my uniform one day and went to Fehrbelliner Strasse to see if I could claim my rations. It worked. The official left hand knew so little of what the right was doing that it was tacitly assumed that I was still a serving member of the Corps and no questions were asked.

Naturally I went again, and again. I was standing around there one day when a familiar figure came swinging through the entrance. John! And I thought he had long since gone home! He was equally surprised and delighted to see me, and we left the building together to catch up privately on what we had been doing since we last saw each other.

Neither of us had a great deal to tell. It seemed he was still with the

Kurt Eggers. The transfer to Italy had not yet materialised, but he and Lena still intended to go as soon as the papers came through. They were married now and living at her flat in Dahlendorf.

After that we usually contrived to run into each other most days and spent our time foraging about the back streets of Berlin. It struck me that our preoccupations had changed very little since our Jersey days, although those seemed a lifetime away. The last successful coup we pulled off together in Berlin was when we were collared by a fanatical German SS sergeant to help him load a wagon with provisions, clothes and ammunition. As we worked, he told us with zealous enthusiasm that he was preparing himself to carry out the last orders of his superiors. These were to organise werewolf bands to roam the Russian-occupied territories and raid enemy troops whenever the opportunity presented itself. This would undoubtedly save Germany from total defeat by the Allies, he said with conviction. Our enthusiastic approval of this crazy plan was so convincing that he asked us to join him and, when we agreed eagerly, the deluded fool left us in charge of the loaded wagon for a few minutes while he attended to another small task.

It was long enough for us to disappear with the wagon, complete with provisions and equipment. We took the food, a pistol and an American revolver, and the remainder of the stuff, being of no use to us personally, we dumped in the back yard of a dilapidated house hoping it would be of some assistance to the occupants.

Our scouring of the back alleys and bombed-out houses also led to my acquiring two small, useless but very endearing items: an incredibly grubby little boy and a miniature long-haired Dachshund.

There must have been dozens, hundreds even, of such children living in the streets from hand to mouth, orphaned without home or family by the bombing. They were strange urchins, precocious and old before their time, masters in the game of self-preservation. Those that survived the first few weeks alone became adept at fending for themselves, clever thieves and successful beggars – they had to be if they were to go on living. This particular little brat attached himself to me for a while for some unaccountable reason, the archetypal waif and stray, the pathetic monkey-old face so pale even beneath all the dirt.

This dirtiness was probably the most outstanding feature about him. In the end I took him home with me and put him in the bath. I must have been scrubbing with soap and brush for about five minutes before I came to his shirt! But the urchin had his uses too. I noticed that when it came to food queues or handouts, people were much more likely to make way for you if you had a child in tow, and for a while the two of us did a good trade together.

Then one day he simply stopped turning up at the point near the station where we would usually meet by unspoken and instinctive agreement. I never did discover what happened to him for I had no way of finding out. Perhaps he had smuggled himself onto a train to seek new streets elsewhere, perhaps he was killed in an air raid. I missed the little fellow. He hadn't wanted to come and live in the flat with us – his home had been in the streets for too long for him to feel comfortable enclosed by four walls – but we had enjoyed each other's company. For a long time I looked out for the familiar, grubby little face, but it didn't appear again.

The tiny Dachshund, on the other hand, was delighted to have a home. I found it yapping frenziedly in a bombed house after a raid, the only survivor and terrified out of its miniature wits. I took it back and gave it to Anneliese and it turned out to be a faithful and stouthearted friend to us.

By April the Russians were closing in on Berlin and soon we would be in a state of siege. John said very little but I could see that he was beginning to get worried. If the transfer didn't come through soon, it would be impossible for them to leave. But at last it was approved and 9 April was fixed as the day of their departure.

John and I had nothing much to say as we stood on the platform waiting for the train. We both knew that this time it was final, that the very successful team the two of us had made was about to split up. Together we had dodged the hangman, ducked the firing squad, escaped from prison, stood by each other at times when it would have been easier to have walked out. Now, as we stood on the ruined station, there was nothing to say. Lena tried to make small talk to lighten the silence, her chatter interrupted at regular intervals by the mortar bombs crashing into the shattered streets around Stendal Bahnhof.

149

We were all relieved when the train rolled in. Most of the carriages were packed with wounded and disabled soldiers. Lena dashed to find a compartment, which she soon accomplished with her pretty face and charming smile. John stood fidgeting a few moments more on the platform, young, blond and very handsome in his new field grey uniform of an SS war correspondent. Then in response to Lena's urgent calls he too boarded the train.

He stood near the window and we said goodbye finally. For all I knew I would never see him again. The train slipped away and gathered speed, the waving arm and fair head at the open window became a blur and receded to a dot in the distance.

It was the last train out of Berlin.

Chapter 12

ESCAPE FROM BERLIN

It was nearly May in Berlin. The sun shone, a cherry tree flowered defiantly in the garden of a ruined house, the light breeze riffling the pink and white blossoms scattering the ground like confetti. Anneliese and I walked hand in hand from the Register Office in Charlottenburg, man and wife under the National Socialist law of Germany.

Himmler's dispensation for us to marry had at last come through. Now we were honoured if not with a 21-gun salute then at least an impressive volley of mortar bombs which the Russians encircling the city sent crashing into our vicinity. The well-trained registrar dutifully ignored the disturbance and proceeded with the ceremony, if at a slightly quickened pace. For the first time I stated my real name and place of birth, a fact which caused the registrar rather more surprise than the bombs. Here I was not Erich Doran, the name I had taken on joining the BFC, but my very English self, Reginald Eric Pleasants, born in Norfolk, England.

The formalities complete, the registrar pushed the huge register across the table for us to sign, shook our hands and congratulated us, all just as he must have done on countless other more common, peaceful occasions. Then he courteously opened the door for us and as I made no attempt to give the Hitler salute nor did he, a significant omission for such an official.

Anneliese and I stood in the warm sunshine outside and smiled at each other. 'Let us hope the man is right!' she said softly. I knew she was referring to the registrar's good wishes to us for a long and happy life together. In these days it was more a fervent wish than a polite formula.

Strangely enough, though, the future was far from my mind at that moment. There was only the present, the reality of the instant, the surroundings in which I moved. I was involved in it all without being overwhelmed by it. Because I refused to take sides, I belonged nowhere, unbound by time and place, part of my present world, but not drawn into its suicidal vortex. And despite the hopelessness and destruction all around me, I felt a happiness that was almost light-headed, the sense of freedom that only the escaped prisoner can know.

This was what I had chosen, I was doing things my way; what the end result would be I had no idea, but that had so little significance for me that I scarcely considered it at the time. I was without any fear. I felt only a curious contentment.

At the other end of the scale from me was the once mighty Hitler. He had brought his country up from the poverty line to a nation which had formed the largest fighting front line ever known in history – a considerable achievement, whichever way one looked at it. Now, half-demented, he crouched away in some last hiding place, a megalomaniac dog in the manger compelling his enemy to burn his people from the face of the earth on the 'If I can't have it you won't have it either' principle.

At this moment my thoughts were scattered by heavy anti-aircraft fire. A little scared, we dodged into a nearby machine-gun post where a grey-haired German soldier helped us in, saying with a cheery smile, 'It won't be long now!' At first I thought he was speaking of that particular burst of gunfire, but as he went on I realised he was referring to things in general.

'Have you heard how a written communication is being passed around the troops fighting just beyond the city? It says that England has called a treaty and withdrawn her troops from the approach to the west – so now our third army can march back and defend Berlin from the Russians!'

'That is wonderful!' I said with what I hoped was well-simulated joy, privately thinking, 'You poor gullible fellow!' and hoping that the fatherly old soul would be lucky enough to remain alive, even if it was only to find out how unkindly he had been deceived.

The barricades, traditionally the last bastion of the citizen, were going up in the streets, erected with the desperate courage and remaining furniture of the German housewives. All those last few precious household remnants they had managed to preserve through the bombings they now piled up in a final gesture of simultaneous surrender and defiance, reinforcing the flimsy structures with burnt-out vehicles, iron palings, barbed wire – anything they could drag into this last-ditch stand to keep Ivan at bay. I think it is fair to say that they were motivated more by personal terror than patriotism or fear of defeat, for the reputation of the scruffy, youthful Russian soldiers who surrounded the city had gone before them.

Slowly, inexorably, the strange tattered urchin soldiers of the Red Army were burning their way like a slow fuse into Berlin. Soon they would be in Kurfürstendamm, shooting, raping and looting, goaded on by their officers with promises of a free hand with the women of their now helpless enemy; the prerogatives of a conquering invader have changed little since the days of Genghis Khan.

On the corner of Joachimstaler Strasse we passed a public notice board declaring the execution of an officer and three soldiers for desertion and using false papers, a farcical reminder that even before their defeat the German people had been totally at the mercy of their own rulers. Now the notice seemed anachronistic, even ridiculous, as unreal in the middle of all this instant death as a theatre bill. Whatever crimes the ordinary Germans may be accused of, they had paid for them in full measure.

Crouching, running, sheltering – no journey across the city was ever straightforward now – we returned to Rudesheimer Platz and Anneliese's flat, which still stood erect among the surrounding ruins like a country lavatory. It could not be long before it too was hit and brought tumbling to earth, and we didn't want to be in it when that happened. But now there was nowhere else for us to go but underground – literally, for the streets, as dangerous as they already were, would be plain suicide once the Russians entered the city. We had no option but to stay in Berlin until it fell; once the Russians were in and the roads open again we could reconsider our position.

Something almost like nostalgia crept over me as I looked round the room while Anneliese sorted out essential clothing and provisions. This little place had been a home and a refuge to us both. Here we had loved and talked and laughed, and shut out the harshness of the world; here we had lived, finding sanity and reality in each other and in the ideals we both still believed in, despite all that had happened. Anneliese looked across at me, saying nothing, smiling a little sadly at thoughts which must have mirrored my own.

As we went out, she locked the door carefully behind her, a precaution both of us saw the funny side of, and we made our way down to the street laughing, the little dog tripping along behind us. And then the underworld closed upon the three of us, shutting out the light.

Beneath every great city is a vast network of concrete tunnels and vaults unsuspected by the pedestrian who daily treads the pavements above them. It is not a region he would care to visit even if he did know about it, for the word 'sewer' has about it an emotive ring of filth, dampness and foul air.

The effluent and excesses of generations of the city's people had drained into these sewers: now the people themselves seeped, fittingly, through the manholes, the waste of a crazy society, degenerate and dehumanised. Deserters, escaped criminals, refugees – all of them hiding from German police or Russian invader, all desperate to live at any cost. Friends and principles were dangerous encumbrances. It was each man for himself and if you could stab, shoot, kick and punch a little faster than the next man, then you lived a little longer than he did.

The sewer into which Anneliese and I descended was, if it carries any distinction, next to the Reich Chancellery. The chaos in the streets was reflected below them, only here people knew even less what was happening. Groups ebbed and flowed from one chamber to another, driven by rumours of police or Russian raids. Here the sounds of bombs reached us only as muffled explosions which shook the walls of our cavern. This dismal subterranean world was relatively safe but its gloom and cut-throat viciousness oppressed me and I wondered how long I would be able to stand it.

We pitched our 'camp' upon an empty stretch of the concrete shelf. As far as one could see in either direction there were other similar encampments of whole families, groups who had joined forces for comfort and protection, occasionally couples, but never single people on their own. The reason was simple: those who did come down on their own didn't live long enough to stay that way. They instantly fell prey to the gangs of hungry and desperate brigands who would kill for little or nothing. Amid the apparent chaos was a certain organisation: the weak sought the protection of the strong, the strong went foraging for food and provisions to keep this strange society going. As these foraging expeditions were generally conducted above ground, they were also a means of gathering information about what was happening in the world outside.

It would have been impossible for us down there to know at which point the Russians actually rolled into Berlin, but the time came when there was a deafening explosion in a nearby tunnel and a few severely burned men stumbled blindly into our chamber, gasping that the Russians were using flame-throwers to clear the sewers. If that was true then we would have to get out at once, but I was doubtful. It doesn't take much to cause an explosion underground, and besides there seemed to be no follow-up.

Leaving Anneliese briefly, I went to see if I could find out anything from one of the groups near an exit. As I rounded the last bend on my return, Anneliese's piercing screams reached me clearly through the rest of the noise. I rushed forward, drawing a PPK pistol from beneath my shirt, now distinguishing Anneliese struggling violently with one man while another was bending over our bundle a short distance away. I fired first at him so as not to endanger Anneliese.

As I pulled the trigger a vibrating crash echoed through the tunnel. The crouching figure straightened up and for one horrible moment I thought I had missed him. Then he threw his hands out and with a convulsive jerk twisted round and collapsed, sliding round the wall. The second man released Anneliese and stood hesitating, undecided whether to run or fight. By this time I was near him. He decided to run. I sprang after him, pushed him face down to the ground and smashed the pistol several times onto the back of his head. It was a small weapon and had little serious effect, but before I realised what was happening a sobbing and dishevelled Anneliese appeared near me, a tiny Beretta in her hand. The toy-like gun cracked several times and the half-conscious man on the ground jerked a little then lay still.

Anneliese collapsed sobbing at my feet, clutching my legs. At last I managed to prise her hands loose and lift her up, trying desperately to soothe her with a torrent of words in English and German.

For a long time we stood huddled together in that stinking vault, finding comfort in each other's nearness.

After a while we became aware of the need to move to a less dangerous spot. Going over to the man I had shot first, I searched through the pockets of his tattered uniform. They yielded a few hundred marks, which I immediately transferred to my own, and a Luger pistol, which, luckily for me, he had not had time to draw. It was too big and cumbersome to be of any use to me so I tossed it into the sewer gully and pushed the body of the owner after it. I went back to the second body, picked up the small pistol Anneliese had dropped, and then dropped the dead man in to join his companion.

I stood there a few moments staring down into the blackness and suddenly I was sickened by the disgusting, debased brutality of the whole incident. With my whole being I revolted against being compelled to live like some vicious sewer rat, every human, moral consideration anaesthetised by the foul air that engulfed me. I had to get out. I would take my chances in the street rather than die down there like a poisoned rodent.

As night fell we emerged cautiously through a manhole. I had learned that the city had finally capitulated, that the Russians were now in command of the streets. The air, pungent though it was with the smell of burning, seemed fresh to our nostrils. For a while we wandered aimlessly without a sense of direction or purpose until we realised that we were making towards Rudesheimer Platz, drawn by some irrational magnet to Anneliese's flat.

The building was still there. We watched and waited, then went in.

I wished we had not come. The little retreat had been violated, ransacked and despoiled. The furniture and the less portable of our belongings had been smashed and several people with a quaint sense of humour or sanitation had emptied the contents of their bowels and bladders in the most awkward places, even though it would have been easier and more comfortable to use the still-functioning lavatory. The thefts I could understand, but the deliberate destruction and soiling was like a desecration of our private lives.

(It was not until much later that I found out that the wonders of modern plumbing and sanitation were unknown to many of the backwoods Russians. Some of them were so impressed by the convenience of water on tap that they carried off a few taps so that they might enjoy the facility when they returned home – it never occurring to them that the taps could not function without a plumbing system behind them!)

After a sad and at times tearful hunt among the remains of her home, Anneliese found enough bedclothes to make up a bed for us in the kitchen, where we spent an uneasy night snatching short periods of sleep and listening to the rumble of tanks and the transports of yelling, cheering Russian soldiers.

Obviously we couldn't have stayed there, even if we had wanted to, and next morning, forlorn and heavy-eyed, we set ourselves to thinking where we might be relatively unmolested in a Berlin bristling with the menace of celebrating Russian hordes. There was a hospital bunker near Fehrbelliner Strasse – we could try that. We had no idea what we would do once we got there, but it was enough to take one step at a time.

Rummaging about her scattered wardrobe, Anneliese found the remnants of a nurse's uniform, together with a Red Cross armband. She put this on, tucking her hair tightly out of sight under the uniform cap and trying to make herself look as unattractive as possible. To match this, I had a heavy gauze bandage tied around my head, partly covering my face but leaving one eye uncovered for emergencies. My SS pay book and other papers were destroyed. Anneliese, who had prudently retained several blank forms, produced their equivalent in Wehrmacht type to substantiate our tale of me being an ordinary soldier with a nurse acting voluntarily as escort. Putting the rest of our essential provisions in a rucksack – including the little dog perched on top of everything – we left the flat for the last time and without a backward glance.

Once in the street we saw many dressed as we were and we congratulated ourselves on having chosen an opportune disguise.

The solitary Red Cross orderly on duty admitted us to the hospital bunker without demur. Inside, we found the long concrete passages lined with beds so close that they touched each other. A few doctors, obviously SS, moved among them faithfully carrying out their duty to humanity, saving lives where they could, easing pain and the last agony where there was no hope. The few medical staff were too occupied to challenge us and it was not difficult for Anneliese and myself to find an obscure corner in which to seat ourselves.

We sat together without speaking in the hopeless silence of that underground hospital, waiting. We did not know what for, we expected nothing. We were just waiting. Waiting to cope with the next twist or turn that fate decided to take. I felt calm but unutterably depressed. In the gloom, Anneliese's pale face looked relaxed. We both felt a little tired. The Dachshund slept, curled in the mouth of the rucksack; once in there, we knew from experience that it could be trusted to remain still and quiet.

Suddenly, from further down the passage, the low urgency of a hoarse whisper reached us: '*Ivan kommt!*'

We sprang up, searching frantically among the bunks lining the corridor walls for one which was empty. There were none, but we quickly discovered one in which the occupant lay still and cold. My need was greater than his. Lifting him out, I placed him on the floor against the wall and then stretched myself out in the vacated bed. Anneliese pulled the blanket over me. She had scarcely finished when a youthful figure emerged out of the gloom, the ragged clothing offset by an American helmet. The bright slanting eyes peering from beneath it darted about and came to rest on Anneliese. His grimy face broke into a leer and he stretched out his hand demanding menacingly '*Ure, ure!*', pointing to the watch on her wrist.

With an air of weary resignation she undid the thin strap and dropped it into the boy's grubby paw. He whisked it away into the folds of his tattered tunic and, swinging the well-polished American rifle onto his back, he turned and disappeared along the corridor as softly and stealthily as he had come.

As I lay waiting for Anneliese to give the all clear before I got up,

I was suddenly aware that one side of my body felt wet and sticky. When I climbed out of the bed, Anneliese screwed up her face and pointed to my side, which was soaked in blood. Evidently our dead friend had bled to death in the same bunk which had saved me from the chance of arrest or worse.

The incident prompted once more the instinct to rational planning if we were to stay alive. We could not stay indefinitely in the hospital and there was unlikely to be anywhere else we could take shelter. The Berlin that had once been the refuge and last resort of thousands fleeing before the enemy had turned into a vicious open arena. The stream of people that had flooded into the city now turned its course and throughout the day a flux of travellers plodded down the rubble-deep streets, making their way to the outskirts to join with other similar groups all with the same, simple idea – to go to the west zone, away from Ivan. We decided to join them.

The experience of those few days in captured Berlin have left a deep ugly scar on my memory. Atrocities worthy of the barbarian hordes of Attila were commonplace sights in the streets where bands of Russians roamed unchecked, looting, pillaging, raping. No woman, whatever her age or condition, was safe from violation of the most perverted kind.

One young woman, dragged by four jubilantly cheering soldiers from the cellar of a crumpled building, tried to save herself by screaming repeatedly that she had some terrible venereal disease. When this eventually got through to her captors, who had already partly stripped her of her clothing, the youth at the back drew his revolver and blew out her brains. Dropping the body, they left it writhing reflexively on the ground while they skipped merrily away like a group of mischievous boys in search of other entertainment.

Warned by such sights, Anneliese was now dressed to resemble a ragged and rather grubby boy, of which I was supposedly the father.

'You look the part, *Kleine!*' I said, smiling at her appearance. She grinned.

'Yes – it will be all right as long as we don't meet up with any Russians who are queer!'

It was only two or three days after the fall of Berlin and our sense of humour was returning, albeit in rather a macabre and gallows vein. I laughed.

'We haven't done too badly so far – you've only lost your watch to the Russians!'

'Oh, that!' she said carelessly. 'I put that one on my wrist in case something like that happened. It hadn't worked for years. My good gold one is in my hair under this silly hat!'

Realising it was going to be a long trek, we acquired a handcart and piled our stuff onto it. Then we tagged on to one of the sad little caravans of wearily trudging Berliners, doggedly pushing similar handcarts, prams or barrows loaded with the salvaged remnants of their material goods they had spent a lifetime working for. They had lost nearly everything except the indomitable desire to start again in middle-class respectability in the security of which they believed even now.

Chapter 13

NO HIDING PLACE

It drew near evening of our first day on the road, the time when all civilians had to be off the streets. We stopped at a hostel organised by a group of Germans under the auspices of the International Red Cross. It was a large, comparatively undamaged house, fitted out with sacks of straw to sleep on. The two field kitchens run by four solid German women produced hot soup of unrecognisable origin, which nevertheless had a remarkable effect on the morale of the hungry and footsore gathering.

The place filled up quickly. Some lay outstretched on the straw sacks, asleep with exhaustion or staring wide-eyed at their memories; others sat on bundles of their precious belongings. New arrivals eagerly wolfed the soup. Gradually people settled down and, despite the horror of all they had so recently left behind, the gathering seemed to have an air of relaxation. Children played and plagued their parents and were scolded and loved alternately; people talked and joked and laughed quietly. I marvelled at the resilience of the human being. The continuous air raids, bombing and shooting, the sleepless nights and constant fear of death already seemed miles away in the past.

We were starting to drowse when the street door burst open and two tall American soldiers strode in and pushed briskly through the crowd. Instantly a hush fell and our slumbering anxiety and alarm leapt into wakefulness. One of the soldiers, pale and puffy-faced, shoved his way to where the women were serving soup from cauldrons. Pulling a handful of paper money from his pocket and thrusting it under her nose, he said loudly and arrogantly that he wanted to buy some.

The woman obviously did not understand what he was saying but guessed from his actions what he wanted, or pretended to want. She shook her head and said firmly and politely in German: 'No, sir, this is only for German civilians.'

The young American, realising that he was being refused, answered with his entire German vocabulary.

'*Schise!*' he bawled in pidgin German, pulling a revolver from inside his shirt. 'Me shoot!' Instantly his companion did likewise, moving back to the door, effectively barring it and menacing the room with his pistol. The puffy-faced GI now proceeded through the crowd of refugees taking from them their wrist watches, money and any other valuables that caught his eye or which his victims produced in terror. Now and then he would empty a bag or case onto the floor, fingering through the contents while the owners gazed stoically as their precious trinkets disappeared into his pockets and shirt front. From the woman sitting next to us he demanded the rings from her fingers.

Then it was our turn. He tapped the baggage at our feet with the toe of his boot and indicated with a flourish of his gun that somebody was to empty it out. Anneliese coughed nervously and got meekly to her feet to do as he ordered. I remained seated, my arms hanging limply over my knees, the tips of my fingers only an inch from the small automatic pistol in my boot.

Rage made my stomach burn. I looked into the soldier's small shifty eyes and snarled slowly and distinctly: 'You pox-ridden, stinking Yankee bastard scum!'

The effect of this totally unexpected invective in English was electrifying. He froze. For a few awful moments the world stood still with his pistol pointed straight at me. My mouth felt dry. The American broke the suspense by spinning around and thrusting the gun back into his shirt.

'Let's get the hell outta here!' he snapped curtly to his companion. The other obediently jerked the door open and the two small-time crooks disappeared into the darkness.

The spell of silence was broken. People began to move about the room again. I still felt a little shaky. Several crowded around us wanting to know who or what I was, what I had said, what language it was. It was publicity we could well do without, but Anneliese, who had now recovered her poise, slipped smoothly into an account of my carefully prepared fictitious history. She told them that although I was German I had been born in the Argentine – which accounted for my accent when speaking German – and on a visit to relations in Germany I had been enlisted in the German army, after a thorough investigation by the Gestapo, of course, but I had unfortunately had to be invalided out after suffering severe injuries while fighting for the Fatherland.

The story seemed to capture their imagination and sympathy, but all the same we felt uneasy and made up our minds to get away as soon as we could, which would be at dawn the next day.

The problem was: where could we go? Once more we would be running away from, rather than to, something. There could be no sanctuary for me, a renegade Englishman, in this confusion of American and Russian troops. But obviously it would have been foolish for us to walk aimlessly for long. The little handcart carried, besides a change of clothing, blankets and bedding and a fair amount of food. With luck and a lot of stamina we could walk to Anneliese's home province – a mere 200 miles away. Of stamina and good fortune we both had our fair share, and though we were uncomfortably aware that every step of the way could be full of danger, we believed we could make it. Besides, what choice had we?

Once more at dawn we piled our few essential belongings and the dog onto the handcart and followed in the struggling wake of refugees already out on the road. Many of them were hoping to enter the American or British zones, where they believed some sort of orderly future might be possible.

Time and again we saw the Russians make arrests among the refugees on the road. They needed labour for the coal mines of Vorkuta and timber camps of Inta, and this was as certain a way of getting it as any. Anneliese and I quickly realised that they detained only the physically sound and obviously fit, whereupon my left arm became swathed in bandages and strapped across the front of my chest. The bandage around my head and over my left eye was readopted for good measure. Anneliese did her best to transform herself into an old crone, blackening her teeth and hunching her shoulders into a stoop.

The bandage on my arm also provided a secure hiding place for Anneliese's few valuables and a thick roll of German money.

Once out on the open roads the little knots of travellers grew fewer until it seemed for long stretches at a time that we had the highway to ourselves. Our spirits rose. The weather was glorious, we were walking the road free and we had somewhere to go. We could even put to the back of our minds the constant fear that nagged us night and day: the marauding bands of Russian soldiers, many of them unofficial, who haunted the highways like blood-crazy bandits out for plunder and rape. I feared constantly for Anneliese whenever a group of these heavily armed ruffians approached and I marvelled at her composure. What I didn't realise was that she was more concerned for my safety than her own and was prepared to undergo anything if it would mean saving my life and freedom.

After several days of walking we were nearing the border. We had left the general stream of people heading for the American zone and were now deep in Russian territory. Night was falling and we were trudging along looking for a place to sleep and rest our aching legs and feet when the dreaded apparition of three Russian soldiers loomed up out of the dusk.

They were a frightening picture in the failing light. Sturdily built youths with hard, unsmiling faces and Mongol-slit eyes, they purposefully barred our way with rifles at the ready.

'*Stehe!*' growled the leader, demanding in bad German that we hand over watches and money. The other two circled about us, repeating, '*Ure, ure!*' ('Watches, watches!'), their guns pointed steadily at us. I stood still, the smell of their unwashed bodies and dirty uniforms overpoweringly close. One of them peered impudently at Anneliese, tilting up her chin with his filthy fingers.

The leader grew impatient and stretched out his hand. The soldier standing by me slipped off the safety catch on his rifle slowly, deliberately. Little Anneliese, with a timid, imploring smile, slowly spread out her empty hands and shook her head, indicating that we had nothing of value. Then she pointed to my bandaged arm and head.

They seemed to understand and to accept that we were penniless and harmless for they slung their rifles onto their backs, muzzle down in the traditional Russian fashion, and began to sort through the contents of our handcart. After tossing things out and finding nothing that interested them, they spoke briefly together. Then one of them came slowly over to me.

I went cold. I knew that all our valuables were hidden in the bandage on my bogus wounded arm and I thought they must have tumbled to the fact. But to my astonishment he didn't touch me and in fact offered me an American cigarette from a packet. I was so amazed I simply accepted it, not troubling to make him understand that I didn't smoke, and put it behind my ear.

While this was going on, the other two had positioned themselves on either side of Anneliese and when I looked up at the sound of their footsteps I saw them walking her up the road between them. Their intentions were suddenly horribly clear.

The third soldier, who was trying to distract my attention with pleasantries in broken German, had clearly been left behind to stop me getting in the way. I suppose that but for the bandages they would simply have shot me or clubbed me over the head to prevent my giving them any trouble. As it was, they didn't seem to think that I, a wounded, one-armed and slightly built man, constituted any threat, for my guard was now searching through his pockets with both hands for a light for our cigarettes, the rifle still slung harmlessly down his back. That was his mistake, and I have never felt any regret for what I did next.

Silently and carefully I measured the distance between us and with lightning speed I brought my right hand up to catch him a hammer-like blow on the side of his round, flat face. As he staggered and crashed to the ground, I drove the heel of my boot several times into his neck and face with all my force. He lay still, making no sound.

Ripping the bandages off my left arm I ran frantically along the road in the direction taken by the others. Even as I ran I felt a fierce surge of pleasure in my own strength and litheness and in the power of my limbs, and then there was in me only the cold inhuman killing rage of the animal whose family have been snatched away.

I came to the nearby farm-like building and stopped for a moment, listening. I caught the sound of voices – Russian voices. Desperately I searched for an entrance. It was almost dark but at last I found a door and hurled myself through it.

In the dim light of the pocket lamp on the ground I saw Anneliese spread-eagled on the ground, her skirt pulled up to her neck, pinned down by one of the Russians kneeling on her shoulders. The second one was kneeling, trousers off, between her legs, which he forced apart by his hands on her thighs, his penis erect in front of him.

I was moving swiftly even as I took in the sight and my actions were sure and unhesitating and unthinking. I seized a length of heavy iron lying within the circle of light. I raised it and crashed it onto the head of the soldier crouching on my woman's shoulders even as the second youth looked up and saw me for the first time and froze in immobile terror of his certain death. The heavy iron in my hands rose and fell, rose and fell rhythmically upon the upturned face contorted with fear, my brain still seeing the eternal image of the half-naked youth spattered with the blood and brains of his comrade and his penis erect before him long after he lay in a bloodied heap on the floor.

An insistent whining filtered through to my consciousness. I realised for the first time that the little Dachshund was there. I don't know how long I had stood there, the iron bar still in my hands, but I saw that Anneliese had dragged herself a little away and crouched low upon the ground. There was a terrible silence and stillness about her. The dog whined and looked at her with a slow inquiring wag of his tail. I flung down the bar and put my arms about her but she did not move. I tried to reassure her, to elicit some response, for I could not bear the vacant staring of her eyes and her utter muteness, but she said nothing.

I could feel myself beginning to feel shaky and sick. If I did not pull myself together quickly, I would be unable to do anything. With a tremendous effort I gathered myself. I knew it was imperative to put as much distance as possible between us and the scene of carnage, for to be caught anywhere near there by Russian officials would undoubtedly have ended with us being shot, either on the spot or with the benefit of one of their farcical kangaroo court trials. Worse still, another similar band of wolves could be in the vicinity.

I gathered Anneliese in my arms and lifted her bodily, staggering back along the dark road to where our handcart stood. Setting her on it as carefully as I could, I found a blanket slung out by the rapists and covered her up. Scrabbling about in the region where my discarded bandage showed a dim whiteness, I managed to locate the roll of money and one or two items without much difficulty and then, without pausing to collect anything else, I gripped the handles of the cart and made off as fast as my shaking legs would allow me, the dog trotting soberly alongside.

Fortunately for me, I met not a soul and after about 20 minutes I came upon an isolated cottage. In the light from one of its windows I saw the figure of a woman working at a small bench. Softly, hesitantly, I called to her and she spun round holding her hands apprehensively to her face. With a trembling voice she asked me what I wanted, adding quickly that she was only a poor old woman and had nothing of value.

I managed to convince her that I was not a Russian and said that I needed help for my wife, who had met with an accident. She was still suspicious: where did I come from? If I was a Berliner as I said, why didn't I speak like one? She seemed finally to accept my explanations and at last asked where my wife was. Not wanting to waste another second, I dashed up the short path and fetched the cart with Anneliese still lying prostrate on top. The sight of the girl's bruised and bloodied face swept aside her last reservations. I carried Anneliese into the house and the woman helped me lay her on a couch in an adjoining room and quickly busied herself attending to the injuries.

It wasn't long before she turned to me enquiringly and said: 'Son, this is not an accident!' I did not answer. We looked steadily at each other, then slowly she nodded her head and I knew she understood. She asked no further questions.

I knew it was dangerous for us to stay at the cottage, which was relatively close to the scene of the incident, but it was some days before Anneliese recovered enough strength and nerve to continue the journey. For her sake it might perhaps have been better to stay a little longer, but neither of us wished to endanger the old peasant woman by staying on any more than was strictly necessary.

Early one morning she walked with us to the cottage gate. There were tears in her faded eyes as she took an affectionate leave of Anneliese, and I must admit I could scarcely trust myself to speak. I loved that old woman for her courage, her kindness and for the truly selfless charity she had shown.

The road seemed a little more lonely and empty once the cottage had fallen back from sight and we were both quiet for a long time. We walked steadily through the day, and the next and the next, and little was said between us. Although she walked stolidly and uncomplainingly beside me, I saw that Anneliese had been deeply affected by the experience. She had changed, withdrawn into herself, and I felt so helpless, unable to reach into her shell and coax her out. I pinned my hope on the reunion with her family and pushed up our travelling pace as much as I dared.

It was an emotional homecoming, for, of course, her family had had no news of her for several months. I fidgeted awkwardly in the background but I felt the relief of Anneliese's tears as she embraced her mother and sisters. I don't know whether she ever told them anything of our grim experiences during our last days in Berlin, the flight from the fallen capital and that final, searing incident on the road. Some people find release in talking, others cannot bear to speak of events they would rather put behind them. However it was, I began to notice after a few days that Anneliese was recovering her spirit, her old *joie de vivre* gradually edging out the frightened look that lurked behind her eyes.

Her family never asked questions – not of me at any rate. Their natural courtesy forbade that. But the doubts were there and if they did not raise them there were others in that little village to set tongues wagging. Who was this new son-in-law the Nitzschners had suddenly turned up anyway? This was the heyday of the great Nazi purge and Nazis were suddenly as prevalent as witches in the Middle Ages even, or perhaps especially, in small rural communities like Wilmsdorf. Strangers, particularly those with unfamiliar accents, were immediately suspect. From there it was a short step to denunciation to the authorities, who were at this stage the Russians.

The motives for these accusations, true and false, were as varied as the informers. Petty intrigue, the chance to settle old scores, gaining favour with those in power, revenge, fear – it didn't matter, the result was the same. It wasn't long before it became obvious that the inquisitive glances in my direction were going beyond speculation to investigation. I was rapidly becoming persona non grata not only in the community but also in the Nitzschner household, and I wasn't the only one either. Of course, it had occurred to me to consider whether Anneliese might be better off without me, and that if I were to disappear quietly she would be able to live peacefully and comfortably with her family. However, it soon became apparent that she would not be very welcome as a long-term guest.

Anneliese's parents were postmaster and postmistress at Wilmsdorf, a station in society that carried with it a certain solid respectability. In the past, Frau Nitzschner had boasted to her neighbours, as proud mothers will of their children's material success, that her youngest daughter held a well-paid government post in Berlin. In popular opinion now this added up to only one thing, since no one could have held any government post without being a member of the Nazi Party, however unenthusiastic they personally may have felt about their membership. The vaunted daughter was now something of an embarrassment, and her husband a positive hazard.

It had to happen sooner or later. There was a family council, a few more tears, and we left quietly. Our little Dachshund stood on the porch whining as we walked away. I wished the tiny fellow was coming with us but it seemed unkind to condemn those short legs of his to an eternal life on the road when he had been offered a good home there.

For Anneliese and myself there was no such choice. Our rucksacks loaded with food and a change of clothing, we made once more for the railway station, where we caught the next train out. It went to Dresden.

It didn't seem a great deal to ask, to vanish from sight until the Germans had stopped witch-hunting the Nazis, the Russians had stopped punishing the Germans, and the Americans and English had stopped digging for 'traitors'. On that reckoning I was a much-wanted man, and for the likes of me to remain concealed until the cry for scapegoats was over was rather like expecting an elephant to remain undetected under a tablecloth. Dresden afforded about as poor a cover as I could have chosen.

The reorganised German police worked with the enthusiasm of the proverbial new broom. To get ration cards you needed residential papers and to get those you had to undergo an interrogation that would have done credit to the Gestapo. Without me, Anneliese did have some small chance of getting papers and work, but my record would certainly not have stood up under the enquiries. I began to feel something of a burden to her and turned to my only alternative means of livelihood – theft and black-marketeering. It was back to the old routine, only this time the stakes were higher and the hazards greater.

The chances of being caught as a black-marketeer were so high that after several very narrow escapes I began to think that there would be less risk in trying to get work. But it didn't come off. Despite my convincing yarn, the official who interviewed me still wasn't satisfied and detained me so that he could get in the police to question me more thoroughly. I had no intention of making their close acquaintance and rapidly escaped from the office where I was being held. I ran straight back to the place where Anneliese and I were staying.

She looked up in some alarm as I came bursting in breathing hard.

'Come on – we're getting out!' I said shortly. She was too familiar with the situation to waste time on questions and as we got our few belongings together I told her what had happened. In less than half an hour we were on the road again. We had tried the Germans and the Russians, now we would try our luck with the Americans.

The US-occupied zone lay on the opposite side of the river. We made for the official cross-over point, a wrecked bridge temporarily repaired by the American pioneer troops. As we approached, we could see that the bank on our side was crowded and the traffic all in one direction – towards the American side. Jostled by the anxious throng of refugees, a small group of Russian soldiers made a random scrutiny of papers and personal belongings but it was merely a pretext to confiscate articles of value, which, they would tell the protesting owners, one was not permitted to take from the country. On the opposite bank two bored-looking American soldiers watched the scene with nonchalant indifference.

Merging with the crowd, Anneliese and I were eventually shuffled and pushed to the bridge like grains of sand sifting to the waist of the hour-glass. I tried hard not to show the nervous agitation jangling inside me as we filtered slowly past the guards and onto the bridge. We were not challenged, but with every step I took over that bridge I could feel the back of my neck tingling in anticipation of the imperious command to halt, the volley of shots.

But they never came. The relief as we reached the opposite side was almost physical.

We were in the American zone. If safety and freedom were possible for us, we stood as good a chance of finding them here as anywhere else.

Chapter 14

CIRCUS STRONG MAN

E rich Doran, Englishman and one-time member of the British Free Corps, was now dead.

In his place there emerged a new character: Hans Sandau, native of Sachsischen Schweiz, who in peacetime earned his living as a strong man.

I had for so long spoken, thought even, only in German that it came as something of a shock in the refugee clearing station to hear people openly speaking English, and when they addressed me in bad German it was no effort to reply in that language rather than my own.

It was not until Anneliese and I were transferred to the established camp near Halle on the River Saale, not far from Leipzig, that I felt safe enough to disclose that I did speak English. Here I made myself useful by acting as interpreter for the harassed American authorities who ran the camp, and the many compliments I received on my good command of the English language gave me a lot of simple amusement.

It was a good life, relatively speaking, while it lasted. The food was plentiful, the accommodation comfortable. As my services proved increasingly useful and reliable, the officials with whom I worked were glad to let me get on with things on my own and in my own way; sometimes a few days at a time would pass before any of the staff bothered to put in an appearance, which of course suited me fine. Quite incidentally, I began to build up quite a nice little sideline in curios and souvenirs too.

It started by accident one day when an American, who was returning home the following day, commented upon the rather unusual inkwell standing on my desk.

'Well, it would be unusual, wouldn't it, considering it was Hitler's,' I said with a completely straight face but intending it as a joke. To my amazement, he took it seriously. He was thrilled and picked the thing up almost reverently.

'You don't say! You mean to say this was actually Hitler's own inkwell, the one he personally used? You – er – you wouldn't be thinking of selling it, would you?'

I couldn't believe my ears. But, if he really wanted to buy Hitler's inkwell who was I to ruin his chances of acquiring a unique inkwell? Because it was such a singular item I had to drive quite a hard bargain, of course, but he was delighted – and so was I.

I sold Hitler's inkwell several times after that, or rather, replicas of the original on my desk and, growing quite bold, I branched out into daggers, helmets, old watches, paperweights – anything that could conceivably have belonged to some notorious Nazi official. My stories grew more fantastic too, but the more farfetched these were, the more my gullible customers seemed to appreciate them, and my fertile imagination embroidered incredible tales for their benefit.

For a while Anneliese and I were content to live each well-fed day as it came, recuperating slowly. For me it was enough to see the strain and anxiety fade slowly from Anneliese's face and to have her smile and laugh easily and readily once more. But we were realistic enough to know that this pleasant state of affairs could not continue indefinitely, so that when the Russians replaced the Americans as the officiating camp authorities it was no great blow to us.

It meant that we had to leave the camp itself, for the Russians were not as easy-going as the Americans and it would only be a matter of time before they got round to investigating my background. I felt, to put it simply, that it would be unwise for me to hang around while the administration staff and border police made their enquiries.

During the fruitful days of the American administration, Anneliese and I had been able to get down to some long-term planning, and now for the first time we knew what we were going to do. I had decided to settle permanently in Germany. I liked the country and there was nothing for me to return to in England. We would buy a farm in the mountains of Bavaria, and we would run it ourselves. In the winter we would take in tourists, I would act as ski instructor and Anneliese would operate the necessary taxi service to and from the nearest railway station.

It was a good plan and one worth working for. All we needed was the money to buy the land. A large sum of money, and quickly.

I knew that there was a regular traffic in illegal border crossing and frontier guides were in constant demand. The Allied authorities tended to turn an indulgent eye but the Russian view was very different. It was, consequently, a dangerous operation, but one which paid the frontier guide handsomely if he didn't stop a bullet. Some people willingly paid fabulous sums to be taken safely from the Russian frontier and across the no man's land that lay between it and the Allied side. When there was no cash, furs and jewellery were passed over without a murmur. The refugees put as high a price on their freedom as the guides did on their lives.

When we left the camp at Halle, therefore, we moved to Blankenstein, a little town not far away and situated right on the frontier between the American and Russian zones. It was not difficult for us to find somewhere to live, for we simply moved into one of the many hastily evacuated houses in the vicinity. Since the end of the war Blankenstein had become notorious as a crossing point for people engaged in the shady business of refugee smuggling. It was not just the war-uprooted who were trying to get away, but even the settled landowners and wealthy farmers. Despairing of ever being able to prosper again under the Soviet system, they sold everything they could, stuffed the proceeds into their coat linings and corsets, hung their jewellery around them and made tracks for the Allied zone. And all along the frontier there were shepherds, gamekeepers and foresters ready to cash in and show them across – at a price.

As soon as I got to Blankenstein I suddenly developed a passionate interest in botany, gathering herbs and chasing butterflies daily along the frontier. It wasn't long before my country-bred senses knew every tree, bush and blade of grass on a couple of winding patrol-free paths. Obviously one could not advertise one's services, but word would get round discreetly. A casual approach would be made in the local inn, times and terms discussed and agreed. My price was high but it was always paid. Sometimes I would refuse to take German marks and accept instead jewellery, watches or gold coins as a better long-term investment than paper money. I must have accumulated half a sack of these precious baubles, which I buried for future use. Some day somebody will dig them up and congratulate themselves on their good fortune, or perhaps the sack will continue to lie there, because I never got the chance to recover it.

The illegal emigrants came in all types and numbers, from single people to whole families. Generally they travelled light with all their worldly goods stowed about their person, but there was one notable exception. God knows, no one can accuse me of being sexist, but it had to be a woman. This one was well equipped to make her way about in the hazardous days following the end of the war in Germany. The men she couldn't persuade with her swaying hips, slender waist and arrogantly up-thrusting boobs she could easily buy – she was loaded in both senses of the word.

I was sitting in the Biergarten one day when she walked in accompanied by a young lad and I wasn't the only male in the place to run my eyes very slowly over her. After a bit, the lad came over to me and said the lady wanted to talk to me. I walked over as casually as my weakened knees would allow and sat down at her table. She looked up at me, the twin souls of eternal Eve lustrous in her eyes.

'Somebody told me you could take me over the frontier to the Americans . . .' The husky voice was half appealing, half a provocative challenge.

All right, I was disappointed, even though I don't know what I had really expected, but it was caution rather than pique which made me answer shortly: 'That somebody knows too much.' It was an ambiguous role; on the one hand one had to make one's services known, and on the other, one had to remain anonymous to avoid the investigating authorities. But she persisted.

'But if it is possible, you will help me . . . please?' Now there was only the damsel in distress, but something in my expression must have made her realise she'd need to back up the appeal to my better nature with something more substantial. 'I do have money, of course . . .' she added slowly.

I named my price and a bundle of her German marks found a welcome home in my pocket. Arrangements were made for me to take her across the following night.

When we met at the appointed rendezvous the next night I simply could not believe my eyes. The woman had six or seven huge, heavy suitcases she wanted to take with her! I protested, I got angry, I reasoned, argued and pointed out the extreme danger and near impossibility of taking all that baggage. It made no difference. She would not budge an inch. They contained, she said, her entire wardrobe and were irreplaceable and absolutely indispensable to her career as an actress. There she touched about the only sympathetic spot in me, since having moved in theatrical circles myself I realised how much importance stage performers place on their costumes and props. To cut a long, argumentative story short, I gave in eventually and we compromised on a higher fee. Anneliese's services were enlisted to chaperone the woman over by my safe secret path, while I scoured the district for the only available horse and cart to transport the suitcases. The journey seemed to take hours as I rumbled my way nerve-rackingly across by a different, dangerously Russian-infested route with those blasted suitcases under a loaf of hay. It was a terrible risk and one that I should have known better than to take, and my relief at seeing the Allied uniforms as I reached the far side would have done credit to a patriot.

As previously arranged, I met up with Anneliese and our two troublesome clients at the house of a friend in the American sector, who agreed to put us all up for the night. I stowed the hefty suitcases in an outhouse at the back and then joined Anneliese. She looked thoughtful as we sat drinking a well-earned cup of coffee in our room.

'You know, *Kleine*, that woman must be either a very great actress or very crazy to risk her life for some dresses and costumes. I don't believe she is a great actress, and I know she isn't crazy . . . but there must be something important in those suitcases for her to be so concerned about them . . .'

I stared at her. She was right: it *was* an absolutely crazy risk for anyone to run over a theatrical wardrobe. I took the hint. In the early hours of the morning I went to the outhouse with my enormous collection of keys and a flashlight. Every single one of those cases was packed with priceless and exquisite furs. I'm no expert but even in that brief flashlight examination I could see that they were of a quality rarely seen.

It took me nearly an hour to find enough soft rubbish and rags to replace them. Dog eats dog; tomorrow it might be my turn. Dawn saw Anneliese and myself tramping back across no man's land to meet the sun rising over the eastern sector.

Although my smuggling activities made it unnecessary for me to have to work at anything else, I realised that I must be seen to have a job so that nobody would ask awkward questions about how I made a living, and now the fictitious character of Hans Sandau came into his own.

The name Sandau was no accidental choice. It reflected the great German strong man, Sandow, whose feats had so inspired me in my early training days. The proprietor of the local Biergarten had just started a cabaret for the amusement of his clientele, mostly Russian soldiers, who dearly loved a show of any sort, and I offered him my act as a strong man with Anneliese as my assistant, looking very fetching in black tights.

I varied the act, of course, but it was always pretty spectacular. One of the favourites among the Russians was watching me catch a 56 lb cannonball, dropped from a crane at considerable height, on my stomach. Naturally it fell with such force that the table upon which I lay smashed beneath me, and they would gasp with wonder as I nevertheless got up unscathed from a blow which would have made a large hole in anyone else. It was, though I say it myself, an impressive feat by any standards and in due course it attracted a totally unexpected invitation.

One evening, as I wiped the greasepaint off my face, there was a knock on the door of the makeshift dressing-room and a middle-aged man hunched into a faded caricature of a theatrical impresario limped in. He eased himself down into the only available space in the jumble of clothes and, leaning forward on his cane, slowly removed the cigar from his mouth. He introduced himself by some name that I have long forgotten – let us call him Schmidt – and explained that he was the proprietor of a small travelling circus that was due to open in Blankenstein very shortly – had I heard of it? I had not, but now knowing what the man wanted I merely said rather noncommittally that I had noticed posters about the town advertising a circus. But the answer seemed to satisfy him for he expressed a wish that I attend, as his guest, their opening performance in Blankenstein.

'You are a good performer – good act!' he said approvingly. 'And when you have seen what we have to offer, I hope very much that you will wish to join us. We are not very big or famous yet, but in the future – who knows!' He shrugged his shoulders and spread his arms expansively, the world his oyster.

I paused in my cleaning-up operations, staring at his reflection in my mirror. At last I said that I would be pleased to accept his invitation to attend the performance as his guest, and after that I would give him my answer.

The troupe turned out to be typical of many such groups that must have sprung up in Europe after the war, a small patched band of performers, remnants of mediocre talent washed up from happier and more prosperous times. If I decided to join, it certainly was not for the glamour or for the money. There was very little of either. It can only have been for the whiff of circus sawdust, talc and animal pee – the smell of the greasepaint, the roar of the crowd, as the saying has it. The lure of the fairground, the booth and the sideshow, the skill and the sham, the art and the artifice, have always drawn me as surely as a magnet a nail. I hadn't been sorry to use that youthful affair with the squire's daughter – after which I was persona non grata in the district – as an excuse to leave the village where I was raised and seek my fortunes elsewhere. I had no trade or marketable skill except as a tree feller. I had only a splendid, disciplined physique, considerable potential as a boxer, and an 18 year old's lust for life. I joined a travelling boxing booth, the sort that toured the country, frequently tagging onto fairs, challenging all-comers.

When I did return home after about a year, it was scarcely surprising that I was unable to settle down in the electrical apprenticeship which my father, using his influence as a freeman of the city of Norwich, had managed to secure for me. The day I threw away the pliers and kicked my tin lunchbox over the hedge and ran away to London, I finally capitulated to the showman in me. I scarcely knew where my next meal or lodging was coming from, but I lived in a paradise of my own making, a world away from the never-ending rows of terraced houses linked by miles of electrical wire. My entire fortune was packed under my vest into the well-trained bunches of muscle, and with hard work and determination the talents I had been given grew and developed.

But while there yet clung to me the sweet scent of Norfolk hay I allowed – not too unwillingly I admit – three slick city boys to talk me into joining their tumbling team and we eventually got a job with a small family circus about to tour the British Isles. I floated entranced in this aura of adventure and skilled physical effort, a small muscular Ulysses on the first lap of his voyage, and though the money was poor, it was to me of little consequence.

Watching Herr Schmidt's little band in Blankenstein that first night, with the stale sweet odour of sweat nostalgic in my nostrils and the remembrance of resin rasping my palms, I had no doubt that I would join. When the circus left town, Anneliese and I went with it. The tour would not be long and the circus intended to base itself in Blankenstein for the winter.

Irrespective of nationality, children from six to sixty love circuses and the Germans and Russians were no exception. If they loved the tinsel splendour, they appreciated, too, the presentation of artistic physical skills, even though these were limited in a troupe as small as ours. The performers were fairly run of the mill. A family team of acrobats and jugglers, whose main post-war problem in life seemed to be the fact that they could no longer obtain the skin dye to maintain their disguise – necessary to the professional image – as Arabs. The wife was getting a bit past the gymnastic stage but she made up for this by doubling as universal wardrobe mistress. Somehow she had managed to hang on to the remains of a collection of stage costumes and these she guarded with her life, patching, repairing and making do with threadbare outfits that would in former times have been used only for rags. But under the glaring lights the darns and patches scarcely showed, the eye attracted only by the garish colours, the sequins glistening on the high wire as the two trapeze artists went through their competent but ordinary routine.

I always felt sorry for the female half of the high-wire duo. Somehow she seemed to me the sort of young woman who would have been happier in some mundane occupation like serving in a sweet shop rather than flying through the air propelled by the strength and influence of her partner. He was several years older than she was and seemed to have over her a kind of fascination which effectively bound her, soul and body, to him.

Occasionally they would double up with the acrobats to make for some variety, for, apart from the dwarf clown, there was only one other act – a team of performing dogs whose handler wistfully hankered after a tank of seals but had had to abandon the idea because of the difficulty of getting fish to feed them on. Before I joined there had already been a strong man of sorts, a Pole of the big, dumb muscleman type, whose lack of intelligence and imagination were obvious in his very pedestrian dumb-bell-lifting, leotard-posturing routine. His principal role was really as general hand and odd-job man, to which he quickly found himself relegated when I came in. This was unfortunate for us both because, although I had no direct part in destroying his aspirations, he naturally resented me and, I believe, looked for opportunities to get rid of me so that he could be reinstated.

The apparent good humour with which we all mucked in together was largely a façade and the mutual suspicions were never far below the surface. Travellers and circus people have always been objects of mistrust. No one ever really knows where they've come from, where they're going, what they've been or done. Traditionally they have always played up their 'foreign-ness' as part of the mystery, and so I did now. But in the prevailing circumstances it was a bad mistake, particularly as I had made an enemy of the big Pole. He did not know precisely what my nationality was, but I do believe that he tipped off the Russian authorities that I might be worth keeping an eye on. Additionally, I was healthy, well fed and very strong – they might care to speculate on how and where I had spent the war years to come out of it so well. However, I suspected nothing of all this at the time, and even though I was aware of the general undercurrent of mistrust and watchfulness among the circus folk, and maintained my usual caution, there was no particular thing to prompt me to make another immediate disappearance.

Curiously enough, despite, or perhaps because of, the recent war, we encountered less hostility than I had as a youth in my first circus tour when, after struggling through one or two shows, our little troupe had crossed the sea to Ireland. I was thrilled – my first time abroad! – and so entranced was I by the musical babble of Gaelic as I sat in a pub one evening that it never occurred to me that the Irish might have a tendency to xenophobia. Two cloth-capped fellows came over to my table and sat down.

'You English, sonny?'

I resented the 'sonny' but let it pass. I nodded cheerfully. Their response left me dumbfounded. One of them leaned confidentially across the table to me.

'Then just you piss off out of here, you filthy English bastard!'

I had it in mind to knock the hell out of the pair of them, but in the event I merely drained my tankard, replaced it carefully on the table and walked out. That night stones as big as hens' eggs rained down into our encampment, most of them aimed at the huge Union Jack painted on the side of the boss's caravan. Our fodder tent was set ablaze and we all braved the hail of stones to rescue the animals. The police finally arrived but didn't break their legs trying to catch the culprits. Early next morning we were on our way out of Ireland and soon after back in Liverpool, the tour a flop. It was time to part company with my Cockney mates: from here on I would go solo.

I kept it that way throughout my career as a showman while I worked the halls in England and Europe building up and developing a strength act. Contrary to what most people think, you don't just make up an act once and for all and leave it at that. The moment it becomes simply a routine it loses something – vitality, energy – and audiences are always quick to sense that. No – an act must be worked on constantly, the details perfected, altered, the sequence oiled to an imperceptible smoothness. At that time it was also a highly competitive business with a large number of performers trying to make the grade in too few music halls, clubs and circuses. You had to be good to get in; and to get on you had to produce something different, more arresting and spectacular than your rivals in the same field. It was not necessarily the artist with the most skill who got the highest billing because, in the main, people want to be thrilled by sensation rather than appreciative of artistry. If two trapeze artists can perform exactly the same feats of skill and daring, the one who works without a safety net will attract the larger crowd.

My act, although without the polish of the one I had worked the halls with in England, nevertheless appealed to the less sophisticated Russian and German audiences. One thing I did stick to, however, and that was to perform in evening dress. I would walk on in my black suit, frilled shirt and bow tie, a small, apparently slightly built man, which for a start whetted their incredulity as to my ability and billing as the circus strong man. It wouldn't have been half so effective if I had come on in leotard and tights flexing my muscles. Quietly, demurely, I would submit to a thick rope being put about my neck and merely stand there while two teams of five a side hauled on the ends in an effort to strangle me. The soldiers among them appreciated that, knowing how easy it is to break a man's neck.

I was the antithesis of the popular image of the strong man and I gave the crowd what it wanted: something to marvel at, to excite their wonder and distract their thoughts from the daily round, and I succeeded where the traditional approach failed. Mind you, I had learnt a lot about showmanship and crowd handling from Alf Stewart, the little fellow who owned and ran the boxing booth I'd joined all those years ago.

In appearance it would be difficult to imagine a less prepossessing publicity man than Alf Stewart, a sort of walking skin bag in which a collection of bones jostled at random, but he had a tireless mouth that worked with the skill and tempo of a politician, making black white and grey no colour at all. Somehow he managed to convince audiences that his team of five broken-down has-beens and never-made-its were glamorous warriors of the square ring, every one of them a George Carpentier in skill and style. Looking back now, I can see them for the pathetic bunch they were, but even though I had my suspicions then, my 17-year-old experience was not yet wide enough to stand aghast at the silk purses Stewart managed to conjure out of his four other sows' ears. There was the massive black man Antoni Christian, 15 stone of muscle and fat that could just be taken for human, with his hairline starting at his eyebrows and the brain inside that ape-like cranium well and truly scrambled. He walked on his heels and spoke thick and indistinctly, the large puffed-up mouth moving slowly and the saliva always glistening in the corners.

His only claim to fame was that he had once been sparring partner to the famous Jack Johnson, a fact which Alf Stewart of course played up to the hilt. But in fact, poor Christian had been little more than a human punch-bag and the terrible beatings he had taken had completely wrecked his brain. They had, however, failed to make him unfriendly or unkind and the big broken hands were always willing to fry you an egg or make toast if you were pushed for time or unwell. Not so Red Pullan, a ten-stone, alcohol-soaked jackal who would hover around to beg or steal the price of a drink. But a pair of cauliflower ears like miniature boxing gloves, kept apart by thin, wispy red hair, made him an awe-inspiring showpiece to the uninitiated. He must have learnt to box in prison for it was there that he seemed to have spent most of his career.

Tony 'Spider' Malone, by contrast, was completely honest – even if he was the only Irishman I have ever known to carry a prayer shawl in his kit bag and refuse to eat pork. It must have been the effect of all those years he had lived in Golders Green. With all this he had a Cockney accent you could turn a handspring on, but whatever his ethnic group he threw punches with business-like dexterity and saved every well-earned penny. But I never took to Malone the way I did to 'Dolly' Grey, a one-time merchant seaman, who to my 17-year-old mind seemed to have read every book written and who also took as much pride in bodily fitness as I did myself.

At first he annoyed me with the contempt he felt for the rest of the team – the cream of boxing hall shithouses, he called them, and said if we continued to listen to Alf Stewart both of us would wind up battered and discarded has-beens like them. I found this difficult to understand, for to me they all had the aura of ancient Greece or the gladiators of Rome clinging to their stale-sweat-smelling bodies, and at that time I adored and believed too implicitly in the glove-slinging world to recognise its punch-drunken darkness and exploitation of human weakness.

While Dolly punched a rattling tattoo on the speed-ball at the front of the booth to attract the crowd, Alf Stewart went to work with a flurry of words as to the wizardry of our fighting abilities. The flatties gathered round and gaped. Big old Antoni Christian rolled the whites of his eyes, Red Pullan scowled, Spider Malone stood relaxed, feet apart, arms folded across his chest. I would be secreted in among the crowd ready to accept the challenge that Alf Stewart eventually flung out. Two guineas to anyone who can stay three rounds with Red Pullan! (Here, of course, Stewart would display his blinding eloquence describing Pullan's past and prowess, while Pullan himself began to look positively ferocious.) At this I would push my way through the crowd, a fresh-faced country lad with straw still in his hair, and as I caught the gloves thrown to me by Stewart and walked to the front of the booth I felt the sympathetic surge of the audience. They would pile into the tent after me, paying sixpence a head, and watch eagerly while Pullan went through the motions of fighting a strong, enthusiastic novice. Eventually I would knock him out with a lucky punch – here the crowd roared its approval – whereupon Stewart would leap into the ring with a heart-rending appeal to the audience to show their appreciation by tossing the rubbings into the ring. More often than not a rain of coins would land on the dirty canvas to be gathered up later and shared between us at the end of the day, everybody watching Red Pullan to make sure that he didn't pocket more than his due.

Sometimes there would be a genuine response to Stewart's challenge. As a rule these were fairly easily disposed of, but when the local champion – who was like as not some giant miner or rock-hard quarryman – took up the gloves it was as much as we could do to keep out of the way for three rounds. I was battered a few times but still unbowed at the end of it all. And I think I might have gone on believing in the romance of the boxer, despite all the evidence to persuade me otherwise, for a lot longer if it hadn't been for Dolly Grey. Not so much for the things he said, the warnings he gave me about ending up 'like one of them', as for what he turned out to be, the only muscular pederast I'd run into so far. At first I noticed only that he paid more attention when we were dressing and undressing than he usually did, but his proposition when we were once sharing a bedroom so shocked me that it changed my attitude not only to him but also to all the others around me. He was something quite new in my experience and I suppose I felt that he had betrayed the god of physical excellence whom I thought we both worshipped. From then on I scarcely spoke to him and, apart from brief conversations with the rest, I strolled around alone. Looking at them all from a distance, and with more understanding, I realised that the only one among them with any brains was Alf Stewart himself – and who wanted to finish up like him? It was time to move on, even though the magic of the fairground, the travelling tinsel, still remained for me bright and untarnished.

Sometimes while I toured East Germany with Schmidt's circus I would find an echo of those far-off fairground days in some of the tales told by Kleinekin, the clown, the only one of the troupe with whom I formed any friendship. Offstage the four-foot dwarf hid a generous and gentle heart under an apparently cold and humourless exterior, but he was always ready to help me, to explain if there was something I didn't know about or understand. He had spent a lifetime with circuses in various parts of Germany and, once you could get him talking, proved a good raconteur with a marvellous fund of stories and anecdotes. Sometimes as we travelled through places like Düsseldorf and Königstadt where accommodation was difficult to find, Anneliese and I would smuggle the little old fellow into our lodgings where he would sleep in a travelling trunk in our room, and on a Sunday morning we would lie abed till nearly lunchtime listening to his tales.

The world of the fairground and the circus vary little from one country and nationality to another, and he was able to throw light on a wonder which had caused me some amazement at a fairground in the north of England many years ago – the dancing duck. As Kleinekin told it, he'd been drawn to a crowd gathering in increasing numbers around a sideshow where a man standing on a box hustled them with the German equivalent of the 'roll up, roll up, ladies and gentlemen' harangue. The man went on to explain that he owned and trained the only dancing duck in the world, and on payment of a small admission fee they could have the privilege of seeing this rare and wonderful creature. Intrigued, Kleinekin paid his fee and went in.

Inside was a small raised stage with the front curtain down. When the tent was full, the showman left the door, made his way to the front and raised the curtain of the miniature stage by pulling a cord. Then he took a small flute from his pocket and began to play a slow, melancholy tune, and onto the stage waddled a plump white duck. At first it stood peering and pecking around as ducks do, and then slowly it began to lift its feet to the time of the flute music. Quicker and quicker went the music and faster went the duck's feet until its movements resembled a tap dance. The little show ended after a few minutes and the audience left amused and full of admiration for a showman with the ability to train a duck to dance. Young Kleinekin was fascinated and for days after that hung around the show tent – which was how he discovered that the showman was close friends with the hot potato seller, who always stood with his barrow and coke-fired portable oven alongside the dancing duck tent. But once the tent was full and the door closed, the potato seller would push his barrow round the back of the tent, where the duck's little stage protruded out of the tent wall. Then he would take the glowing coke brazier from his oven and place it under the tin floor of the stage and sit down to smoke his pipe for a few minutes while the floor of the stage grew hotter and hotter – and the poor duck naturally hopped from one warm webbed foot to the other!

Even though working and travelling with Schmidt's circus was not an easy or comfortable life, it fulfilled something in me. I suppose it was, in a way, completing the life of fantastic reality – or real fantasy, however one prefers to put it – that I had set out to find as a youth. But I never allowed it to obscure my primary aim at the time, which was to make a large enough sum of money to buy a sizeable estate to farm. When the circus completed its short tour of several East German towns and returned to Blankenstein therefore, I resumed my equally fantastic but infinitely more dangerous role of frontier guide.

In all I must have made about 18 successful crossings. The money I made I handed to Anneliese, who, with her keen business sense, had already bought the farm. One or two more crossings were all we needed to be able to complete the stocking and equipping. Of course, I was well aware that refugee smuggling is not a long-term occupation: one should make a few good, high-priced crossings and then quit the business. I knew that, but I decided to gamble my luck just a bit longer. It had held so long. But I did not make allowance for the big Pole, my rival as circus strong man, who must have been watching my every move and just waiting for a chance to get me out of the way.

Soon after what was to have been the second to last trip, Anneliese went to visit her parents, taking the money with her to dispose of safely. Returning to our lodgings after seeing her off on the train, I had just opened the door of my room when the janitor's door at the far end of the corridor opened and two heavyweights moved up to me with surprising swiftness. One of them flourished some sort of identity card at me and said in German with a thick Russian accent: 'Russian State Police.'

So it had come at last, the spectre that I had been half expecting for so long, its realisation more chilling than the cannon-sized revolver with which the other security man was threatening me. It was all over in the space of a few minutes. I was hustled out of the building and into the waiting car faster than it takes to tell it. There was no way to get a message to Anneliese, to tell her what was happening.

Not that I knew very much myself beyond the fact that I was at first taken back to Halle. There, the relentless interrogation began, and from that day I was completely cut off from the world outside and the prison walls closed around me. And if I had known on that day what was going to happen, the only way that pair of Russian heavies would have got me out to that car would have been as a corpse.

It was to be my last day of freedom for seven years.

Chapter 15

TWENTY-FIVE YEARS' HARD LABOUR

In a cell, 6 x 8, alone.

I pace it out, measuring my steps, counting my steps over and over. I have time, day after night after day. But time stops counting and I cannot count hours when there is neither daylight nor dark, only the 25-watt bulb that stays on and on and no window to shame it pale or burn it bright. Concrete walls, concrete floor, a plank bed, one blanket. One ragged blanket to cover my sleeping and dreaming and waking and dreaming and shoulders shaking for misery and cold when winter pierces the thin shirt. One shirt, one pair of trousers, changed, as I reckon it in bread rations, every 12 days. Sometimes they fit approximately, but most of the time they don't fit at all. No shoes, my feet bare on the floor as I pace the cell, the cold coarseness of the concrete on my naked soles. Feeling with my hands the roughness of the wall, the smoothness of the planks, fingertip contrasts for the reality of touch, tactile reassurance to anchor my senses.

Slipping from my bunk into the warm waters of Norfolk's River Yare . . .

Take from a man the certainty of night and day and you take the cornerstone of his sense of reality, of time.

Living on the endless plain of timelessness in a damp cell, the river lapped my tanned skin as I trod water, aware of the muscular nakedness of my body and the lady in the big house by the river aware of it too, exchanging morning pleasantries with me as she looked through the glass water. Come up to the house, she said, and I said, although she knew, I've got no clothes on, and she said I won't look, lying of course. And looking and grasping and frantically lying with me on the old sofa she kept upstairs in the boathouse until the guard dog, frantic for his moaning mistress, jumped in clean through the window and the noise panicked me in my vulnerability and I dived through the shattered pane back into the river like a leaping fish in the morning sun, not feeling the jagged glass on my skin till later . . .

Now the pain cuts across my face, my head, felling me. Taste of blood and stink of stale urine. The floor of the interrogation room, my eyes focusing dimly on booted feet and stained pisspot. An incredible weariness flooding me. I have told them again and again. Yet again. Jerked upright, standing swaying unsteadily. Again. I am not a spy. My name is Eric Pleasants, I came to Germany in . . . On and on through the blurring and the pain, shouting and mumbling, screaming. Suffering, numbness, insensibility. Waking in my cell, a cell, any cell, but always alone. My bruised and broken body wakes me, clamouring its outrage, congealing to the blanket. Lightheaded release, the stain darkening on the blanket then on the canvas . . .

Not my blood now but his, for I was the victor and in me the surge of triumph as the referee raised my gloved hand and the crowd in the Norwich Corn Exchange roared and cheered its approval. The gnarled quarry-rough hands of old Clarkie, my second, slid with motherly tenderness over my young shoulders as he slipped my robe round me. 'You did good, boy. A right crowd pleaser you are, boy, you'll go a long way . . .'

Ironies. My knuckles tap painfully on the cell wall, spelling out every letter of every word. Slowly, painstakingly, we prisoners struggle to communicate. We have no other way. We never meet, never even glimpse one another, scarcely ever see our jailers. A disembodied hand pushes food round the door, bread in the morning and thin soup in the evening. At least I reckon it's that way round because the bread comes soon after the daily slopping out. The door opens and I emerge, pisspot in hand, and make straight for the washroom, turning neither to right nor left, but neck-pricklingly conscious of the warder a few paces behind me. We pass no one. In the long dim corridor there are only his soft-shoe steps and my naked feet.

Once in every two days – reckoned in bread and soup and slopping out – I wear a pair of wooden clogs. These clogs stand by the door leading out into the 'exercise yard'. I thrust my cold-pinched feet into their unreceptive hardness and am released into the yard, the warder remaining behind the door, which he locks after me. I am left entombed alone in a kind of concrete well where I must shamble about exercising myself as best I might for ten minutes. Jesus Christ! How many wretched human beings must have had to shuffle those miserable clogs round that well of a yard? Better not to think of it . . . human beings cannot stand much reality.

Be strong, boy, you've got to be strong. Pushing my exhausted body on, shambling to a half run, running, sweating. The sweaty smell of the gym, athletes training to be fit and strong and I among them striving for an overall physical excellence. Not just hand strength like Elliott with his ambition to tear a tennis ball in two after he'd torn two packs of playing cards put together. I wouldn't give a pinch of shit for such over-estimated finger strength. I only needed a hand strong in keeping with the rest of me. To hold up my opponent long enough to deal with him in the wrestling ring. To hold an axe and fell trees at break of summer dawn so that I could earn my bread and still have the day free. Lazy sod, the factory workers would jeer at me sitting on the wall watching them go in, enviously self-righteous, uncomprehending of anything outside their shift-rooted, bench-narrow existence. They would never know what freedom was, poor yoked buggers, never know the fierce joy of living free, of running for the pure pleasure of it, of swimming, fishing, lying in the sun, except when their masters gave them leave. Sensuous enjoyment of being alive – disgusting, sinful! Even their copulating was a secretive, inhibited act, begetting fettered children. And now I, who had been free . . .

Oh, that intense longing, yearning to be free, can drive a man insane! I reach out with my mind into the richness of my vivid freedom, living it all again in slow motion, lingeringly. There is so much that I have no need of fantasy. *This* is the unacceptable, fantastic unreality, that I should be in here, counting not-counting the days in bread and soup and shit. Always the same question tapped from cell to cell: how long have you been here? Five years, ten, perhaps twenty. What if they forget me! It's so easy for them, all those people with power of life and death over us, to forget . . . A sense of creeping despair, a spectral emptiness . . . No, not that, not me, I'd rather be dead than that.

Be strong, boy, be strong. If you're not strong, you're as good as dead.

Here they come for me again. I know they're coming because I hear booted footsteps and our warders wear only soft shoes. Is it night or day? I can't be sure in here. I might know in the interrogation room because sometimes there's a window and I can see out. I can even see what time of year it is and if I can't see out I might be able to hear the screech of the high-flying swifts. It's not always in the same place, interrogation, and it's not a regular thing. Oh no! They're too clever for that! Sometimes I go through many plates of soup without hearing boots outside my door and I half-relax because I am not being kicked around and half apprehensive in case they have forgotten me. Then they go through phases of coming after me as though there was no one else in the prison, sometimes keeping me for an hour and sometimes, as I can see by the light and dark of the window, for several days, half-conscious with fatigue and suffering and lack of food. Once they give me salt fish, which I eat hungrily, greedily, but afterwards I am thirsty and there is no water and for days they will not give me any until I go crazy with thirst.

Once I glimpse a face in the darkened glass of the interrogation room. Haggard, pinched, beard greying over sunken cheeks. It takes a few minutes to register that the face is my own. And I could not have looked again into those eyes nor described the depth of their misery.

Sometimes there are many interrogators, sometimes only one. One day there are three of them. Sizing up the opposition, I note indifferently that one is in naval uniform, one in army red and grey and one in civvies. Then my eyes wander wistfully to the window. I can see it is spring, the sun is bright on the hawthorn and sparrows squabble and chirrup in the blossom. There is a silence in the room. Why haven't they started the questioning? Reluctantly forcing my attention back to the three, I see that they are seating themselves with ponderous formality behind the table, on which stands a stack of paper. I notice for the first time a fourth man a little to one side. He clears his throat and addresses me in German. Gradually it dawns on me: this is a Russian troika and I am being tried! This is my 'trial' and that stack of paper is the 'evidence' against me!

The realisation brings neither fear nor relief. I feel only a weary contempt. What a farce, with its military baubles and spangles, big pot-bellied boys playing a cruel game with me as victim. I have no doubt they will find me 'guilty' – of something, anything, what does it matter? What could they do to me? Nothing that was worse than what I had already been through. They could free me, which would be expecting too much; they could hand me over to the English, have me executed or, worst of all, condemn me to a loss of freedom for life. After two years of the mental and physical torture of solitary confinement, little things like dying had taken on what could well be the proper dimension.

After a slight indignation that the one-sided bastards have provided me with a Russo-German interpreter, knowing right well that I am English, the window reclaims my attention and I lose interest in the proceedings . . . Blossom, whiteness, Anneliese, snow, a December night in the suburbs of Berlin when we rolled and wrestled like kids in the snowdrifts, lay warm and breathless looking up at the stars, the cold air fresh in our nostrils before Ivan changed that for the smell of burning flesh and carbolic and urine. The offensive staleness of the inevitable pisspot in the corner of the 'court room' and the droning officialdom intrude themselves upon me, an interruption in my life.

The sentence, when it eventually comes, makes little impression. For alleged espionage, sabotage and demoralisation of Russian troops: 25 years' hard labour.

So there it was, after two years' interrogation and solitary confinement, those important officials were going to stuff me away for 25 years in some remote part of Russia. Which part they did not say, but meanwhile it was back to prison, except that I was moved from Höhenschauenhausen, where I had been incarcerated for most of the time, to a jail in Lichtenberg. But prison conditions were now so different that on my return I realised that the trial had had a stunning immediate impact on my life after all.

Gone was the solitary cell. This time a huge – no, vast – room containing strange, unreal people actually walking or sitting about, as many as three or four in a group. I had forgotten there were so many people left in the world. Ragged, washed-out, with a gaunt look of frightened bewilderment in the eyes. I had seen that expression in the eyes of dogs and of one other human being – my own, in that unforgettable dark-glass reflection. Intuitively I recognised them all. I was one of them, a shadow man, a moving figure with something missing. At the core of my relief at being again in human company was a chilling apprehension like a heavy ice lump in my stomach. How much had I missed? How could I judge, how could I know if my judgement had been twisted by those mind-bending years? At least, so far as I could tell by comparison with some of the others, I was still sane.

At least, unlike the German ex-policeman, I didn't carefully mould and knead my bread into dozens of small animals before pounding on them and eating them. Nor, like the Polish lad, did I spend my time kneeling in the corner crossing myself and bowing to the wall, lips moving in incessant invocation.

If I had ever prayed it must have been so long ago that I could not recall it at all. In this pantheon of man-made gods and causes, so vast that there is no room for simple goodness, I found not one to pray to or trust in. I put my faith in myself and I have never lost it, even though at that point in my life it was about as severely shaken as it has ever been. But gradually there were the small reassurances that come through being with people, learning again to accept and be accepted.

At first my speaking was reserved and halting; it was easier to let others talk to me even though I found it difficult to concentrate on what they were saying, for I had first to break the habit of silence and closing my mind to its alternative, the bullying voices of the interrogators. But hesitantly I learnt to communicate, even to like people again, and to learn from them. Even if it was only a matter of improving my German grammar with the German student who eagerly practised his English on me. It seemed strange to speak English again. I spent a lot of time in his company, for I liked him. Equally, I quickly learnt to dislike others: the self-pitying erstwhile bank manager who battered the ears of any unfortunate listener with a recital of those who were much more deserving of his unhappy fate than he was. Nor was he deterred by lack of an audience, tediously bewailing his misfortunes to the endless refrain of 'Why me – I ask you, why me?'

Obsessions were commonplace, only the form was different. The wiry little Berliner who would walk round and round the cell with impatient little steps, leaning slightly forward, his hands in his pockets and a faraway look in his eyes, only stopping to recount in vivid detail one of his many and varied sexual experiences. I felt sorry for him, obsessed as he was with sex, but he did give me a sound piece of advice. 'While you're in here don't give too much thought to the dames you've screwed or you'll go out of your head. Think about those you nearly had but somehow you never made it or something happened so you lost it.'

Towards the last of my stay in Lichtenberg prison there were 30 of us, who managed to fill daily a large drum with evil-smelling crap from the 250 grammes of bread and litre of thin soup each. The two of us who took the stinking bucket out each morning certainly carried out much more than the cook carried in. We all took turns at this, except the silent German-born Italian who moped all day in a corner speaking to nobody. He was the last to be thrust into the cell and the first to leave. At some time in the night, with a strip torn from his blanket and incredible determination, he hanged his six-foot self from the post of the five-and-a-half-foot bunk and his feet did not touch the floor until after he was dead. It was the same kind of determination which the rest of us shadow men were using to keep alive.

I spent about six months in Lichtenberg prison, but I have never grudged those six months because while I was there a strange and marvellous thing happened. A letter was smuggled to me from the women's block. Incredibly, wonderfully, it was from Anneliese, of whom I had heard nothing since my arrest. To my great sorrow, I learned that she was serving three years. Apparently she had, on my arrest, gone to the English sector of Berlin and reported the affair to the English authorities, but on her return to the Russian zone she was also arrested and sentenced to three years' hard labour. I have never seen or heard anything of her since.

With the letter she sent me a piece of bread. It was the most precious gift I have ever received. I treasured it because she, so short of food herself, had sent it, because she had touched it. I was half-starving, but I kept that piece of bread for three days before I ate it.

The first move from Lichtenberg was to the prison camp Sachsenhausen, a name synonymous with German crimes against humanity. That is a worn phrase now, but alongside those German crimes there are Russian crimes, French, American and English crimes, Chinese, Japanese and Italian – all of them pay lip-service to humanity, yet they all continue to commit the crimes.

Actually, the Russians had improved Sachsenhausen: the cells designed by the Germans for one person now held six, and the two-man cells held twelve – the Russians had their arithmetic right – and never a window in them for ventilation.

There was no room to move in our sardine tins. I lay like a stuck pig comparing it with those two years on my own. That German engineer is on the bucket again. With six of us the lid is a laugh, but as we never go outside the stink is unnoticed. Man is an animal that grows accustomed to just about anything. Or does he . . .? I slip away from the foetid cell down a Bavarian valley pathway through endless acres of pink cherry blossom, Anneliese a little ahead. I am just about to catch her up when the fat little doctor lying next to me turns over onto his elbow and I hear he is telling me about the last boyfriend in Munich. He is a nice harmless little fellow so, with an effort, I stop myself from hammering my fist into his round genial face and feel curiously flattered that he has chosen me to sleep beside. Except that I realise now that it was no accident his hand rested nearly all last night on my thigh. I like him, but not that way.

I go back to Anneliese, her soft little hands glide over my chest and stomach and the sweet smell of her body fills my nostrils. To hell with the big stinking feet and long legs of the fellow on the other side of me, who professes to be a hotel chef and talks about nothing but food all day, kicking me as he writhes in self-imposed agony. Eventually I kick him back; we don't speak with each other any more but I still have to listen to this food-crazy shadow while I'm so hungry that my stomach feels as if my throat has been painlessly cut. One hundred and fifty grammes of bread a day. The fat Pole pinches my bread. I grab his testicles and smash my head into his mouth. He speaks Russian, I don't, so his explanation to the guards is understood better than mine, despite his broken teeth, and I finish up alone in a perishing cold stone hole without food or covering for 24 hours.

So ends lesson one as a convicted prisoner: do what seems right at the time and do it quickly, but don't think about it or expect justice, either private or mortal. Be strong and you might survive.

Outside, steam engines hissed and puffed. For years the rail siding of Sachsenhausen had sounded like that. It was not so very long since groups of ragged and vacant-eyed Poles had been chugged into the siding, dejected, uprooted people, each one still living because of the tiny glow of hope hidden in their souls that had kept them alive until they got here, unlike the Italian in Lichtenberg who held his feet off the ground until he choked his own life way. Curiously enough, it was only in Sachsenhausen that I ever felt any serious desire to be done with it all. When we disembarked and stood herded into a cowed group in the siding waiting to be put in our cells, my attention became irresistibly drawn to the high barbed-wire perimeter fence and I suddenly felt a powerful urge to make a break and run for that fence, to climb and claw my way up it, knowing that the guards would instantly open fire. But it was a momentary thing, probably partly the result of being outside after so long, a kind of brief insanity, and others I spoke to later said they had experienced a similar sensation.

A rumour that we were to be moved rippled through the tightly packed cells. A female doctor examined us for fitness to work. The backless chair on which she sat disappeared in her gigantic arse. She must be a fixture, I thought, staring at her, fascinated. She was too fat to walk – a huge pile of female clothing with a little head on top, a pale flabby face with two round weasel eyes scuttling about in it. She sat busily looking on while the orderlies divided the jumbled mass of naked males into two groups, the plumpest to the right of the female heap, the tottering skeletons to the left.

While waiting our turn to be examined – no, judged – one ageing weed with a contemptuous eye on my shoulders sneered with a note of self-satisfaction: 'Well, comrade, they will certainly make a splendid coal miner of you!' If he thought his feebleness gave him an advantage, the truth would have killed him on the spot; a pity for him it did not – it might have saved him a lot of suffering later on, when life became a struggle that only the fittest survived. Still, he'd managed to get by so far by exploiting his weakness. Good for him, but not my idea. In me there still somehow survived the eager-faced 12-year-old boy tripping along beside the man in worn gamekeeper's tweeds, listening to the slow Norfolk drawl: 'It's best you be strong, boy, it's sartain if you eant strong you'm weak and this 'ere world eant got much use for weak 'uns!'

'*Du richts!*' snapped the orderly, giving me a push to the group right of the female hulk. '*Du links!*' he ordered the ageing weed, who was already tottering to the group on the left.

The rumour they were going to move us was right. The wooden shelf-like bunks of the crammed cells were cleared of the bodies that now moved as a slow chained mass at the rail siding and lumbered slowly into the waiting trucks. At last we pulled out of the siding. The hissing and clanging and smell of hot oil changed to the rhythmic clatter of train wheels speeding over track that had carried the Polish, Russian and Jewish prisoners in the opposite direction, herded from their homes, perhaps by somebody on this train with me now, somebody who had only been doing what he had been ordered to do. Everybody does his duty without questioning the authority; more crimes are committed in the sacred name of duty than through wicked intent.

In the semi-dark wagon the manoeuvring and fighting for the best positions now began. The weakest got shoved nearest the hole in the corner, through which we all pissed and squatted with trousers around our ankles. The cold pierced up through the hole, which stank revoltingly, and through it one could see the track racing past, speeding us on into the hard land of Dostoevsky and Tolstoy. Russia. In the past I had read about it, its prisoners, its suffering and its mysteries, all remote and so distant then. Even now it was unreal, the only immediate reality was the problem of staying alive in the gloomy wagon. Power groups formed for mutual protection. The 24 hours I had spent shivering half-naked in the punishment cell at Sachsenhausen for working the big Pole over now paid off because I did not have to fight for a place – people readily made way for me. Oddly enough it was the Poles, the strongest group, who offered me their companionship. I quickly accepted and found myself lying beside the big Pole whose balls I had twisted. He still talked with a lisp through a gap in his front teeth but appeared to bear me no malice and, like the others in the group, shared his food with me.

I was in a position to feel sorry for the weaker ones, like the little Jew who sat next to the icy, disgusting hole. His thin neck seemed too weak to hold his large head upright. He rested it on his drawn-up knees. His clothes hung on him like the feathers of a wet crow. I said hello to him in German and the big burning brown eyes which looked up from under the huge military cap said everything in reply. Slowly we got talking. He had been a master engraver and had managed to live through his imprisonment in Himmler's camps by using his considerable skills to make excellent forgeries of English and American paper money for the Germans, with which they hoped to flood the market and upset the Allied economy. Then came the Russians, he was mopped up as a 'war criminal' and his last gleam of survival went out.

The second day of twilight with two issues of bread, two bowls of soup and six salt fish. The little Jew had died in the night. We said nothing to the guards and threatened with death anyone who did. We drew his ration and we six strong ones ate it between us. I felt glad to be with the strong. Somebody with a conscience covered the little Jew's set face with a coat and folded his long thin hands on his chest, hands that had rained pound notes down onto the British Isles. Somebody stole the coat an hour later.

Three long twilight days passed and three menacing stretches of inky darkness with its dangerous stupor and dreams through which some slept fitfully and some watched with alert, hungry eyes. At last a grinding halt. Brest Litovsk. We disembarked.

At the transit prison they herded us through the bathing and delousing like sheep through a dip. More bread, more soup, and we were locked for two days in a huge cell crowded to its limits.

I lived in a world where there was nothing but prisoners, manacles, barbed wire and guards, a world of sheep-dip bathing, bread, fish soup and cabbage. But my mind, so accustomed to its solitude for so long, still glimpsed sideways from the crushing present out through a gate in a field where a man in sun-drenched tweeds leaned, his gun crooked over his arm, and the scent of summer blew over the clean fields. And in the large packed cell with its three-tier bunks we clambered like apes and plundered each other's petty belongings and abused our own kind like humans, while elsewhere invisible gods with power of life and death over us sorted through our records hoping to find something their almighty kind had missed or failed to find even after years of tortuous interrogation.

'*Gavay! Gavay!*' ('Hurry up!') We're on our way again. Get up, get moving down the corridor, rubbing shoulder to shoulder like cattle down a loading chute to the trains. Freshly swabbed, heads shorn, we wait in the loading bay by the tracks. Among the new ones joining us are six tall Ukrainians who stand out like pearls in a heap of dross, followers of Stepan Bandera, the Ukrainian freedom fighter. That was their crime: they believed in and followed him with their tall muscular bodies and steady blue eyes. Something in their gaze reminded me of that man in tweeds as he looked out into my distance and slowly nodded approval.

The coat issued to me was comparatively good. A guard beckoned me furtively, fleetingly fingered it and offered me a whole loaf of bread for it. The nights were cold and would become colder, but thanks to the strength of the Polish gang I was not terribly hungry, and I was able to refuse with malicious glee. The guard said nothing, but later I saw him talking to my Sachsenhausen Pole.

I continued to walk up and down in the loading bay watching my feet and hoping nobody would break into my world where Anneliese was telling me how things could have been with our inn on the side of the Bavarian mountain, the swish of the skis, the sun on the snow. Then suddenly the sun blacked out and there was stifling darkness as a blanket was thrown over my head from behind and pulled tight around my neck. Thinking stopped. I ducked and turned in the darkness like a wild animal on the end of a rope. Twisting under it, I kicked in the direction of the pull, then was crashed to the ground under a rattle of blows and weight of bodies. Screams, dull heavy thuds, then shouts of *Banderos! Banderos!* The blows ceased and the weight was lifted from me. Light returned as the blanket was whipped from my head. I blinked up at the six terrible angels, blond symbols of freedom and strength standing among a litter of prostrate bodies and cringing men with bloodstained faces. The outside ring of curious faces murmured respectfully.

'You fight like a wildcat!' said one of the giants with a wide laugh, speaking German for my benefit. 'They say you are English?'

'They say what is correct,' I answered shortly.

'Why do you speak German if you are English?' enquired another curiously.

'Because none of you speak English!' I snapped back, too preoccupied with my bruises to feel properly grateful for my deliverance.

'By the Holy Mother, he's nobody's doormat!' they laughed, and I sensed their approval of me. I was right, for they advised me to get into a wagon with them when we boarded, if I got the chance.

This attack had been the revenge of the big Pole, who, it seemed, was not as disposed to turn the other cheek as it had appeared. The man collected defeats like a punch-drunk boxer did bruises; if he carried on like this he was not even going to make it to Russia. But it started my acquaintance with the Banderos, a piece of good fortune to which I would certainly owe my life again later on.

Back in the twilight with the stinking cold hole in the corner that graced us all like a judge. The further you lived from it the more powerful you were. All over the world dung carriers are despised and untouchable; it may make potatoes big and tasty and roses smell sweet, but it's a sad lot for those who are forced to bring them all together.

The six Ukrainians and I lay on coats near the door, a position most prized of all. Sharing their food, sleeping safe. Me lying together with a bunch of Banderos while the train rattled rhythmically to a place near the Arctic with deep snowdrifts and deep prisons all lit by the Northern Lights. It seemed like some fantastic fable. But it was happening to me – each clang, each guttural German word and incomprehensible Russian syllable was real and happening. But so far so good. At least it was an improvement on the solitary cell.

We clattered noisily along with periods of twilight and darkness. Boredom came with the security that the Banderos' friendship gave me and we passed the time sleeping or talking. Mostly they talked and I listened. I heard and learned more about the Ukraine in those two rattling twilit days than many have in months at a university. Through their eyes I saw Russia opening before me and, at the same time, an entirely new Germany. They were part of both countries, yet neither Russian nor German. Tough and pliable as rain-soaked rawhide, they were misleadingly called Little Russians by their neighbouring nations to distinguish them from the other inhabitants of Russia, who had hammered them unmercifully for years without breaking them. They spoke a language different from the Russians and were proud of it, fighting stubbornly for its preservation and their independence both before and after the 1917 revolution. During the war years, the Germans would have found them sturdy allies, but their unsympathetic handling of the Ukrainians only served to create partisan groups and characters like Stepan Bandera, the likes of whom made nearly as much trouble for them as the Russian generals did. The German retreat in 1945 was followed by a flood of arrests by the Soviet secret police for collaboration. Some of these charges were true but many were just an excuse, and the mass deportations quickly depleted the working strength of the country to the benefit of the many convict colonies, where most of these partisan fighters now found themselves.

For a time I held the mistaken impression that Ukrainians were of remote German origin. Their national costume has a resemblance to that of Austria and their sound command of the German language gave me a good understanding with them. To me, they always appeared more west than east European, unlike the other Soviet nationals. Later, I discovered that there were amongst them many German immigrants who had settled and farmed the Ukrainian soil for several generations.

As far as the Russian language was concerned, I fumbled along in a fog but I was learning fast. '*Blatnoy*' – 'thieves in law' – was a word which frequently cropped up, mostly when certain well-dressed prisoners, the elite of the prison hierarchy, were around. They kept a good distance from my Banderos, but otherwise lorded it mightily over the rest. I asked Pyotr Usilof, the leading Bandero, who those impressive-looking fellows were.

'Godforsaken Blatnoy!' was the laconic reply. I knew from the tone of his voice that something displeased him, but out of curiosity I pressed the point. I was told they were a criminal brotherhood, a freemasonry of criminals that made its own laws and had corrupt police and officials in its pay. In prison or out, a Blatnoy is a grafter and does no work, living from blackmail, robbery, prostitution, intimidation and violence. The brotherhood gave powerful protection to its own members, but it also operated a harsh discipline over them and each member had a rank which remained the same whether he was in prison or not, his lifestyle correspondingly changing very little. The history of the Blatnoy is as old as Russia and some of its activities made the Mafia, which it resembled in many ways, pale by comparison.

We clanged slowly into Orshave. The same herd-like movements of bathing, taking in food, sleeping, digesting, eliminating, enveloped me in the thick, stifling miasma of stale urine, sweat, garlic and carbolic that I never got used to. The few days in the transit prison were spent in a large, well-lit cell with about 60 of us crowded in. A brawl in the cell. A huddle of prisoners in the centre sways to and fro then parts. A limp body slips to the floor with foam and blood on its mouth. A young German who made two mistakes. He didn't keep quiet about the fact that he had some tobacco, and he had started an argument. It pays to be popular, even when you are strong.

After Orshave, our form of transport changed, the big boarded-up cattle trucks being replaced by the Stalypin wagon. Stalypin was, it seems, a Czarist minister who had invented this particular means of transport especially for prisoners to Siberia. The wagon was a wooden cubicle seven feet square and ten feet high, with three tiers of bunks on which we crouched and slept. The locked, iron-barred door opened onto a corridor, along which an armed guard patrolled ceaselessly. There was no lavatory, not even a hole in the floor, and if you couldn't wait until the one daily lavatory stop it was too bad for you and the rest of the occupants of your wagon. Outside it was cold with a coldness I never thought possible, but in the cubicle the heat and stench were nearly as unbelievable. Prison life is made up from monotony of extremes. The only place any of us could stand upright was the six-foot square in the middle of the carriage, and the impossibility of moving without disturbing at least three people brought the animal to the fore in us all. Muscle was necessary to get and keep a comparative comfort, and reputations were constantly at stake.

From the comparatively comfortable spot that I had won, I watched a young German lad die. When and from exactly what he died was not clear. Nobody else had noticed him dying and there was nothing I could do. The fact was that nobody had noticed him living. A fight broke out over the bread in his pocket. I got a bit. Dead man's bread tastes just the same as any bread when you are hungry.

The next transit stop – the Lubyanka. Prison of a thousand solitary cells, a monument to Russian history and symbol of its inhumanity. I'd read about it all long before I even dreamt I might one day have the doubtful distinction of being an inmate. I felt I should have some sense of occasion, feel like some Dostoevsky character ready to laugh, grieve or fight. But in fact I felt nothing. To me, it was just another prison and by now they all filled me with the same sense of hopelessness and desperation without the slightest tinge of adventurous thrill. And yet when we left I knew I was part of Russia's nightmare history. I took with me the murmuring echoes of its solitary cells and the vibrations of countless agonised souls, the living and the dead; there wasn't much difference between the two in the Lubyanka. Like the grey-haired mumbling shadow of a ghost who gave out the daily ration of bread. A German prisoner from the First World War, he still went from cell to cell whispering enquiries of his home in Bavaria as if he had left it only a month or two ago. He had already entered that prison at the time I entered school. What crime had he committed to warrant such a punishment – or had capricious authority simply overlooked him, lost his records? Did this often happen in this soulless, crazy world? That ghost from all those prison years stuck icicles in my bowels and panic froze me like a terrified cat. Stop – in the name of anything that may be holy or sacred! Moscow was far enough from Norfolk and here were these fanatics trying to improve their world by dragging me further away into their panorama of torment and hunger with only the promise of a short unhappy life ahead of me. Dostoevsky had made it all good reading: being one of his characters was straight bloody hell.

Back into the Stalypin wagon, you rootless scum. Was I without roots, was I just scum now? The iron wheels rocked and swayed on and on over miles of line laid through territory peopled by prisoners and fur-coated zombies with rifles and red stars on their hats, of women pushing barrows of earth or carrying pit-props like forlorn crows building a nest.

For five days more we rumbled and rolled then slowed down, stopped. The name of the camp was breathed down the train of subdued prisoners. It sounded like a curse. Inta. We had arrived.

Chapter 16

THE ARCTIC SLAVE MINE

Inta. A prison town in the Arctic snow waste, named for the river on which it stood. A strict-regime slave labour camp in the Komi Soviet Republic, and one of the toughest and bleakest in the entire Gulag forced-labour camp system established by Stalin across the whole USSR. A panorama of rough-hewn timber buildings and barbed-wire fences, a mingling of dirty snow and coal and watchtowers rearing up into foggy grey sky and in the top of them hunched fur-muffled sentries like dangerous and watchful teddy bears.

Clambering down from the train we stumbled stiffly together in groups surrounded by hillocks of coal. The cold was so intense it closed my nostrils, making it difficult to breathe. Stamping our feet and flapping our hands, we tried to bring warmth and movement back to our inappropriately clad bodies. The guards were in no hurry. Like true teddy bears, all furry material and no brains, they counted us over and over again, trying to agree how many of us there should be, how many had died since leaving Moscow. It was the numbers that were important, not those thinking moving forms called prisoners. They disagreed noisily while we froze silently. The Soviets owned our bodies now; we were theirs to dispose of in the course of their obscure search for an ideal way of life.

Yelling and pushing, the brainless bears at last got us into a column of fours. We crunched slowly off with armed guards and snarling dogs on each side, each of us hoping soon to be somewhere out of the stinging cold. The tall bent coat and hat in front of me stumbled along without seeing or hearing where we were going, the hanging head muttering '*Mein Gott! Mein Gott!*' I couldn't tell whether it was a despairing curse or a plea for aid and comfort.

The further we stumbled the cleaner became the snow underfoot. Tall spiky black pines lined the road, thrusting themselves darkly into the heavy sky, but we passed little in the way of human beings or habitation. My eyes were beginning to hurt from the glare of the snow when after what must have been a couple of hours we arrived at our camp. The barbed-wire gates of Camp V opened and we entered upon an entire village of prisoners and row upon row of barrack huts.

After a hasty roll call we were all hustled into one of the huts to await medical examination and allocation to work groups. Three-tiered bunks lined the wall, a sack of straw and a blanket on each. The scramble was on for the bunks nearest the stove – the '*pechka*', as I was to find out, is about the only thing that makes life possible in North Russia, belching out constant heat like a squat silent foster mother. The smell of sweaty bodies, heavenly after the bitterly cold march, mingled with the steam from two wooden buckets of soup which were now carried in to an accompanying rattle of tin bowls. We ladled the two pints a head down our throats until the feeling that we were human started to return.

Clearly the news of our arrival had flashed through the camp. From all over it prisoners crowded in on us, creating a tower of Babel with men seeking news of friends and relatives in dozens of different tongues. Nobody was interested in me and I was allowed to enjoy a temporary isolation which ended all too soon. A German doctor with our party had a woollen vest which, miraculously, he had managed to keep on the journey, and which he now traded for a large amount of bread and sugar. In a state of near ecstasy, with the precious food clutched to his chest, he scurried squirrel-like back to his bunk. But in the hungry eyes that followed he recognised the threat to kill him for his food. He turned to me in the next bunk from his.

'If I give you some will you stand by me?' he pleaded. I nodded agreement and ate with him under the wolfish eyes. Had it been his official ration of bread it would have been different: here among this horde of cast-off men, many of whom would steal at first chance anything you did not actually stuff up your anus, the only rule which stood fast was that nobody stole another's official portion of bread. That was sacred and it went badly for anyone who was even suspected of stealing another's manna.

A respectful murmur of 'Blatnoy!' distracted the hungry eyes from our eating and heads turned to observe the latest entrant to the hut. He looked like the popular romantic image of a Cossack, white fur hat over a ruddy face, thick well-fitting coat and trousers and polished top boots. I stared at him in amazement as he passed my bunk glancing at me arrogantly. His neatness, pride and self-assurance were totally out of place in this lost rabble. He was greeted by a bearded member of our party and they gabbled together excitedly. After a few minutes, they flung their arms around each other, kissing on both cheeks, then left the hut together arm in arm.

When I next saw the bearded man it was several weeks later and he too strutted in top boots and fur hat, obviously a Blatnoy recognised by his organisation. A murderer from Moscow with a sentence of five years. Five years for murder! I had 25 for being in the wrong place at the wrong time! I did not like what I had seen and heard of the Blatnoy but, looking at the transformation in the bearded man, I made a mental note. If one had to be in this place, it seemed a good thing to be a Blatnoy – they were the strong, and here you very definitely had to be strong to survive.

Medical examination for fitness to work. A simple and foolproof system. The doctor asked you your age and whether you had syphilis and then passed you as fit for the mines (what happened if you did have syphilis I never discovered). Nobody took his job more seriously than that doctor, a prisoner himself with a ten-year sentence all but over. He was taking no chances of having it lengthened for sabotage against the state. In his book if you could stand you could work, and who could blame him!

We were allotted to work groups headed by a foreman who qualified for his job by being the receiver of good food parcels for a well-placed Blatnoy. If you had food parcels, you in turn gave some to the foreman for favours and light work. I had no food parcels. I was assigned to work at the coal face.

On the journey out, the Ukrainians had given me some idea of what life was like in a soft-coal mine. It meant premature ageing and ultimate death from exhaustion before many years had passed, sweating one's life away on an inadequate diet, making up for those who did nothing, for the production target still had to be met. But if I did not work I would get no food, for I had no powerful friends to protect and feed me. What a choice! I stretched out on my straw mattress and pulled the blanket over me in hopeless despair. Whatever future I may have had stretched as bleak and sombre as the snow-cold waste outside. It all seemed so vast, so lost and empty that my tired brain couldn't comprehend it. I rolled my newly issued *bushlat* (military winter coat) into a pillow and slept while the frost spun intricate patterns on the tiny barrack window.

Clang, clang! The iron-cold early morning bell urges us from the warm barrack to make our way slowly to the main gate to take part in the ritual of the daily gathering and march to the mine in rows of four, the warders counting us out while the soldiers count us into the column ready to march. The prison 'prayers' are recited as usual by the officer in charge of the escort: keep in line of four, look straight at the back of the man in front of you, keep your hands clasped behind your back, no talking, anybody leaving the formation will be shot. The incantation never varies, even though the final threat is completely superfluous. Who in his right mind would want to escape into that white waste of nothingness! As a jailer, Jack Frost has no equal.

With two in front, three on each flank and the officers behind, we crunch forward, the flanking boy soldiers looking more bored than the prisoners; in fact, their lot is not so very different from ours. Those of us who don't converse in whispers out of the sides of our mouths sink into ourselves. Hands drawn up the sleeves of our coats, cold stinging our unprotected faces, we trundle along like a flock of thoughtful penguins. After half an hour, the tall watchtowers and barbed-wire surrounds of the mine come into sight against the snow, a blight on the land of Father Christmas. Under that sky with Jack's lethal fingers waiting – there is no escape here. You have your choice: die of cold, be shot or fester away beside the warm stove after a short eternity of coal dust and toil. An armed soldier opens the mine gate and we go through into the comparative freedom of steam-driven machinery and oily-smelling wooden structures, and each one makes for his allotted job.

The pits in which I worked were, by any standards, primitive. Working at the coal face was cramped, dangerous and decidedly unhealthy. Automation was all but unknown. Every ounce of coal had to be manhandled from the face to the surface. Even pit ponies were considered a luxury. Our task was to shovel the coal by hand in stages along waterlogged pit shafts no more than five feet high as far as 50 yards to the main shafts, where it was thrown into iron trucks or bogies which were pushed by two men to the erratic lift that took it to the surface. Protective clothing was a joke; an assembly of miners ready to go down looked like a gathering at a tramps' ball. Lamps and helmets were officially supplied, but without bribes they were devoid of straps, linings and buckles so that it was impossible to wear them successfully. More often than not one got soaked in the mine and in the few yards' journey from pithead to tool sheds and baths the ragged overalls froze stiff and one had to use a hammer to break out of them.

There were shower baths, but so bodged that only cold water ran with any success – hot water was a lucky event. Nevertheless I had to admire the ingenuity of the engineers and plumbers, all prisoners of course. They were magicians who conjured up from old buckets, tyres, tins and odd scraps of this and that anything from a shower bath to a set of false teeth. But the showers were few and at best four men shared one at the same time. Everybody was always in a hurry. If, through no fault of his own, a man was late and kept the shift waiting with the guard at the gate (where the counting process was repeated before the return to barracks), he could get himself kicked almost to death by his freezing, irate fellow prisoners.

Sometimes I rebelled against my troll-like existence doubled up underground and managed to sneak off to the slag heap. I would sit halfway up the sulphurous burning mountain enjoying its warmth and look past the top of the barbed wire into the distance of snow and sky and it seemed that the very thing that confined me gave me a sense of freedom. Once I sat there the whole shift, joining the men only when they assembled at the gate to return to camp for food and sleep, but my absence had not gone unnoticed. That evening I was hauled hitting, kicking and biting from my bunk by a small gang of prisoners and hustled, battered and bloody, to the hut of the foreman. It looked as if he was going to continue the beating-up personally when suddenly the door burst open and Pyotr Usilof, my Ukrainian saviour from the transport train, brought a quick change in their attitude with a torrent of Ukrainian. Then, grabbing me by the shoulder, he propelled me out of the room and back to his own barrack. Seated on his bunk, he explained to me that the foreman, a Ukrainian Bandero, was following the customary procedure for work dodgers but was now full of apologies after it had been explained to him who and what kind of fellow I was. However, Usilof cautioned kindly, I should try to do a little more work and meanwhile he would try to find me an easier job. May that fellow find favour with every god man has thought of! I had need of friends like that, and even though he didn't manage to come up with a soft spot for me, it gave me something to think about for a few days.

There was one short, lunatic period when I went to the other extreme and took it into my head to astound them all by using my stamina and muscle power in the pits to achieve a 'Stakhanovitch' performance. The gangers and foremen sat up and took notice but quickly lost interest when I dropped back to my usual dawdle.

Stakhanovitch was, apparently, a Russian minister for labour who devised a scheme to increase work output, which, in theory, was simply to set a production target, a level to be recognised as the normal, which came to be known as the work norm. When this norm was reached or passed, it naturally gave way to a new, raised norm. In the labour and penal camps the new work norms were posted up every week and everybody exhorted to strive to at least equal it. Those successful in equalling or surpassing this were known as 'Stakhanovitchki', earning official approval and the contempt of their fellow workers, most of whom were busily engaged in devising new methods of making convincing gestures to cover the tricks they used to get through their work with as little physical effort as possible. Many, including myself, became experts in work evasion – that way you didn't die of exhaustion so quickly. Stakhanovitch struck me as having much in common with Jesus Christ: there were conflicting statements and theories as to the origin of each, and both probably set out with the best of intentions only to have their ideas and teachings twisted out of recognition by politicians. Like the name of Christ in so-called Christian countries, the word 'Stakhanovitch' was on every citizen's tongue in Soviet Russia, while in both cases the actual practice of their ideas was carefully avoided.

The forced manual labour was unpleasant, hard and dangerous, but it took several months for the fact to sink into my poor washed and scrubbed brain that if a life has a high measure of danger, then it must also have a high proportion of pleasure to balance it. The truth was that, after the years of misery in the interrogation prisons and solitary confinement, arriving at Inta penal settlement was, for me, like entering heaven. Everything is relative. Being able to walk in a straight line for more than eight feet without encountering a wall, being with people, being able to talk to them most of the time, having the occasional opportunity to obtain a little extra food, simply breathing fresh air – at first I felt a happiness I had forgotten. Compared with the captivity I had known, life in Inta was one of relative freedom, its very routine almost comforting.

At the end of our eight-hour shift, lengthened by the waiting and searching and counting processes at the gates, we mine workers rushed for the warmth of our barracks in winter where we could wait, stretched out on our bunks, to be assembled and marched by the foreman to the dining hall for the almost invariable meal of soup and daily issue of bread. Sometimes one was lucky enough to earn a little extra food, and to my good fortune I discovered among the prisoners a few who were eager to learn or improve their English. In return for food or articles of clothing, I would help them to read and write my language. Somewhere in Russia today I am sure there are still Russians capable of speaking English with a pronounced Norfolk accent, just as my camp-acquired knowledge of Russian would scarcely be comprehensible in drawing-room circles.

The one dining hall served the entire camp, so that we literally ate in shifts and had to leave as soon as we had finished, after which we were free so far as the barbed wire and prowling warders allowed. Not being allowed to visit other barracks was a rule frequently broken and it was downright bad luck if you met a screw who disliked you when inside a barrack where you did not belong. Even on the one day off out of the seven we were supposed to keep to our barrack. In the winter we were pleased to be able to do this, but it was then that the battle against monotony and melancholia began, similar to and yet completely unlike that which I had seen in the prisoner-of-war and internment camps during the war. Then there had been the swing of the nations' fighting to follow, the conviction that it was for a limited period, the hoping and wishing for an end, any end, to restore normal life to the prisoner. But here, a forgotten vegetable in the Soviet stew pot with the Arctic Circle for a neighbour, what hope was there, what escape! Nothing existed except life within the camp, staying alive and making the best of it. Living in the overcrowded hut, you learned not only the other fellow's language but also how to tolerate his nearness, how to fight and win a place in the pecking order of this human henhouse, crowing and scratching from twilight to twilight all the hours of the Arctic night.

The deathly cold, and dark cramped monotony of those first winter months echoed the blackness inside me, for I could see no escape from an eternity of unrelieved danger and hardship. For the lucky few, there was a temporary respite in the camp hospital, a paradise with clean beds and decent food, but like all promised lands it had its avenging angel at the door barring the gateway with flaming sword. The entry to this particular one was effectively blocked by the bulging stomach and hindquarters of the presiding female deity. You had to arrive carrying your head under your arm before you were considered deserving of a few drops of the hospital's panacea, iodine, with which she treated everything from sore feet and septic throats to conjunctivitis. A prisoner nearing the end of her sentence, our fat doctor was careful not to have it lengthened by pronouncing too many of us unfit and in need of hospital treatment.

It was not long before the effects of the inadequate diet upon which I had lived for so long began to show, aggravated by the extreme climatic conditions and heavy labour. The scurvy from which I suffered – a condition bringing with it pain, irritation and an unconquerable lassitude – grew so bad that my teeth began to fall out and my raw tender gums bled constantly. If I had had to rely upon the medical system, this state of affairs would undoubtedly have continued until I fell apart completely, but, very fortunately for me, there existed a compound of camp and folk wisdom, a remedy as effective as it was vile. Some nameless, gnarled old prisoner, who had spent three-quarters of his life in prison in North Russia, took pity on me and advised me to boil handfuls of pine needles and then drink the water in which they had been boiled. This resinous draught certainly came within the old belief that the efficacy of a medicine increases in proportion to its unpalatability, but my perseverance was well rewarded not only by my scurvy being cured but also by my being able to prevent its recurrence.

Although my chronic scurvy, bad as it was, did not merit official medical treatment, let alone hospitalisation, I was not prepared to go to the extremes to which some prisoners resorted just to get a break from the hard labour and the crowded barracks. Self-mutilation was not uncommon and there were indeed some who became experts at the practice. There was one in particular, a good-looking, rather frail young Blatnoy of about 25, who took a great pride in his heavily scarred stomach. White and hard, the many stitch-crossed weals ran from the lower part of his chest to the top of his pelvis. When life became too much for him, he would stretch himself out on his bunk and, after a period of contemplation, would quietly produce the knife which all Blatnoy members seemed always to secrete somewhere, and then slit his abdomen open. It was obviously done with great skill for the angle and depth of the cut were exactly calculated to produce a wound that, while not fatal, nevertheless produced such a ghastly mess that his entry to hospital was assured. Others, with less surgical skill but perhaps more desperation, would hack off fingers or thumbs, but they bought their brief respite at greater cost than the young Blatnoy, who never seemed to suffer any long-term hardship or ill-effects as a result of his gory blood-letting.

I could not contemplate such desperate measures any more than I could seriously consider suicide as a way out, although there were many who chose that as their final solution. The only thing I could do was to keep plodding from one dreary, miserable day to the next. I had been through worse – and everything passes. And the passing of the Russian winter into the sudden spring, when it eventually came, was truly unforgettable.

None of my long experience of the cycle of the seasons in the English countryside had prepared me for the Arctic spring. At home I had been accustomed to the gradual approach, the first snowdrops through the snow (when there was any), the faint green fuzz on the willows, the fat buds in the hedgerows heralding the leaves, the subtle change in the air and in the quickening smell of the earth. In Inta there had been some preparatory lengthening of the day, or rather a decrease in the constant night, but there was one definite and particular morning when one emerged from the barracks and felt immediately that it was several degrees less cold. There was an almost overnight change in the ice-bound surface of the ground and an ensuing rapid thaw, although a foot below the surface it remained eternally frozen like a permanent ice-core. The inevitable slushy interim when the snow in the vicinity of the mines resembled a dirty, gooey pudding, was not long in clearing, and it seemed that no sooner was the ground bare of snow than it grew warm and green.

From permanent night we moved to unchanging day. Endless days of light that gave the wheat and weeds the power to grow an inch in 24 hours but not the time to ripen; of heat when we handed in our winter clothes for flimsier rags; when the camp scavengers got double rations and dysentery and the latrines stank for miles. Now the timber-felling crews worked three shifts in every 24 hours like the mine workers, and the Blatnoy and work dodgers with influence changed their warm jobs in the mine to laze around in the timber-hauling gangs, and even the sparrows left the mines to chirp and peck and mate in the sunshine.

The door of paradise stood ajar for all of us for a few glorious weeks and the golden sands of Norfolk beaches burned hot under the feet of a small lone Englishman dreaming in the sun by a pile of pit-props near the Arctic Circle.

Generally speaking, the fact of being the only Englishman in the camp was something of a burden to me, and a dangerous one at that, for it made me a total outsider, an albino blackbird to be pecked by its fellows – although they pecked at their peril. In the crowded barracks fights were common, but generally I managed to keep out of them or, when they were unavoidable, to give better than I got, using my fists to good effect to assert myself, establish my identity and my right to be left alone. But my 'foreign-ness' and slowly growing reputation for being useful with my fists made me a natural target. On one occasion I was picked upon by an ambitious prisoner with some authority over the rest of us, who tried to increase it by beating me up. The fact that he ended up dazed and bleeding on the ground earned me the grudging respect of those in the barrack who might have harboured the same idea. But I felt terribly alone, vaguely comprehending that it was only a matter of time before I would be found dead, face down in the latrine with several inches of homemade knife in my guts. Murder was commonplace and many a fight ended with one of the antagonists being killed. A body floating in the shit pit scarcely raised any more than a passing interest, so frequently did it occur. I had little doubt that there was a very good chance that one day that body would be mine, the inevitable end of a friendless, unprotected misfit.

Then one evening, as suddenly and dramatically as the transition from Russian winter to spring, my life in Inta changed overnight.

Big, brutal Sostachenko was dead. The little Englishman had killed him with a single blow. Not with a knife or an axe when his back was turned, in customary camp fashion, but square on and face to face, striking him to the ground with his fist. The story flew from mouth to mouth like the fairytale achievement of the valiant little tailor, embellished at every telling.

I had not intended to kill Ivan Sostachenko but the humiliation had hurt just that tiny bit more than usual. He was a '*soka*', a Ukrainian in charge of the dining hall. I had gone there with my gang to eat and receive rations. They, like good shadow men, had finished eating and with their portion of bread tucked under their arms, had left to make way for the next shift. But I stayed behind in the huge food-steamy barrack on the lookout for anybody wanting to practise their English and willing to reward me with a bowl of gruel or a chunk of bread. Sostachenko spotted me. He ploughed battleship fashion through the jostling men and made in my direction. I hastened to get out of the door but he caught up with me there and planted a hefty kick on my arse that sent me sprawling out into the snow. Picking myself up, I saw him lumbering towards me. There was a burning rage inside me and I knew this would be where I made my stand. No more running now. I had had enough. Suddenly the whole situation felt familiar and I quivered with the thrill of anticipation.

His big hand reached out for my shoulder. My right hook passed over it and met the side of his face. His head jerked back, the bulky body arched and his shaven skull crashed back onto the frozen ground. He twitched and convulsed a little, then lay very still, and my life as a Russian prisoner changed.

As I walked away, the crowd of onlookers parted in respectful silence to let me pass. I made my way to my barrack and stretched myself out on my bunk, dimly aware of the faces full of wonder and curiosity that peered round the door at me. They wanted a glimpse of the small volcano that had spewed up fire and fun in their midst. Suddenly the eager faces disappeared and a warder walked in and called out my name. I sat up and he came over to my bunk and said in a kindly fashion: 'You had better come with me. They say Sostachenko is dead.'

For a warder to behave amicably towards me was extraordinary. Friendliness was the way the warders showed respect for a prisoner out here in Russia. I went with him to the cells, where I spent two days with blanket and full rations. Even more remarkable: it should have been no food, no blanket.

I slept most of the time, pondering over events in my waking moments. That I had killed Sostachenko worried me very little; I had lived with the choice of killing or being killed too long for that. But how was the camp authority going to take the incident? I had no way of knowing and the uncertainty made me feel trapped and uneasy. I was relieved when they released me with the information that I had been given an additional five years for killing Sostachenko. It was almost laughable. I lost no sleep over that extra five years. Twenty-five or thirty years – what did it matter? It was still a lifetime of shovelling coal on cabbage soup.

But as soon as I left the punishment cell I found that Sostachenko's death did matter. I walked out into a much improved world, still surrounded by barbed wire it is true, but the people on the inside couldn't conceal a grudging respect and admiration. I had a new name. No longer was I called just plain 'Englishman', or '*Anglichanin*' – and that with superior condescension; now, with studied courtesy, it was 'English Sledgehammer', or '*Anglissky kuwaldo*'. Back in the barrack, my bed had been moved next to the stove. I was definitely on my way up. The next step wasn't long in coming.

The wintry sun had struggled through, a welcome stranger. With my back against a pile of pit-props I let its watery warmth creep through my clothes while I listened, head bent, in my mind's ear to Anneliese as she tried to make me understand a rule of German grammar. Her voice changed. It was deep and masculine and Russian, saying: 'Eric Georgeovitch, may I have the pleasure of your attention for a while?'

I looked up. Between me and the tired sun stood an opera bandit straight off the stage, complete with huge sheepskin hat, gleaming knee-high boots and theatrical courtesy. I stared at him in disbelief, as much because of his appearance as for the fact that he had addressed me formally by my name and patronym. He just smiled and continued, requesting the pleasure of my attendance at Barrack 7 that evening. I recovered sufficiently to accept and to take the hand he offered as he bade me 'Goodbye until then', clasping my hand in both of his as if I were a long-lost brother.

As he walked away, I gazed after his upright striding figure, waiting for some kind of warning alarm to sound in my head but there was none, only the quiet echo of my father's voice as he knocked out his pipe on the heel of his boot and said softly as he gazed into the bowl: 'There can't be much else yer kin dew, boy!' Slowly I nodded my head in agreement. I had no choice but to go. My theatrical visitor had not said who he was or who had sent him but I knew without asking, for the flashy figure of the Blatnoy strode unmistakably through the snivelling, fawning prison community.

When I got to know these Russian spivs better, I had nothing but contempt for them, but still their lifestyle undeniably had something very attractive about it. For one thing, they were never hungry, ill-clad or overworked. The Blatnoy – 'grafters' is probably the best translation – were organised on lines similar to the Mafia. How it originated nobody seemed to know, but they certainly formed an integral part of life in the prison colonies of Russia. I did hear it said in all seriousness that Stalin was at one time a member of the brotherhood and that the Blatnoy produced funds for the party by robbing banks and jewellers. How true this was no one could say, but I do know for a fact that while Stalin was in power the Blatnoy practically ruled the camp I was in, and it was only at his death that their power declined, to give way to the more politically oriented Banderos.

It was a brotherhood bound by oath and strict discipline based on rank, inside prison and out, and membership was for life. Obedience to a superior within the organisation was unquestioning, but in return for this loyalty the pack protected its members from outsiders and saw to it that they did not want. But if most of the rules governing them were harsh and uncompromising, some appeared almost childish and whimsical, although it was apparent that they sprang from the arrogance of the strong. No member was allowed to open or shut a prison door or gate or accept an extra helping of prison food from a warder or trusty. Under no conditions would they return a stolen article. If a member was struck by an outsider, the assailant would be killed, even if the Blatnoy had struck first.

Gambling at cards was an organised and serious business. If one of them lost and could not pay his debt, the creditor was allowed to beat him with a stick (without hitting his hands, which might ruin a skilled pickpocket), after which the debt would be satisfied. If, when playing cards, one of the school lost everything, he could play for the life of somebody the others chose for him, that is, his debt would be paid off by him killing that person. Usually he approached the victim and said, 'Comrade, I have lost you.' The victim, knowing what was happening, usually simply said, 'How much?', whereupon the Blatnoy would name the sum, enough to clear him of his gambling debt. The victim invariably produced the price speedily, for he knew he was a dead man if he did not.

Taking everything into consideration, I saw it would be better, if the chance presented itself, for me to have the Blatnoy as playmates rather than adversaries, whatever I might think of them privately. I knew that I wanted to survive and in this environment there were no morally good or bad methods – only results decided that.

Barrack 7 was a nice, clean, well-situated barrack; its distance from the guardroom earned it the description 'well situated'. A muscular orderly got up from his seat just inside the door to challenge me as I entered, but a quiet word from one of the reclining figures on the bunks round the walls was sufficient to tumble him back into his seat, from where he stared inquisitively at me. The group around the stove rose from their stools. The opera bandit of this morning – minus his hat and coat – advanced to meet me with his hand outstretched in a gesture of welcome, overdone, unreal and childishly theatrical. I felt a desire to laugh and would have done but for the realisation that I was in the presence of the biggest gathering of irresponsible killers that it had been my bad luck to meet, a closely clustered hive of wantonly cruel drones unsoftened by their crucifixes and religious superstitions.

Aware of the scrutiny of my audience, I felt uncomfortable and scared that it might show. I stared out into the hazy black void where they sat beyond the blinding glare of the footlights, waiting as the half-hundredweight cannonball was slowly raised to its highest point. The audience was hushed, a roll of drums, and then the compact mass of iron hurtled down on my stomach. My trained muscles caught and repelled it, the crowd roared approval, the unnerving suspense was over and I breathed easily. I bowed, smiling slightly, as the haze cleared from my vision and I took the opera bandit's large soft paw. I took my seat within the circle about the stove and a mug of sweet tea was handed to me. Then the questioning started, Vasily Oblinken, as I now discovered my opera bandit to be called, translating into German for me, as my knowledge of Russian was still very elementary.

The questions were a mixture of the curiously naive and dangerously loaded. Could I read and write; was I a professional criminal in England; what sort of crime did I specialise in? In this gathering it seemed wisest to have a criminal background and I hastily invented one. My business, I said, speaking slowly to give myself time to think, was safebreaking. I picked it at random, thinking it was the skill I would least be called upon to exercise in Inta, but it seemed that I had chosen well, for there was an awed silence for a moment. If the Soviet system was classless, their credentials were not. Safebreakers apparently formed the elite over the rank-and-file pickpockets, horse thieves and black-marketeers. I began to enjoy the approval of these self-styled connoisseurs of crime.

After an animated discussion among themselves, in which I took no part, quietly relishing the unaccustomed luxury of another mug of tea, Vasily Oblinken leaned over to me.

'We like you and we think you should be one of us. It is soon to be decided. We shall meet you tomorrow in the mines. Goodbye until then, *tavarish Anglichanin!*'

This time I did laugh a little. Goodbye, Comrade Englishman – *Comrade* Englishman! It was the first time I'd been called that. It sounded silly, but I can't deny that I liked it. It gave me a hazy feeling of pride and sense of belonging that I hadn't known for years.

They went one better the next day. I was sitting halfway up the warm slag heap, turning over the meeting in my mind, when a small, sallow-skinned fellow wearing a nearly new *bushlat* and *valinie* came up to me and addressed me respectfully as '*Tavarish Anglichanin gaspoda*'. The *tavarish Anglichanin* bit I grasped all right, but I thought I must have the last word wrong. It meant 'sir'. That really was going from the sublime to the ridiculous – or was it the other way about? Either way, I didn't care. I wasn't going to argue.

I got up and followed the man as he threaded his way through the untidy jumble of grimy buildings with the certainty of an old lag. Finally we arrived at a large shed, where he ushered me in and shut the door behind me, then disappeared like a trained flunkey. The atmosphere inside was oily and warm and clearly it was some sort of repair shed, lit by several naked electric light bulbs whose brilliance came and went with the panting efforts of a generator struggling to power various other pieces of machinery as well.

Taking in my surroundings at a glance, I noticed with some alarm that there were about 50 men present. If yesterday's gathering in Barrack 7 had made me feel nervous, this one was plain frightening. As though at a given signal, they stopped playing cards as I entered, turning as one man to stare fixedly at me, the unsmiling faces menacing in the fitful light. I doubt a film director's imagination could have conjured up a more villainous-looking bunch, only this was no celluloid drama, it was real, it was happening to me. I felt like stopping the world and getting off. The sight of Vasily Oblinken coming towards me with his paw stuck out in the now familiar, exaggerated gesture was a welcome relief. The gathering began to put away the cards and reassemble in what appeared to be an order familiar to them, some seated around the long wooden table near the centre of the room, the rest standing around at the back of them.

Suddenly I got the picture. A committee or tribunal or something of the sort was convening. Vasily Oblinken guided me to the end of the table, which had obviously been reserved for us. Opposite me at the other end sat a truly remarkable figure. Close-shorn dark hair, a long sallow face, black beard well shot with grey, the fullness of which did not hide the wide, thin-lipped mouth; but what nearly stopped me breathing regularly were his eyes, burning cobra eyes, unflinching, merciless. I forced myself to look straight into them – why not, I had little to lose. I like to think that my own cold blue gaze countered effectively.

Somebody rapped sharply on the table. In the silence that immediately followed, the bearded man rose to his feet, his clear and surprisingly pleasant voice stopping after every few words to give Vasily Oblinken, standing at my elbow, time to translate for me.

'Eric Georgeovitch, we have gathered here to invite you to become one of us. Before you accept and take the oath, I must ask if you are aware of what that signifies.'

He then recited from memory the rules governing the Blatnoy. As I listened, it struck me that this man would have brought dignity to a brothel keeper's wedding party. All around, blurry suspended faces watched attentively. A large pointed dagger appeared on the table before me.

'Please pick up the knife in your right hand, Eric Georgeovitch, and repeat after me: I swear on the lives of my parents, on the lives of my children, on the lives of all I hold dear, to observe until I die these rules which bind and guide all members of our great family who live outside the law of the general establishment. Should I break this oath, may I die by the knife as certainly as I will bring death to any who betray or injure one of us.'

In that badly lit, metallic, oil-sweating shed the drama and solemnity of that moment struck deep. The image of a body face down in a pool of human shit was vivid in my mind. Melodramatic as it may sound now, it was at that time only too real. The oath inspired in me no sense of loyalty to the Blatnoy as such, but it would also make me very careful to cover my tracks if ever I transgressed against their code. All the same, when the strange ceremony was over, there was in me a renewed sense of belonging. I felt less lonely in my real aloneness and the warmth of being wanted, extinguished for so long, rekindled the zest for life which Siberia had all but frozen to death. From now on things were going to be different.

Chapter 17

THE ENGLISH SLEDGEHAMMER

The English Sledgehammer was now a Blatnoy and something of a camp celebrity. The image of the debilitated, fastidious Englishman so deeply engraved by propaganda into the naive Russian mind was shattered by the same blow that scrambled poor Sostachenko's brains, and I was enjoying the results. The prisoner in charge of the clothing store ran after me: did *gaspoda Anglichanin* wish for a pair of top boots? It was several degrees below zero this morning: *tavarish Anglichanin* could stay in bed if he felt unwell. The *Anglissky kuwaldo* must eat well: the cooks cheerfully ladled out extra soup for me.

Could I live with these creeping, ass-licking hangers-on? You bet I could, when the alternative was working wearily cold, ragged and hungry at the coal face, slogging at the so-called honest toil that was supposed to dignify. I felt no dignity in it, nor did I see any in my workmates. Now I was one of the drones, one of the powerful polished parasites, and I was more than willing to gamble my worker's dignity for a share of the Blatnoy glamour and good living.

Even in this godforsaken place there was good living of a kind – everything is relative. Things that are common and taken for granted in the outside world were luxury goods here, but still they were to be had – at a price. Tobacco was allowed into the camp, but because prisoners were only allowed to receive one parcel a month from the outside there was always a shortage and many of the free workers, who came in to work in the camp from the outside each day, did a good trade supplying it to the prisoners at moderate prices. Vodka, on the other hand, was completely banned, which, of course, made it even more desirable and sent prices sky-high. The vodka looked as clean and innocent as its name – 'pure little water' – but to the unaccustomed throat it was like the contents of a car battery, despite which we all drank it greedily whenever we got the chance, which was not very often.

The vodka had to be smuggled in by the free workers, who had to be paid in cash. This was the first stumbling block as the cash had first to be obtained from the outside. Even in a Communist state money is money, so only those with influence in the world outside could manage to get it brought in, and even then a percentage had to be paid to the person bringing the money through the prison gate. It was always carried in in small but frequent amounts so that the carrier could say it was his own if enquiries or a search should happen to be made.

In most prisons there will be one or two warders who can be persuaded, for a small consideration, to smuggle things in. Here in Inta we were watched over by guards who were soldiers, and warders who were prison officers: two separate and distinct bodies of men, but both, for different reasons, were virtually incorruptible. We had personal contact only with the warders, whose duties lay within the camp, although they lived with their wives and children just outside in long army-type huts. There were approximately five families to a hut, with two rooms to each family, all sharing the lavatory at one end and the kitchen at the other. Their brown uniforms, trimmed with red, were styled on military lines and the red Soviet star adorned winter hats and summer caps alike, while the three-inch-wide leather belts and brass buckles owed not a little to military spit and polish. Like the vast majority of their profession, they were not blessed with sensitive natures or outstanding intelligence, but they were shrewd enough not to jeopardise what was more a relatively comfortable way of life than a job by accepting bribes from prisoners, especially as they had little to gain by it.

The warders were never armed for the simple reason that, working as they did in constant and close proximity with the prisoners, there was always the danger that they would be overpowered and their weapons seized. Only the guards, who were soldiers, carried weapons, and for that reason we were never allowed to approach them, let alone get close enough to offer them a bribe. It was their job to supervise us outside the camp on working parties or as an escort to and from the mine, and every five soldiers were accompanied by a dog handler, who also held minor political rank and was therefore a government informer. If it was necessary for a guard to approach a prisoner, he always handed his rifle to one of his colleagues before doing so, but generally in the event of some disturbance the guards would fire into the air to alert the warders, who then came running from the camp to deal with the situation. Most of the guards were shaven-headed, brow-beaten young men who, like all soldiers, had had the ability to think for themselves systematically drilled out of them, leaving them well fed, randy and bored. But if they were always ready to shout at the slightest pretext, there were also times when they were prepared to turn an indulgent blind eye, for instance by slowing down a marching column just enough to enable a prisoner to pick up a bottle of vodka that had been hidden in a prearranged spot by the track.

Oddly enough, the easiest 'luxury' commodity of all to smuggle into the camp was sex. Any free woman worker (and there were a few in the mines) could, if she felt so disposed, easily manage to bring in enough to satisfy several fellows. Most of those coal-grimed courtesans were kind hearted beneath the tough exterior, for nearly all of them had been prisoners themselves at one time.

One night shift I was making my way along an unfrequented mine shaft when I heard the muted but unmistakable commotion of a group of excited men and a shrill female voice rising above it all, which left me in no doubt as to what was happening.

'Fuck away as much as you like, lads, but by the Mother of God will you keep my naked arse off this cold wet stone!'

Obviously, the woman dynamiter for our shift had been grabbed by three or four of the prisoners with the idea of making her perform one of her natural functions, and, equally obviously, she was not raising any unreasonable objections. I retraced my steps the way I had come.

I felt no desire to get in on the act. Not only were the wrappings awfully tatty but the commodity itself had also experienced a long and active career and should have been rewarded with a more dignified retirement.

But the prisoners from a nearby women's camp – now they were something else altogether. We seldom saw them but when we did it was an occasion.

'There's plenty of fanny about but the trouble is the girls have it all!' Vasily Oblinken observed with a wry grin one morning as we were working side by side felling trees, my new status as a Blatnoy having manoeuvred me into the most prized of jobs. I stopped swinging my axe to follow his gaze as the rest of the gang started hopping from one foot to the other, excitedly chanting *'Baba, baba!'* ('Crumpet, crumpet!'). At first I failed to recognise the muffled-up figures trudging slowly between guards as women until the low-tension hysteria got to me and I stared along with the rest and saw that the waddling bundles had shawls covering their heads instead of *shapkas* (hats) such as we wore. Women prisoners from the nearby camp had arrived to load the pit-props we had cut and every male that was near stopped to watch their mummified movements. Even our guards showed interest; what a great leveller is the need for the opposite sex!

The wagon that the women were loading stood in a part of the railway siding out of bounds to us, but Vasily Oblinken suddenly noticed that the siding sloped slightly down to us. He held a shouted conversation with our guards and on some pretext got them to extend our 'no entry' area to include the end of the siding, where buffers stood to stop shunted trucks. Signals, not always of the polite variety, were already being exchanged between my party and the women, who had caught on with alacrity. More than one willing little boot helped to kick the blocks from under the wheels to set the wagon rolling towards us. Several of the clothes bundles showed surprising agility in springing up into the moving wagon, sometimes in their eagerness tearing down those already climbing up.

The wagon arrived with a clash against the buffers, the girls clinging and squirming in the open doorway. Several had already taken off their outermost garments, displaying glossy hair and pretty faces burning with excitement. Blatnoy and those sheltering in their favour were first. The lesser mortals crowded into the doorway, now empty of girls. The dimly lit interior was filled with a hubbub of sounds, rustling straw, voices hoarse and shaking, giggles, grunts and tearing cloth. I found myself in a moving maze of arms and legs, a bonanza of bottoms, breasts and smooth thighs with nothing between them but tufts of short curly hair, hot searching mouths and clinging arms. Such a long time with so little, now so little time with such a lot! Ability came and went, came during a lull and went when most needed. If only I knew one of them by name, if only a pair of arms would hug me just for the feeling of closeness for a little while first, all would be well. I buried my face in a pair of breasts. Anneliese's arms closed about me and for a short while I floated above the smell of sweaty female bodies, earth, pinewood and damp straw.

A large, strong hand closed carefully on my shoulder and I heard a man's voice saying urgently: 'Hurry, Comrade Sledgehammer, the guards have tumbled and the warders should be here any minute now!'

Pandemonium of struggling back into clothes was all about me and the venomous cursing of authority, now grinning in the doorway. Resistance was out of the question, so we all clambered out and with peasant resignation the women pushed the wagon back to its official position.

Our working party was placed under arrest, marched back to camp and jubilantly plonked into the cells for three weeks, with no mattress, no blanket and eight ounces of bread a day, the misery of which our very memories made fun of. What a wonderful thing is this body of mine – a glimpse of paradise, a generous portion of hell and still it's ready for more!

Desperate or depressed as I may sometimes have felt, never was I bored. I would have appreciated books to read but they were much more difficult to obtain than vodka or women. In general, the demand for books among the prisoners was not great and the reading matter required by those who did have a need to read would probably have been difficult to get even outside the camp, since the need was more for serious reference works than story books. It was no good asking the free workers: imagine asking a man who could hardly write his own name for a book on philosophy or art or economics. Requests for vodka or tobacco he could understand, but all that book crap only made him suspicious because it was completely outside his world. Even if books were sent in parcels, the political officer would be certain to confiscate any literature beyond his limited understanding. About the nearest I came to a book was a sort of notebook I put together from odd scraps of paper I found or stole. In this I would write Russian words and phrases, adding to it and poring over it in the evening idleness.

In the winter-cramped barracks, talents buried deep in the least promising were forced to the fore, pictures sketched with self-made charcoal, tales told and poems sung by souls that were free inside the cages and bars, things modelled and carved with pitiful materials and vision that still saw beauty everywhere.

I don't know where the ability comes from or when it started but I seem always to have been able, with a sharp knife, to chip from any available piece of wood figures and shapes that please me and are often admired by others. The main prerequisite is time, and as a Blatnoy I now had that. The knife was a piece of hacksaw blade I had picked up in the mine one day and hidden in the sole of my boot to avoid its discovery on the gate search when returning to camp. The German blacksmith honed it to an edge that I could and did shave with, and a scrap of rag wrapped around one end served as a handle. After I found the bit of blade, I chipped away contentedly for several weeks at a collection of small figures that multiplied into an elaborate chess set, and each night I would hide them in the *sushilka* (drying room) with the connivance of the *sushilnik*, who was a minor Blatnoy.

The time came when, polished with wax stolen from the mine, the set gleamed in battle array on the board I had also made: tiny pawns, knights on rearing horses guarding solemn bishops and regal kings and queens, as proud as I was of the admiration they excited, particularly among the Russians, who are passionate chess players. Warders cast covetous eyes on the little wooden army they had no power to destroy, for even in Siberia a prisoner has some rights, and one of them was an entitlement to the pitifully few personal possessions he might have. I cannot play chess and personally I think all such games a waste of time, but I lent the set to friends and looked on as they played until I became accustomed to the sight of the little creatures I had created and they faded into a commonplace, making them primarily a bargaining counter, for I intended to barter them with the free workers for butter and vodka. Trading with the free workers was forbidden but it was done every day to the benefit of both sides.

Information travels fast in the prison world and word of the beauty of my chess set having reached one of the more prosperous free workers, back came the offer of butter, vodka and tobacco – I didn't smoke either but I could always trade the tobacco again. Throw in a couple of Russian grammar books as well, I said, and it's yours. He must have thought the last addition slightly crazy, but he agreed, and everything was set for the exchange, which was to take place in the mine.

The night before the deal was to be carried out, the warders decided to hold one of their sudden midnight barrack searches. This involved hauling us from our beds at some ungodly hour and while we stood in a shivering cursing crowd at one end, a whole army of screws emptied our mattresses and pillows in heaps on the floor, ransacking our entire quarters, including the *sushilka*. The tornado produced the usual couple of daggers and a wicked-looking club, but they could have been brought in by the screws themselves to justify their action and gain their superiors' approval. At last, calling on several different gods in a variety of languages to witness the mixed-up sexual habits of the prison staff's parents, we rearranged our beds and belongings and crept back thankfully to the warmth of bed and forgetfulness.

Next morning, happily occupied with thoughts of the coming treat, I went to the *sushilka* to get the chess set. The sight of the abject *sushilnik* wretchedly wringing his hands stopped me dead in the doorway. The set had disappeared and he had no idea where to. Incredulity, anger, outrage all trembled through me in successive waves, settling finally into a crushing disappointment. It did not take long for the old lags to convert me to their opinion that, after mother fucking, stealing prisoners' prized possessions was the chief occupation of all Soviet prison officials, and this explanation, which seemed the most plausible, smouldered dully in my jail-besieged mind.

Several weeks later I was in a gang repairing the barrack homes of the warders. Engrossed in the strenuous task of avoiding work, I sauntered round the barrack and wandered over to an uncurtained window, peering in curiously to see how the other half lived. As I gazed into the cramped living quarters of a Soviet jailer, all criticism of the mean furnishing was chased from my mind, for there on the meal table were my little black and white children on their chequered playground. The smouldering resentment in me flared up into a terrible anger, raging in frustrated helpless impotence, the sense of blind injustice that provokes violence. Something exploded in me. I clawed frantically at the frozen ground, gouging out hard lumps of ice and snow and in a frenzy I smashed every fragment of glass from the window. I felt no desire to climb through and reclaim the set, only to lash out in anger and revenge, to give vent to the deep sense of injury that I was powerless to redress. A distant rifle shot echoed the crack of the splintering glass, the guard on the boundary summoning the warders to come and deal with a prisoner who had apparently taken leave of his senses. Wearily I sat down to await their coming. There was no point in defiance or resistance now.

I shivered alone in the cells for a week, trying to keep out the cold on 100 grammes of bread a day and without blanket or mattress to cover the bare concrete floor. There were many to whom a week in the punishment block was tantamount to a death sentence because even if they managed to survive the period their health was so impaired that they didn't last long afterwards. But wretched though I was, I felt a warm glow of satisfaction each time I thought of that thieving warder trying to keep the cold out of his quarters, for it was already several degrees below zero and there would not be another consignment of glass until the spring. Each morning, prisoners would shout encouragement to me as they doubled past the block on their way to assemble for work, giving me a staccato report on the temperature and the latest device being employed to stop the unglazed gap. I was starving and near freezing myself, but as I listened to the crunch of their boots dying away I laughed softly, enjoying my small revenge.

I did my fair share of time in the punishment cells, one way and another, for various misdemeanours, sometimes alone and sometimes with others. Generally I preferred to be on my own because you never knew who or what you might get for company. However, it was in the cells that I came across the only person I met who was mad or desperate enough to try to escape from a Siberian penal settlement by simply walking out into the tundra. He was a member of one of the many strange, Eskimo-like tribes who inhabit northern Russia, their language as alien and uncouth as their way of life.

I had been put in the cells this time not for any offence, but because it was the anniversary of the Soviet revolution, a time when all prisoners thought by the authorities to be a political risk were locked up. Why, I don't know, any more than I know why I was considered a political risk, but I always found myself confined on that date. Apart from the principle of the thing, I had no great objection, however, since I was allowed normal rations and a bunk to sleep on as I was not in for any offence. And it was a pleasant respite from the crowded barracks. I was lying on my bunk enjoying my own company when the cell door opened and a ragged animal-man was thrust in. His little eyes burned briefly in my direction, then he grunted and limped over to the other side of the room and squatted down on the floor. As he passed me, I was aware of a nauseating smell that stuck in the back of my throat. A repulsive smell quite unlike the sweaty smell of crowded human bodies, which I had grown quite accustomed to; it seemed vaguely familiar and yet I could not place it.

Through half-closed eyes I looked covertly at the man. His clothes hung in filthy rags about him – could that explain the smell? – but I was most intrigued by the fact that the hair on his head had grown about an inch long and the emaciated face was streaked with a sparse beard. Obviously, he had had the shaven head and face of a prisoner and, equally obviously, he had managed to evade a razor for some time. (The rule was that if you were over a certain age and came into a convict colony with a beard you were allowed to keep it, otherwise you remained clean shaven for the duration of your stay.) I started a conversation with the usual opening gambit between prisoners: what are you here for? He replied slowly, as though he had to think about his words, addressing a spot on the wall somewhere to the side of my bunk, for the coal lumps of his eyes never once rested directly on me.

It seemed that he had escaped from a similar camp further south and was simply walking until he could find a few of his tribe, but he had injured his foot, which had become so painful that he had been unable to go on and had surrendered himself to the guards at Inta. He fell silent, as though the effort of answering my questions had exhausted him. Sliding my hand under my mattress, I felt for the chunk of bread I had hidden there and passed it to him. Stretching out, he grabbed it from my fingers and wolfed it down, cramming it ravenously into his mouth. Then he eased himself onto the bunk and, after sitting on the edge a moment while he adjusted the disgusting rags bound around his feet, he swung his legs up and stretched out full length. As it didn't look as though he was going to volunteer any more conversation, I might have dozed off myself if a slight movement on the scrubbed floor hadn't caught my attention.

Opening my eyes wide now in disbelief, I stared hard at the floor near his bunk, but, no, there was no mistake. On the floor where he had loosened his foot rags there was a small, greyish-white heap that writhed and crawled: a bunch of fat, soft maggots.

The sight was so unexpected and so repulsive that almost before I knew what I was doing I had slipped from my bunk and was hammering on the cell door, yelling its number at the top of my voice. A disgruntled screw ambled down the passage demanding what all the goddamned noise was about. My Russian vocabulary did not run to maggots and my roundabout way of trying to explain what was troubling me sent the warder into such a fit of laughing that he refused to take me seriously until I recommenced thumping on the door, swearing loudly and fluently and demanding to see the officer in charge. He was eventually fetched and the cell door opened. With a dramatic gesture, I pointed to the heaving heap on the floor. Now it was my turn to laugh at the look of pure astonishment on the guards' faces. There was a brief exchange between them and the maggoty prisoner, who had lain on his bunk totally uninterested throughout, and I was moved to another cell for the rest of the day.

The following morning, when I was released back into the camp, I made a few enquiries among my friends, which led me to the medical orderly who had been detailed to bath and attend to the escapee. The orderly, who had managed to get the full story out of the man, told me that he had escaped from a working party. He had acted on impulse and completely without preparation, living on roots, lichen and tree bark. Quite early on, he had lost the sole of one of his boots so that his foot was badly cut and grazed. Coming upon a dead hare, he had eaten most of it raw and then wrapped the skin around his injured foot to give it some protection. He had continued to wander about until his foot became so painful and his situation so hopeless that he finally gave himself up. The maggots, said the orderly, had certainly saved his foot and perhaps even his life. The cuts on his foot had started festering and blood poisoning would have set in, but the maggots which had already been in the decaying hare skin had lived on the decomposing flesh of his foot, keeping it clean of gangrene.

I realised now what the smell had been and why it was familiar to me. It was a faint reminder of the stench that had oozed up from the ruins of Dresden, and that was a lifetime ago.

Inta was crammed with people from all walks of Soviet life, ex-government leaders, scientists of national fame, pimps and pickpockets. Most would talk willingly about themselves and their past, and here in Russia, where the tradition of story-telling was still one of the most popular ways of whiling away idle moments, a good raconteur always found an eager audience. But there were some who kept their memories to themselves, living in a private, vanished world that no one could touch, mumbling conversations to themselves that only they could interpret.

Alexander Dutkin fell into the last category. Old, shrivelled and bent, few people knew how long he had been a prisoner or why. Old Dutkin was a barrack '*navalney*' (labourer) but, since he was also a Blatnoy, a *navalney* who never carried water or scrubbed floors, lit fires or dried clothes in the *sushilka*. He did, in fact, spend most of his time in the *sushilka* but that was only so that he could doze in its constant warmth, waking to stare distantly into the past or eat the food brought to him by the Blatnoy. All his *navalney* chores were done by the numbskulls that formed the lowest ranks of the brotherhood.

Enjoying my Blatnoy leisure one day, I walked into his *sushilka*, greeting him from politeness although I never expected him to acknowledge it. We were alone in the *sushilka*. Old Dutkin turned his faraway eyes onto me, focusing steadily on me as I sat down to warm myself by the stove. The toothless mouth mumbled itself round silent words and then, haltingly but quite clearly, he said in English: 'In London they called me Peter. Peter the painter. Yes . . . Your policemen are brave, foolish men . . .'

Or so he claimed. I was so astonished I couldn't say a word, not even to prompt him from the silence into which he now lapsed. Then he started to talk again, mixing English and Russian, the unfamiliar words creaking from him like the rusty hinge on an unused door. It was a long time ago, a long time . . .

London, 1911. A handful of members of an international Communist movement, Dutkin among them, had planned and executed a robbery from a jeweller's shop in Houndsditch. The proceeds were to swell party funds. Something had gone wrong; the police had moved in and a constable was shot dead by the gang. They had holed up in a house in Sidney Street, to which the police had laid siege, and army marksmen were called in. The 'Sidney Street Siege' had made newspaper headlines for days, the 'foreign anarchists' obligingly shooting three more policemen. Eventually, realising they could not sit there indefinitely, the gang had set fire to the house to prevent incriminating evidence and documents falling into police hands. Under cover of the resulting confusion, most of the gang managed to escape, and only two bodies were found in the burning house. Dutkin himself made his way back to Russia to rejoin the revolutionary cause he had so enthusiastically championed abroad, only to be rewarded with a lifetime's imprisonment for treason.

When I knew him he must have been nearing the end of that long lifetime, by now probably a forgotten man. And yet he had made some sort of life for himself here in Inta. In all probability he had no family or comrades to go back to on the outside and, anyway, times had changed. Here, being a Blatnoy, all his small needs in the way of material comfort were provided, and it was a way of life which could become quite acceptable.

That life in the colony could become acceptable I knew for myself only too well and the realisation, when it suddenly came over me after a few months as a fully fledged Blatnoy, frightened me rigid. Accepting the situation and finding it acceptable may sound like a fine distinction, but there was a world of difference between the two, as I sometimes had to struggle to remind myself. I had to, and did, accept the position I was in: after all, there was no escape from Inta and to pine for the impossible quickly wears a man out. But to find it acceptable in the sense of palatable, pleasurable even, to be one of the strutting camp top dogs – that would mean that I had turned my back on the hope, which was so powerful in me as to be a belief, that I would not end my days there like old Dutkin. That was something I must never allow myself to lose sight of, as if by believing in it I could influence it to happen.

In a way, I suppose that belief was to me what religion was to others, a sort of cornerstone to one's camp survival. Religious belief still persisted stubbornly in Inta, even though the only freedom of choice was the same as that which had faced people in Nazi Germany: adopt the teaching of the Party and be allowed to live a comparatively normal life, or practise your religion and starve. Despite the official condemnation of religion in the convict camps, a bundle of rags bobbing up and down in front of a crude homemade icon was a common sight; a prisoner kneeling with cap clutched to his chest, with his forehead on the ground appealing to the God of his fathers. Warders nearly always turned a blind eye to these performances; it was clear that most of them were intimidated by such devotional ardour, and I suspect most of them secretly felt the same as the prisoners. Down in their peasant souls Christ stalked with the same whip with which he drove the moneylenders from the temple, and whips were things the Russians understood. Occasionally I would catch a glimpse of a small crucifix through a torn shirt, hanging about its owner's neck like a furtive talisman.

It took a brave man to declare his religion openly at Inta and for that reason, if no other, Father Paul, a Lithuanian Catholic priest, had a place in my heart. Brave by any standards, he did much time in the punishment block for carrying out religious rites and rituals at the request of anybody who felt need of them, and when he was at liberty within the camp the officials seemed to go out of their way to make life as humiliating and difficult for him as possible. He was made to work under the worst conditions, but despite this he would always give away the food from his splendid parcels to those he thought needed it, rather than as bribes to get himself soft jobs. He was, very simply, a good man and, when not wasting his time trying to redeem my misguided soul, as he called it, he was interesting and amusing company. Ironically, it was through one of Father Paul's religious gatherings that I became involved in a Blatnoy murder.

One Christmas time, Father Paul, at his happiest and best, organised a clandestine gathering of his countrymen in the barrack to celebrate the festival with prayers and carols, complete with smuggled-in Christmas tree and simple gifts. I can't pretend the scene produced in me any nostalgia or sentimental longing to be 'back home with the folks'. The last Christmas that I can remember of any significance was one when, as a very small boy, I woke to find in the pillowcase at the foot of my bed a large monkey that climbed up a stick, the result of many hours of loving work by my father, but since then I have found it little more than an irritating interruption in the pattern of daily life. So I was watching Father Paul's little celebration with rather detached interest when the lookout posted at the door to watch for warders appeared at my elbow. He was a Blatnoy, a young thief whom I knew well. The Blatnoy themselves were for the most part religious with a kind of superstitious fervour, seeing nothing incongruous between their professed faith and chosen way of life.

'*Tavarish* Sledgehammer, give me a hand,' he murmured urgently. 'There's a grass hanging about outside and we suspect him of tipping off the screws. I've been asked to deal with him. Will you help me?'

Such a request from one Blatnoy to another was not to be ignored and anyway I had no desire to do so; as far as I'm concerned, informers are the lowest form of life. Pulling on our padded jackets and felt boots, we left the warm room. The cold outside struck us like a solid wall, closing our nostrils and freezing the breath on our upper lips. Four moons linked by bars of northern light glistened crystal in the indigo sky, shedding an uncanny brilliance over a noiseless snowscape with barrack chimneys forcing white columns of steam and smoke straight up to the stars, and I felt momentarily the same shock of awe and wonder that I always experienced at the sight of that strange, unworldly sky, however often I saw it.

But our man was nowhere in sight. It seemed as though we were too late to stop him. Slipping silently from cover of barrack to lavatory, from lavatory to another barrack, we kept up our search, when all at once we noticed from a doorway in which we stood that the guardroom was in view. A yellow streak of light slid over the snow as the door of the guardhouse opened and a man stepped out onto the path. Pulling on his hat and hunching his shoulders against the cold, he headed in our direction.

'That's him – that whore's son has been singing!' whispered my companion. We waited until he drew level with us and then stepped out to meet him. A guilty conscience or some instinct for danger made him spin round and make off back in the direction of the guardhouse, but he only managed to cover a yard or two before I brought him face down in the snow. I intended working him over so severely that he would never forget it. He twisted and struggled so frantically that I all but lost my hold and had to throw my whole weight on him, when suddenly I felt him go limp under me. Turning to see where my companion was, I saw him drag a long knife from the man's side. I stood up slowly. I cast a long shadow across the snow, livid in the weird light, the slack body of the dead man crumpled in blackness at my feet, the whole world frozen in a deep primeval silence that pressed upon my ears.

Then from nowhere came three quick-moving figures closing in on us, who, after the first shock, I recognised as Blatnoy friends. The five of us lifted the large limp rag doll and carried it to the nearest lavatory. We uncovered the pit and slid the body in. It floated face down, the arse of its trousers blown out like a slimy balloon.

Back in the barrack they were still quietly celebrating the season of peace and goodwill to all men, the hushed voices singing the eternal Christmas message. No one seemed to have noticed my absence. Making my way to the stove, I sat down. I seemed to see my father sit down opposite me, placing his game bag and gun by the fire and shaking his head slowly. 'I just don't know what to say t'yer with all them bad 'uns, boy.' Christmas trees, murder and hymns. A tall Estonian pressed a new pair of raw wool socks into my hands with a smile, a precious gift with the smell of the sheep still in them. '*Dobroy nochy!*' he said quietly. '*Dobroy nochy!*' each man wished his neighbour with sincere warmth. The cautious celebrations were drowsily ending; the hot soup tasted pleasantly of garlic. I lay down on my bunk and pushed my feet down under the blankets to sleep alone with 200 others. The ice on the windows was four inches thick.

In the mine next morning the latest killing was already being talked about. Nobody knew who was responsible. Sitting next to me in the engine shed, Father Paul, his face sad and worried, asked if I knew who had killed the snoop. Perhaps he was more of this world than he let us believe. For the sake of his peace of mind it was easy for me to lie; anyway, a dead man in a lavatory was nothing to worry about. Father Paul was troubled by my lack of concern and retreated into trying to save my soul as usual. I heard him talking without hearing his words; watching his earnest face, I thought how ludicrous it was to call a young man of 25 'Father'. But then Father Paul was one of those people who are born old because they are born with the care of others on their shoulders.

Stalin was dead. Old Shagdad Stalin, father of Soviet Russia, was dead, poisoned (so it was rumoured), his doctors under arrest.

The shock waves of uncertainty and rumour rippled even as far as remote Inta. There would be a revolution, it was said, political prisoners would be released/executed; we would all be home in a few weeks/have our sentences shortened/lengthened/reviewed. The camp seethed and bubbled with whispered, suppressed excitement and expectancy, and in due course the wind of change blew over the camp.

Prison life improved once the turbulence died down. For the majority, that is, but not for me. I had thrown in my lot with the wrong bunch. All work dodgers, killers and Blatnoy of every rank were sifted in the camps and placed in a compound together. Ours at Inta was immediately and fittingly labelled 'the Devil's Compound'. To my astonishment, I was one of the first to be locked up in that den of iniquity and there was absolutely nothing I could do about it. To create this prison within a prison, a barrack was strengthened in the corner of the camp nearest the guardroom at the main gate, secured with iron bars on the windows and locks on the doors, and then surrounded with a high barbed-wire fence. On the day of its inauguration I found myself landed in it along with an ancient Blatnoy godfather, a pair of Blatnoy killers, a short man with a long knife and a reputation to match, a Bandero and, surprisingly, Father Paul of all people.

Obviously he was seriously taken as a subversive influence, but he and the Bandero were quickly transferred into a section of the Devil's Compound strongly separated from our half.

For the next four days the rest of the cut-throats and I lay on our bunks watching our half gradually fill up with the putrid cream of the camp. In they came: the killers, the light-fingered artists, the vicious, the notorious and the work-shy, and among them a fair sprinkling of potential gods and religious prophets bent on putting a new world into orbit. At the end of two weeks the compound housed the finest collection of dangerous misfits the devil ever amused himself putting together – the result, apparently, of new rules attempting to give the penal settlement a touch of respectability. It seemed that the authorities taking over after Stalin's death reasoned that if they were to establish themselves, they must herd the most troublesome inmates into a bunch where they could be kept under strict control.

I was never sure why I was sifted out in this political shit-shovelling exercise, unless the fact that I was English gave me a notoriety I would not otherwise have merited. It could not simply have been because I was a Blatnoy, although I seemed to hear inside my head the hollow echo of the German saying: '*Mit gefangen, mit gehangen*' ('Caught with them, hang with them'). My world was growing smaller. The Arctic sun was smothered by an icy grey mist that reached down inside me, chilling the wail of a lonely Norfolk spirit: 'All this ain't nuffin' t'do wi' me!' I could have done better for myself than get stuck here in this sanctum of Satan crammed with the criminal good and bad, the majority bad and each one with as touchy a code of honour as King Arthur and all his knights, and less regard for human life than an ancient Samurai. If I had to die at this ass-end of the world, I would rather it were with the Banderos as my companions. They had been the first to befriend me and were much more European in their thinking than the unpredictable Russian Blatnoy, with whom I found it difficult to communicate. But at the time when I had to choose with whom to throw in my lot the Banderos had been in the minority and my single concern was to survive. However, I always remained on good terms with the Banderos and tried to avoid any conflict with them. Fortunately, I was never forced into the position of having to prove my Blatnoy loyalties as I would certainly have refused to fight or harm the Banderos, whatever the consequences. It may be that I do the Blatnoy an injustice; possibly the more intelligent of them understood where my sympathies lay but were prepared to tolerate that for the sake of the prestige of having among them the only Englishman in that raw colony of living corpses hidden away in an Arctic graveyard, although some of them resented me precisely because I was a foreigner.

Fights between prisoners had always been a common occurrence, but here in the Devil's Compound they took on an unparalleled frequency and viciousness, generally starting over some trivial incident that was just an excuse. Typically, a quarrel would begin with insults and abuse – I always did admire the richness and imagery of Russian cursing, so much more colourful than our own.

'Stinking Englishman, you were never born – some whore pissed you against a brothel wall and the sun hatched you out!' This time it was young Sacha, a thief and a henchman to a Leningrad godfather, who was calling me out. Earlier that evening there had been a fight during which somebody had been stabbed in the shoulder – why not, here in the Devil's Compound there was very little else to do and him with the hole in his shoulder was well pleased now he could stay in bed for the next few days. I had been busy trying to read my Russian primer so had seen nothing of that fight, in which Sacha had evidently been involved. I'd always had a feeling he disliked me but up until now he had never openly done anything to offend me. His earlier victory must have gone to his head because here he was, using a fight I had not even seen as a pretext to call me out for cowardice in traditional Blatnoy style.

'Piss off, I don't want to fight with you, Sacha!' His childish antics bored me.

'Don't want to fight – don't want to fight!' he mocked. 'Afraid to fight, you mean! Fuck your whore mother!' He was working himself up in Russian fashion to a near frenzy. The whole barrack hugged itself with suppressed excitement at the prospect of a bit more entertainment. Obviously, I was expected to do something to provide them with a show. I got up from the bunk and closed my book with slow, deliberate care. Still moving slowly, I turned as if to place it on the bunk then spun round, smashing it at his face. Although surprised, he swerved and the book thumped into his shoulder, even as he reached inside his *bushlat* and whipped out a knife. Still a split second in front, I tore a blanket from the next bunk and managed to entangle the lunging arm and knife. With my other hand I grabbed at his free hand, which was searching my face for the eyes. I caught only the little finger and bent that back until it snapped. He howled and was off guard long enough for me to knee him hard in the balls. He went through the gyrations all males do when struck there; if God made man in the likeness of himself then he should have put such tender organs in a safer place. Sacha was some weeks in the hospital block with a scrotum like a football.

I myself landed in hospital on one occasion as the result of a fight and, to my mortification, it wasn't a knife but a weapon as homely as a floor swab that put me there. I was with a gang of Germans who got into an argument with another group of their countrymen suspected of being informers. Feelings ran high and the scuffle became a bitter battle involving about 12 of us. It was typical of Germans that no knives were used, but brooms and swabs wielded by mine-toughened arms can cause a hell of a lot of damage. I found the fight exhilarating and got carried away. Contrary to moral teachings, the informers were winning and we were put to flight. I was covering our retreat using handy lumps of coal as ammunition and did manage to make our opponents take cover long enough for my side to reassemble, but seeing their anticipated victory slipping from their grasp, the opposition suddenly made a massed attack and rushed in flailing swabs and brooms like clubs. I got caught and went down under a hail of blows and by the time my side dashed back to save me I could hardly stand for the pain in my lower back and had to be carried from the scene. I lay immobilised on my bunk for two days. It took these two days to convince the staff that I was seriously injured, and when I was finally admitted to hospital it was found that my lower back was so severely battered that the sciatic nerve was all but severed. I was allowed two weeks in hospital, but for a long time after that I continued to drag one leg slightly. Even to this day I often feel the effects of that swab clubbing that I was too damned slow to avoid.

It seemed as though a trip to the hospital block was the only escape any of us was going to have from the Devil's Compound, but one day the compound suddenly and abruptly ceased to exist. Why, none of us ever knew; all we knew was that the uniformed gods ruling the lives of 13 million caged soup slaves had decided on a change of politics. I never reckoned up how long we were inside the compound. Time simply passed, slithering away with surprising speed in numberless bowls of thin gruel, fits of despair, fights, laughs and the head counts that seemed interminable as we stood in the incredible cold.

Released into the camp outside, I found there had been a subtle change in internal politics as well, as the death of Stalin brought the decline of Blatnoy power. Their loss was the Banderos' gain; maybe they did not have the swaggering impudence of the Blatnoy, but there was no doubt now which was the ruling faction and I was glad I had kept a foot in their camp. Not only because it made it possible for me to perform the delicate balancing trick of sitting on the narrow fence of camp power but, more importantly, because without the Banderos I know I would never have left Inta alive.

Chapter 18

GOING HOME

I held it in my hand, unread, for a long time. A single sheet of blue-lined paper that might have been torn from a child's exercise book. A letter. For me. The first letter I had received for seven years.

About once a month prisoners were allowed to receive letters and food parcels. The excitement of mail day no longer affected me because I knew there would be nothing for me; so far as the outside world was concerned I was dead. At first it had hurt a little when the others received mail and I was passed over each time, so I had simply blocked out the monthly event and for all practical purposes my home was non-existent, hovering only as a happy dream.

Until the day I too received a letter. I turned it over in my hands, just looking at the words uncomprehendingly, in such a state of confusion that I couldn't actually read them at first. I recognised the writing as my mother's, familiar and yet unfamiliar after so long, the words carefully formed in her elementary school script. At last I began to read slowly, line by line, the words dragging me back to a world I had left nearly 16 years ago. 'Dear Reg,' she began. No one had called me 'Reg' for more years than I could remember. Only my family knew me as Reg. I had almost forgotten that was my first name, as now I only used my middle name, Eric.

Dear Reg,

I hope you are well. I am in fairly good health myself. We may
be seeing each other again soon as there has been an effort by
the local Member of Parliament to have you released. Dad died
last September, from tetanus, I do miss him. I shall write again
as soon as I can.

Love,

Mum

xxxxx

I read it and reread it, that most significant letter of my life, those few
lines, from my name at the beginning to the row of kisses at the
bottom, even when every syllable was indelibly printed in my mind,
as if by repetition I could grasp its contents as a reality. The small
world in which I now lived convulsed about me in the seismic
shockwave from home. Mother's handwriting, father dead, old
freedoms, manacles, possible release, cold flashes of hunger and
death. The seconds banged urgently on the ring floor, my reeling
senses caught the shout: 'The time's nearly up – hold on and you'll
win!' But was it? Was it really true?

For days I brooded alone. I didn't know what to think. There was
no way I could find out if I was really to be released, no authority I
could ask for confirmation. I said nothing to anybody but nevertheless
rumours began to worm their way around the camp that I was marked
for possible release. The implications of this becoming public
knowledge quickly made me pull myself together: if I was to be set
free then I wanted to stay alive long enough to make the release date.

I had no illusions about the fact that my mother's letter also marked
the onset of the most hazardous stretch of my Russian prison life.
There were times when the Blatnoy, for all their usual devious
manoeuvring, thought in a completely logical and straightforward
manner. They reasoned that anyone lucky enough to be offered release
before his sentence was finished would be foolish to risk official
displeasure by refusing to talk when asked a few simple questions, so
to save embarrassment all round the fortunate one would have his run
of luck cut short by a knife in the back or an axe through his skull as
he slept. I had heard and seen too many examples of Blatnoy logical

thinking in such cases not to fear for every moment of my life from then on.

Confined together with an unknown number of people intent on killing you plays hell with your nerves. No matter how watchful you are, you have to sleep some time. After three nights trying to snatch some sleep with one eye open and ears pricked like a hunted hare, I became jumpy. Waiting in the bath queue – who were they, edging around me? Those three in the dark of the barrack doorway – were they lurking there for me? How many were following me to the lavatory, to the dining hall? To go to the mine was simply suicidal with all those hammers, picks and axes at hand. At this rate, even if my luck held out until I was released, my sanity certainly would not. I had to have help, someone to 'watch my back', as John and I would have put it years ago, only here I had no friends. There was only one possibility, and I had to try it.

I rarely saw Pytor Usilof, the chief Bandero, around the camp, although on the few occasions we did meet we always exchanged a friendly nod or a brief word. After three nights of trying to do without sleep, I stopped a passing Ukrainian and asked him where I could find Usilof. The man said he did not know. All the same, as I sat in the dining hall the following day, eating my bowl of soup, I felt a gentle tap on my shoulder distinct from the usual shoving and jostling that went on in that crowded Babel of a place. I looked up with a start into the steady blue eyes of Inta's chief Bandero. He was grinning from ear to ear and there was a new air of confidence about him.

'Get out of it, you bastard!' he snarled at the Russian sitting next to me. The man moved without a second's hesitation and Usilof lowered his 15-stone bulk into the vacant seat. He came to the point immediately.

'You, my friend, are fairly well in the shit!' he remarked succinctly. I nodded agreement. He obviously knew the position and there was no need for me to say anything. Usilof leaned on his elbow, reflectively picking his teeth as he gazed at me. Then he waved his hand dismissively as though there was nothing to worry about.

'Don't you lose any sweat over those shithouse maggots, the Blatnoy!'

'It's not sweat I'm worried about losing, but I do want to keep every drop of my blood where it belongs,' I commented. Usilof's grin widened.

'And by the Mother of God so you shall!' he laughed, clapping me on the shoulder and rising to his feet. We started to leave the dining hall together, that dinner-plate-sized hand of his still covering my shoulder. He stopped at the door and boomed loudly for the benefit of the entire room: '*Tavarish Anglichanin*, you are as safe from now on as a pork sausage in a synagogue!'

Pyotr Usilof was as good as his word. I never moved but there were three or four blond giants hovering by me like protective, terrible guardian angels. Eating, sleeping, working, sitting in the lavatory, playing dice – whatever I did there they were beside me, their watchful eyes everywhere. I began to feel safe, to sleep more easily under their protection. But now, freed from the immediate anxiety of staying alive, other doubts and fears wormed their way into my brain.

Was all this real, or was I losing my grip and starting to live in a private mirage? For the umpteenth time I would pull out my mother's letter from my *bushlat* and mouth over the words I knew by heart, soothing the creased and by now greying paper. The letter itself could be part of the dream. All shadow men have such dreams; their conversation is full of them. Maybe, without knowing it, I was one of them, unable to distinguish fantasy from reality. A sinking sensation flooded over me. Those watchful Ukrainian mates were taking care of me out of pity. Where is the breaking point? How do you notice it after years with only a past that lives, the future a plaything for the mind in a present packed with nightmares of capture, killing, hunger – and always prison.

Early one morning I was called to the camp office. I stood tight-lipped and upright before the official at his desk, totally unaware of why I had been summoned. The official glanced up at me briefly, curiously.

'Nationality?'

'English.'

'What is your sentence and what for?'

'Twenty-five years for subversive activities against the Soviet Union and five for homicide,' I intoned like an automaton, wondering why he was bothering with the questions when he must have all the information already. It sounded uncomfortably like the prelude to past interrogations. But he merely shuffled a few papers together and put a clip on them.

'Ten-thirty at the main gate. Prepare yourself for a journey from the camp. Dismiss!'

I gaped at him. Had I heard right? I was still standing there gawping when my escort hustled me out of the room. Outside I turned to the guard. Slowly, as though explaining to a child, he repeated what the official had said. Prepare yourself to leave the camp at 10.30 this morning.

Prepare for a journey *from* the camp, I mused as I made my way back to the barrack. No word of where to. It is traditional that a Russian prisoner never knows where *to* – and less than half of them are ever seen again. In a preoccupied daze I gathered together the few pathetic possessions I had. My self-made notebook and a charcoal sketch of me drawn by one of the prisoners I tucked into my *bushlat*, securing it with a belt I had made myself. Then I tied my wooden spoon into my square of cloth, knotting the corners and hanging it like a pouch on my belt in traditional Russian travelling fashion and I was ready. My Ukrainian guardian angels, of course, knew instantly that something was up.

'I'm leaving – this morning!' I said to them in disbelief. They laughed and clapped me on the back, glad for my sake.

Now it was 10.30 and a small crowd of Ukrainians stood around me near the gate where I had been waiting for a while. They all shook me by the hand, rejoicing in my good fortune – if that's what it actually was – kissing me on both cheeks in true Slavonic fashion and wrapping me in their bear-like embrace.

The tall barbed-wire-entangled gates swung open. The head warder handed my papers, and then me, over to the escort officer. Our little cavalcade of four armed soldiers with me between stepped out into the trampled earth road leading across the tundra.

I never turned to look back at Inta, not even to raise my hand to the Ukrainians in farewell. They were undoubtedly fine men to whom I owed a great deal, but all the same I felt not the slightest twinge of regret or sentiment at leaving them. Every other emotion was swamped by a sweeping tide of hilarious joy at walking away from

Inta, at the hope of never meeting its inmates again. I walked out of Inta and into the sunshine looking straight ahead of me, stepping out eagerly between my escort.

The day was warm, filled with dazzling light. As the sounds of the camp fell away, I began to wonder where I was going. I stole a sideways glance at my escort. A watery uneasiness squirmed slightly at the pit of my stomach, caused not by the heavy revolver strapped to the officer's side or the soldiers' rifles, but by the trenching tools in their belts. A trenching tool is part of a soldier's kit, indispensable for digging a shelter or latrine – or a grave. But was a grave needed in miles of trackless tundra? No, of course not. The sun was glorious, the sky so blue, the snow nearly gone.

Tramp, tramp, tramp. The soldiers talked, fragments of conversation reaching me in snatches. Now and again their equipment clattered. The Polish victims of Katyn woods must have heard sounds like this as the Russians prepared them to die, victims even in death of a horrible, criminally historic lie. I observed with relief that we were still keeping to a worn track. Shot while attempting to escape . . . how often had I heard that phrase said about others? But no, the sun was shining cheerfully – nobody died on days like this. The warmth of early summer crept through my *bushlat*, my bundle of dried fish and bread swung on my belt, my ration for the coming journey.

The sun told me we had been on the way for about an hour when I caught the whiff of hot metal and oil. The smell grew stronger as we proceeded until I heard the hissing and saw a small, old-fashioned engine panting on a temporary-looking track that dwindled away into a background of leaning telegraph poles and wooden shacks. Two covered-in wooden trucks were coupled to the engine. Sitting in and around them on bundles and boxes were men and women with children playing about them in a way I had forgotten kids do. What a glorious thing it is to be alive!

My arrival under armed escort attracted no attention and in less time than it takes to turn round the guards were part of the gathering, chatting up the girls. I sat down on the track, alone and unwatched for the first time in nearly a decade. I was not hungry; it was pleasantly warm, and around me people talked and bustled in a forgotten lifestyle. I saw the driver, portly and businesslike, climb into the engine cabin, followed by the fireman. A shriek from the whistle started everybody else moving and clambering into the wooden wagons. I remained seated on the track. It never entered my head to move without being told. The guards, suddenly remembering they were in charge of a prisoner, looked around and beckoned me to climb on the wagon too. When I got in, all the bottom benches were taken so I clambered to a top bench and stretched myself out while two of the guards happily squeezed themselves down between a pair of laughing girls. From my perch above it was like watching a large family outing of which I was not part.

The little old train jerked itself into a shuddering start, everybody whooped in mock alarm and we were on our way, with me the only one not knowing where we were going. But somehow I felt happy. Listening to the puffing of the little engine, I remembered the threatening sound of his big cousin pulling me away to the north in a cage a few years previously. I was returning from where it was said only a few ever return.

It took about two hours for our cow town train to chuff its way into a main line siding, where a larger and more modern locomotive with carriages was already waiting. Before we had finished clattering to a halt, the passengers had swarmed down with their jumble of baggage and scrambled in good-natured confusion over to the waiting train. Two of the guards stood with me while the officer and one of the men went ahead to secure places for us. However, when we got there I still found that the bottom bunks were already occupied with people spreading coats and blankets to make a comfortable place for themselves. Having nothing except the clothes I stood in, I simply climbed once more to a place overhead but now, instead of dozing off, I found myself very much awake to what was going on around me.

We seemed to be in a small but busy market town. The platform side was lined with shabbily dressed men and women with baskets of vegetables and farm produce for sale. I learned later that this was a concession from the collective farming system, which allowed the workers to cultivate a small patch of land for their own use and sell legally anything over quota from it. We didn't stop there long. A powerful puff from the locomotive and it pulled smoothly away. My feelings rose high. In this land of the unusual anything could happen, but so far so good. I was still alive and one step further away from

Inta. I unslung my ration of fish and bread and slowly ate some. I grew drowsy with the rocking of the train and after a while I rolled up my *bushlat* for a pillow and slept.

The jerk of the train grinding to a halt awoke me. How long we had been travelling I had no idea. I gradually became aware that there was a great bustle of coming and going, people climbing in and out of the compartment, fetching hot water to brew tea and prepare a meal. Busy with their own preparations, my guards left the compartment. No sooner were they out of sight than I became the centre of interest for the entire company. They crowded around me full of excitement and curiosity, their apparent indifference banished as if by a magic wand, plying me with a torrent of questions. Was I a real Englishman? How long had I been a prisoner in Inta? Was my sentence finished? One young man asked if Russia was at war with England and already in occupation. When I answered that I did not think so, he said he doubted that I was an Englishman. A sturdily built woman snapped something at him, which I failed to understand but which seemed to offend him. Then she walked quickly away, suddenly reappearing with a generous chunk of cake, which she thrust into my hands. Beneath the Russian sheepskin she could have been Frau Schmidt from a Bavarian inn or Mrs Smith from a Norfolk dairy farm.

Their lively interest vanished with the return of the escort officer and every man-jack of them suddenly appeared completely engrossed in his own business. The train guard waved his green flag and shrilled his whistle and for a moment it seemed to me like the half-forgotten echo of a train pulling out of an English country station. The train gathered speed as it hurtled along a sturdy, well-kept track, quite unlike the tenuous lines we had started our journey on earlier that morning. Below me the people talked, some slept, but nobody read – there wasn't a book or newspaper in sight. Once more I was totally ignored; for all the interest they showed in me, the solitary figure perched over their heads might not have been there.

The compartment grew warm, the smell of sheepskin leather and food rose up to me, so different from the prison odour of stale bodies and stale urine. There were probably fewer bugs around here too. As the train rattled on, my spirits rose higher. I had no idea how near I would get to home – assuming that was where I was going, and assuming that I still had a home to go to. Sixteen years had just hurled themselves by and the only possessions I could be sure of were a whole skin and a head full of curious know-how, and those I had only managed to hang on to with some skill and an amazing amount of luck. Several days in the past I thought had been my last. The train rumbled on. I dozed. My body swayed to avoid the knife jab. I heard the lean-faced man curse the Mother of God as he missed. I brought the pick handle round onto the side of his head with a crack and the blood ran down his face as he slid to the snow, clawing my legs. Somebody gripped my knee. *Anglichanin, Anglichanin!* I started gratefully from my dream. An escort soldier with a huge grin across his face handed me half a loaf and some more dried fish. I must have been shouting in my sleep but not the twitch of an eyelid came from any of the passengers.

A whole day's journey ended at another station, which might have been the one we started from; there was the same traffic of ox-drawn carts, bundle-carrying farmers in sheepskins, and weather-beaten women, some buxom and beautiful, nearly all trailing strings of well-behaved children. There was also the same sort of flea market offering vegetables and eggs for sale, the inevitable one-legged or empty-sleeved beggars with nothing to offer but the palms of their hands, mostly men of my age with medal ribbons on threadbare military jackets – leftovers of the ragged, bug-bitten boy heroes who had stormed Berlin.

An old woman, leathern and creased with time and laughter, was doing a brisk trade serving milk from two large churns, asking each customer: with or without frog? Depending on the answer, she would dip into one or other of the two churns. This puzzled me and I thought I must have misunderstood, but I later found out that it was a common practice of the country folk to keep a live frog in their large milk containers, although whether this was to improve its flavour or nutritional value I don't know.

Passengers were constantly leaving the train and new ones joining it, throwing their luggage onto a vacant seat and quickly preparing a place to sit, usually with the cheery help of those already on board. I had been allowed to alight for a while, but now my escort climbed into the train and beckoned me to return. More people must have disembarked than had boarded because there was now a place for me below, which I took because I could see more. Some of the people spoke to me, but nobody pressed me into conversation. As the train pulled away, we left the shanty town behind and gradually I saw stone-paved streets with a sprinkling of motorcars flit past the window, solid stone buildings and overhead electric cables. The escort officer suddenly took an interest in me and began a commentary on landmarks flashing past the window. With a polite but patronising air, he congratulated me on my knowledge of Russian. He was so friendly that I found it difficult to remember that he was the same man who would cheerfully have shot me if I had taken one step out of marching order at Inta.

Judging by the urban appearance of the streets and buildings, we were clearly approaching a major city, and the escort officer confirmed that these were the suburbs of Moscow. The onion-shaped domes and spires of several orthodox churches caught my eye. Out of curiosity I drew the officer's attention to the next one as it came into view. He took the bait, sliding smoothly into a worn monologue of how the people were free to use the churches for worship if they wished but so few felt the need for this and thus many of these beautiful buildings were being preserved by the state at great expense. The engine whistle shrieked and we roared deafeningly over a tangle of points. Above the din I seemed to hear Father Paul's voice comforting a tiny secret congregation of ragged prisoners somewhere in the north, his words so loud, so clear, that surely all the passengers must have heard, but there was no answering flicker on any of their faces.

Gradually the train began to slow down, finally hissing and lurching its way into a huge bustling station. The large, quaint Slavonic letters slid into a word: Moscow. We had arrived at Russia's capital city. Everyone hustled to their feet, strapping and tying bundles and bags, the soldiers buckling on their equipment. Everybody except me. I had no luggage and no labels to say where I was going or where I had been. The children peered expectantly out of the window. At last the train stopped with a gentle jolt, compartment doors crashed open and the passengers poured out to join those already pushing and jostling their preoccupied way along the platform.

Disgorged from the safe belly of the train into this bedlam, my bewildered brain reeled under the pounding waves of the crowding impressions. So many people, and all in delicate footwear and flimsy clothes, washed and neat and unsmelly! I couldn't help noticing that nearly all the men wore the badge of modern man – a collar and tie. It must have been years since I'd seen them, let alone worn them. We must have presented an odd contrast, but not a soul looked twice at our heavy Arctic clothes as we made our way to the barrier. A tannoy blared out, informing the unheeding people that they were entering the capital city of their beloved homeland, but no propaganda posters adorned the walls or the towering red marble pillars embossed with gold-lacquered fish. At the barrier, good-looking girls in immaculate uniforms collected tickets with the polite dexterity of the well trained. The police, wearing what appeared to me musical revue uniforms of navy and white, looked the peak of proficiency, and so did the heavy shooters strapped to their sides. Beyond the barrier I could see the glint of a line of shining grey taxis. I gaped and stared about me like a duck catching flies.

What was it that struck me so strangely about this splendour, what made me suspicious of the obvious efficiency and cleanliness even while they won my grudging admiration? Days later, when I had had time to think and absorb some of what I had seen, the answer came to me. I was not, as is generally the case, a man of Europe entering modern Russia from the place of my birth. No: I was a man of European culture *returning from* Russia's huge, primitive bowels. I had seen its ancient soul and had journeyed here by the time-worn Russian path of the whip, the penal colony and the ability to endure and survive. Of the modern Soviet Union I was totally ignorant; on that day I was seeing it for the first time, even though I had spent what seemed like a lifetime in Russia.

One of the escorts gave me a nudge. I stopped catching flies so we could make our way to the taxis sounding like metallic peas in the pod of their clearly marked rank. A pass was shown the driver by the officer and the five of us climbed in. Off we swept, a look of rapture on the boy soldiers' faces, and I'd have been willing to bet it was their first taxi ride. For the second time in my life I travelled through Moscow without a chance to see it, for the journey was short, less than five minutes at a guess. We stopped outside a building with the word 'Polictreya' in black letters. So I was back with the old firm again. There was a brief exchange and signing of papers between the officer and a smart police official sitting behind an imposing desk, and then the escort walked out of my life, leaving me standing in a police nick somewhere in Moscow.

The usual familiar routine followed. The pig at the desk pushes a button, a subordinate pig promptly enters. A low, short exchange of words between them, the subordinate pig reaches up the wall for a bunch of keys, beckons me out of the door in front of him and down a stone passageway lined with narrow iron doors with spy-holes and numbers. He opens one of them, I go in and the door echoes shut behind me, sealing me in.

I suddenly felt miserable, the euphoria of my journey evaporating like mist on a summer morning. Life was from one sealed tomb to another. Looking wretchedly about me, I saw a bunk with a mattress, a table fixed to the wall with a jug standing on it and, amazingly, a flush toilet in one corner. I'd never been in a cell with a flush toilet before, but the window, as usual, was barred and too high to see out of. Everywhere was as clean as an operating theatre, or a well-run abattoir. That was it! A bloody, well-polished slaughterhouse! I knew the Soviet penchant for show trials and executions. A headstrong, small-time loner I may have been, but Englishmen with little or no regard for the established rules of conduct are not easy to find in Soviet prisons. What would they devise to make use of this opportunity? I slumped down on the bunk, a tiny spark of panic jumping in my stomach. I tried dousing it by wondering what else a bunch of pen-pushing officials could do with a fellow whose record was as distinguished as mine, and by the time the bowl of soup was pushed through the hatch my appetite wasn't very keen. Nevertheless I ate it and felt better; my belly filled, two blankets with mattress and not a bedbug in sight. Luxury piled on luxury. I took my boots off, lay down and slept.

'Vstat!' ('Get up!') someone bawled through my dreams. A uniform hat with a red star on it was pushing a hunk of bread through the hatch at me. It was morning. I obediently sat up and chewed the bread, reflecting on the wonder of not having to slop out. The screw had entered the cell and stood there going through a silent performance of tucking things under his arm like a mime artist until I said in Russian: 'It would be easier if you could manage to tell me what you want me to do.'

He scowled and snapped: 'Get your things ready, you're leaving!'

Getting ready took very little time. I pulled on my boots and took my *bushlat* off the bunk, thrusting what remained of the bread in the pocket. I nodded my readiness to the screw, who conducted me back past the row of little iron Judas-eyed doors to the reception room of yesterday. A different pig in uniform now sat at the desk. By the window stood a pair of civilians. They smelt of tobacco and secret police. One had a thick red neck that made his head and the hat perched on top of it look too small. The other was slightly built with quick-moving eyes. Laurel and Hardy came instantly to mind. Apparently this was my new escort. With their long raincoats and carefully shined shoes they looked embarrassingly like plain-clothes policemen from an amateur play. Laurel nodded to the official at the desk. Hardy scrutinised me like a stoat would a rabbit, then took his hands out of his raincoat pockets and opened the door, motioning me through. No handcuffs in sight. I felt a little less uneasy. With me between them, we made our way to a waiting car. A driver sat impassively at the wheel, obviously accustomed to jobs like this. What sort of jobs would those be, a nervous little voice piped inside me – without God or influence in the right places, I still had only my luck to rely on.

With none too careful handling, the motorcar started and the gears crunched in. We travelled through a different quarter of Moscow, the driver clearly uninhibited by fear of a speeding ticket. We swept through tarmac streets with brick houses and paved sidewalks, but these quickly gave way to uneven roads bordered with humbler buildings, whose crumbling sides exposed their lath and plaster ribs. The slight elation I had felt at the start of the journey rapidly began to diminish.

A few minutes more of rapid driving, a sharp unexpected turn into a shrub-lined driveway and we halted abruptly before large double doors that could be the entrance to a mental hospital or a prison. I got out of the car and was too busy trying to raise my fallen spirits from the arse of my trousers to notice a small side door open until I was through it, standing in what seemed to be a porter's lodge or guardroom, from which we were immediately led across the courtyard. Entering the main building, we pushed our way through half-glass doors until we arrived in what I took to be a reception room with polished wooden bench seats against the walls. I was told to sit down. No clanging of iron doors or grill – yet.

In came a uniform wearing a thin pale face. He took the cardboard folder handed to him by Laurel, who then strolled out of the room with Hardy. The uniform lifted its face from the opened folder and said, looking intently at me: 'Eric Georgeovitch Pleasants,' as if he was telling me, not asking me, my name. I nodded. He continued in the same informative tone.

'You speak Russian.'

'*Nemnozhko*,' I said ('a little').

'Come with me,' he ordered, snapping the folder shut. He shooed me in front of him through the door and down a long passage bright and clean without an iron door or Judas-eye in sight, the floor covered with waxed-polished, dark-green linoleum. Somehow my heart refused to rise from the seat of my pants. I believe a faint whiff of stale urine or the brief rattle of keys would have made me feel better. All this antiseptic brightness smacked too much of hospitals, and I wasn't ill. I began to feel trapped. Peering at me from my boyhood I saw the moist black eyes of the red squirrel in the tumble trap fill with fear, but defiantly it glared up through the wire mesh at me. It froze as I bent over the trap and pulled out the small wooden stake that fastened the door. The sleek red body was through in a flash and disappeared into the undergrowth. I heard the keeper coming down the ride and I too dived into the undergrowth, waiting, still and silent, until he had gone.

'Wait,' said the pale face, unlocking a door with a key hauled from his trouser pocket by a chain, and then I was in a spacious white-glazed-tiled shower room with real soap and fluffy towels and endless hot water. I stripped and showered, the warder sitting there totally uninterested and making no attempt to hurry me. When a tap came on the door, he rose and unlocked it to a pink-faced youth who advanced into the shower room with a bundle of fresh underclothes. As he placed them on one of the seats, his eyes travelled over my naked body and came to rest on my penis, and I sensed the vibration of a frustrated male. Healthy and well fed, he was probably one of the junior staff or a prison trusty. I've come across types like him in all the places of male confinement it has been my sorry lot to spend time in, poor half-and-half sods who screw themselves into jobs in bathrooms and laundries in an attempt to brighten their prison existence. Let him look: there was small doubt he had little else to live for.

The change of clothing contained a pyjama suit and dressing gown and a large pair of carpet slippers. So it *was* a kind of hospital then! Sure enough, after leaving the bathroom I was taken to a doctor, who examined me minutely, tapping, peering, probing and generally carrying out the most extensive medical examination of my entire prison career. Eventually, with a feeling near to relief, I was dismissed and brought to a familiar narrow iron door by another uniform with a Mongol face. This time it was a roomy, dark-green-painted cell with a radiator, two single bunks (with mattresses and blankets) and, incredibly, coloured sheets. So many unusual things were happening so fast that I must have been much more tired than I felt. I fell asleep on one of the bunks without bothering to creep between the sheets.

I was awake before the key finished turning in the lock and watched the lanky figure enter the cell. Thin white legs ending in large slippers stuck out from the bottom of too-short pyjama trousers. The dressing gown was too large to serve for a jacket and too small to be recognised at once as a dressing gown. Clamped firmly under one arm was a cushion. He was tall, over six feet, with a small round face and close-set blue eyes. I neither liked nor disliked what I saw. I must have looked just as odd to him. Prisoner-meeting-prisoner conversation was soon struck up in Russian.

Lanky: 'How is it here?'

Me: 'Not bad.'

Lanky: 'What nationality are you?'

Me: 'English.'

Lanky: 'Don't lie!'

Me: 'Don't call me a liar, you long twat!'

Lanky: 'Well, I'm also English, so if you are, why don't you speak English?'

I burst out laughing. 'Then I could say the same as you!' I said, changing to English.

Lanky grinned and stuck our his hand in true British fashion. 'Pleased to meet you. My name is William Piddington.'

I shook his hand and introduced myself. The conversation continued, rather slowly, in English, as though both of us had to feel for our words. The first question, of course, was how long each of us had been a prisoner. Piddington, a former Guardsman, had been with the Russians for four years to my total of seven, apparently for smuggling goods into the eastern sector. He went on to talk of the only thing that men who have been cut off from the world for years can talk about and consequently subject matter soon ran dry. But about the second or third day he started weaving colour into the conversation fabric, which passed the time pleasantly enough; usually I listened while he talked.

Neither of us could complain of our present circumstances compared with what we had known in the past. The food was good and there was enough of it to satisfy us, the cell was comfortable and we were given one whole hour's exercise a day. There was only the fact of confinement to oppress us, but it wasn't long before both of us had frayed nerves. His were the first to show. He padded up and down the cell with his long legs while I, as usual, took refuge in sleep or daydreams. The train journey of the last few days merged into train journeys past as I drowsed . . . sleepy trains, rocking me back home with the prize-money from the tournament, and however late it was the door to my parents' room would always be ajar as I stumbled in and I knew my father would be lying awake to ask in a half-whisper, 'Did you win, boy?' and I was as glad for his pride in me as he was for my achievement, and then I would sleep soundly . . . What in hell did that fellow want shaking my shoulder and bawling in my ear like that? Piddington was bending over me, anxiously explaining for my benefit why the Russians were treating us so well.

According to him, we were to be put on trial and eventually shot. I agreed it was possible and patiently pointed out that there was little we could do about it, but to soothe him I added a few reasons why I thought the situation was not as bad as all that. He resumed pacing the cell and I slipped back onto another train, this time an erotic transport, and I was just pulling down the blinds when I was hauled off by

Piddington to hear a complicated theory as to why they would never shoot us. I agreed with him wholeheartedly and after watching him prowling to and fro for a few minutes I dozed off once more, to be awakened by him yet again with his reasons why they were in fact compelled to execute us.

After one or two more repetitions of this, I lost all patience.

'For God's sake, man!' I yelled. 'Why don't you stop flitting from one side of this bleeding cage to the other and light somewhere for a rest? There's nothing you can do about it, even if they are going to shoot us!'

I felt sorry as soon as I had said it. He really was suffering.

'Look, Piddington,' I said rather more kindly. 'We've been with these crazy sods for a long time and neither of us is dead yet. But worrying about it like this isn't going to help anybody.'

He sulked for a little but eventually came round and appeared to forget the incident. But I noticed that he did not try disturbing me again if I was trying to sleep.

We were saved from further quarrelling by being taken eventually before the prison governor. He received us in his comfortably furnished office and, to my surprise, treated us not as prisoners are usually treated, but with respect and courtesy. It was his privilege to bestow upon us the parental pardon of the benevolent Soviet state. In good but halting English, he told us we were now free men. Piddington and I received the information without comment. The two free men rose and were escorted back to their cell.

After the cell door closed, we both sat in silence for some minutes, then Piddington broke it with an excited 'I told you so!' Now the roles changed. Piddington sat with a beatific, contented smile on his face while I paced the cell frowning and fretting, my head filled with somersaulting fragments of thoughts, a jumble of England/Mother without Father, Germany/Anneliese. If I was a free man, if I really was to be released, where should I go? I had left England a lifetime ago: what was there for me to go back to now, even my father was dead? But still, it was where I was born and reared; it should be the place I thought of as 'home'. On the other hand, I had grown to like Germany, the people, their way of life. All the plans Anneliese and I had made came back to me. I knew they could never be realised now, but maybe I could salvage from them the impetus to start again. And Anneliese herself – what of her? She must have made a new life for herself. It would be unfair of me to intrude on that life now, I must leave her out of my considerations in deciding where I should go.

As it happened, I need not have troubled myself about making the right decision. A free man I might have been in theory, but in practice I still had to do exactly as I was told. No one gave me any choice of destination. The British government had negotiated my release and back to Britain I would go.

Somehow the knowledge of my release made no tremendous emotional impact on me. I felt glad, yes, but no more so than when I had won a fight or successfully carried out some dangerous task. It was almost as though I accepted it as something that had to happen at some time. It sounds an odd thing to say, but I don't think that in the depths of my being I had ever really believed I would serve my 25 years, whatever the despair I might have suffered on that score. That medal- and braid-trimmed troika had been as much a pawn as I. I seemed to know, not with my brain or reason but in some inexplicable sense, that the court was merely doing what it had been set up to do. It was one of the indifferent, impersonal tools which had shaped my life but something much greater, more powerful, governed its course, and that course would run true to form, whatever the apparent obstacles, as long as I believed myself strong enough to stay on it.

Next day we were kitted out with clothes befitting free men, complete with suitcases to put them in. My first request was for a trilby hat to cover my prison-shorn head on which the stubble was just beginning to grow. I got my trilby, or something very like it. It must have been the only one of its kind in the whole of the Soviet Union, a wide-brimmed felt hat of the 1930s American gangster type, and they must have gone to a lot of trouble to find it for me. Beneath the hat, my face looked even more gaunt and drawn, but it gave me a glorious sense of satisfaction. Even after seven years I had never been able to come to terms with my convict shaven skull, symbol of brainwashed servitude.

Self-consciously wearing our new outfits, we were taken on a taxi tour of Moscow, chaperoned by the two Soviet bulls who had been present in the governor's office the previous day. They pointed out to us the usual tourist sights: the Kremlin, the impressive magnitude of the Agricultural College, the fine Metro entrance, the flower beds and Soviet symbols flourishing in profusion. The wide, tree-lined streets were spotless, kept clean, they proudly informed us, by automatic road-sweeping machine and trained operative. Piddington and I were duly impressed by the splendour and orderliness. London had nothing half so good to show. Nor had it the bent, shawl-covered old woman I glimpsed briefly, sweeping one of the back streets with a birch-twig broom. Suddenly, I understood that the image of that old Russian woman with her broom was to stay with me for the rest of my life.

We stood in the governor's office dolled up in the strange everyday clothes of Mister Man from any part of Europe. I clutched my hat. Our two bulls of yesterday were talking with the governor. One of them was stuffing a fistful of papers into a briefcase. They shook hands with him and he turned to us.

'Well, lads, let's go!' said one of them. We filed out through the doorway to one of those shining grey taxis standing ready in the drive. It whirled us away to the railway station, where we waited a considerable time soaking up the bustle of the station like a dry sponge – the smell of the coal smoke, the bawling workmen and the hum of a hurrying crowd, with its generous sprinkling of overfed uniforms but total absence of limbless beggars. Piddington must have been as giddy as I was from the glut of impressions, for he hardly spoke a word. My feet felt naked in the light shoes, my buttocks bare in Mister Man's thin trousers, and the shirt collar chafed my neck. But there was comfort in the hat covering my convict's crowning indignity.

Eventually, we boarded a shabby, crammed steam train. The four reserved seats were a pleasant advantage. Piddington and I sat facing the bulls, who pulled down the folding table after placing their hats on the luggage rack overhead. The ordinary actions echoed a life years ago. I was on my way back to that life, but all the joy and excitement of such a moment that I had imagined and dreamed of in prison were not there. It was simply happening as it should. The compartment was crowded and becoming stuffy, the sitting cramped my legs and the jabber of Russian conversation was boring. Piddington chatted to the bulls in his best prison jargon but I kept out of it, my natural inclination being to hold all officials at a distance. I wished I had a newspaper or magazine to disappear into.

By now the train had whistled and clattered us well on the way. I dozed.

'It's a long way to Brest Litovsk,' I heard one of the bulls say as if out of a great distance, and the wheels seemed to take up his words, repeating them rhythmically in the background of my confused brain. A long way, a long way, a long way, Brest Litovsk, Brest Litovsk, chanted the wheels; to England, to Mother, my mother, a stranger, without Dad; where shall I live, how shall I live?; Anneliese, Anneliese, Anneliese, my little one, brave little one. A cracker. 'She's a real cracker!' said Piddington's voice close to my ear.

I opened my eyes. The bulls were looking alarmed. Piddington had been to the lavatory three times in the last ten minutes. The next time he went the real cracker came back with him and they stood talking together a little way off from us. She swayed like the neck of a swan with the rocking of the train, long ash-blonde hair, talking blue eyes, her figure a long-term male prisoner's nightmare. The chief bull was behaving like a worried man. Hopping up and down like a frantic frog, he tried urgent tic-tac signals without getting the slightest response from Piddington, so after a brief mumbled conference with his colleague he pushed his way over to the amorous pair and spoke to Piddington's pearl. The high-frequency, come-to-bed look she tried in reply merely bounced off the official shell, so, with a broken-winged smile to Piddington, she drifted away. Our bull returned triumphantly to his seat, shushing a flustering Piddington in front of him.

For the next half-hour I was compelled to listen to his plans to return to Russia to find this female vision. For the first time in my life I felt something in common with policemen. Piddington irritated me. Where he got his feeling of immunity from I don't know. I certainly did not feel safely out of Soviet power yet and I intended to keep very quiet until I felt that I could do what I wished with impunity, so far as the Russians were concerned. Yet here was Piddington, who only a few days ago had worried himself sick about being shot, risking his neck – and possibly mine – by getting involved in some silly scene.

To stem his flow of mad chatter about the girl, I got talking to the bulls, whom I found to be two full-blooded chauvinists. For them Russia was the only place in the world: once you had been there you were bound to return as if drawn by some irresistible magic. When they asked me for my opinion of their country, I conveniently failed to understand and suddenly appeared to fall asleep – a continuation of the conversation could have become embarrassing.

Brest Litovsk. Suspended in the twilight of half-sleep I was plunged for a moment into the gloom and stink of a cattle truck crammed with desperate and despairing men on their way to a lifetime of imprisonment. It had been a lifetime, and yet the years had slithered away as quickly and silently as an eel in mud.

The train pulled into the present with a jerk. Brest Litovsk. No longer was it just a name vaguely sensed from the depths of a closed truck, but a real live railway station with people going about their ordinary everyday business.

From Brest Litovsk, Berlin was only hours away, which I supposed was the reason for the shining blue and chrome train and luxuriously upholstered compartments to which we now changed. But with the disappearance of the previous Russian tattiness went also the jovial camaraderie of the passengers, who seemed to become more sober and less communicative the nearer they came to Berlin. I felt that they must have been drilled in preparation for their contact with the West.

The train hissed like a comet along the track, the sober bearing of the passengers slowly sloughed to apathy as each one drew into himself. One or two heads began nodding to the rhythm of the speeding train. For me, the once-chattering wheels were now silent, as if they had no time to talk to me in their haste to reach their destination exactly on time. One of our bulls dozed with his head thrown back, snoring softly, while the other struggled valiantly to remain looking alert. Piddington lolled to one side, silent, like a tired puppy. Then I too must have fallen asleep.

Waking as we neared Berlin, I looked eagerly out of the window for landmarks that I might remember, but everything had changed beyond recognition from the heap of rubble and ruin that had been my last sight of the city. At last the train slid with clattering chrome bravado into the capital which, despite some leering reminders of the going-over the Allies had given it, was unrecognisable as Hitler's tumbling, bomb-scorched Berlin.

We were met at the patched-up Anhalter Bahnhof by an official car that took us at top speed to a police station, from where we had an unobstructed view of the Brandenburg Gate, which marked the British/Russian sector frontier. Up to this moment I had no idea what the arrangements were, but just being in Berlin, seeing the famous Gate, reassured me. They wouldn't have gone to all this trouble if they did not actually intend to release me.

With our bulls hovering like heavyweight guardian angels, we were hustled into a room already crowded with fat uniforms and sinister civilians, all of whom appeared to have their attention riveted upon the Brandenburg Gate and its garish display of red flags, hammer and sickle and blown-up portraits of Soviet statesmen.

I turned around to make some comment to Piddington and I suddenly realised he was not there. For a split second I felt a sharp stab of panic and then I saw that they intended to deal with us separately, me first – and in fact that was the last I saw of Piddington until we arrived in London.

Sitting before a telephone in the corner was a Soviet official obviously in communication with somebody on the other side of the frontier as he was speaking in English, stopping to repeat it in Russian for the benefit of our side of the room. I caught only a few disjointed phrases, the last of which was '*Vychodit!*' It was the signal to go. Our two faithful bulls indicated that I was to accompany them as they went out of the door.

The 100-yard walk to the frontier was simply 100 yards. I felt partly as though I had been caught stealing apples and partly as though I was going to receive a prize at a garden party.

The famous Gate was already open on our arrival. From the other side came a couple of nine-to-five clerks, complete with white collars, dark suits and attaché cases. Between them walked a tall, pale-faced man wearing an overcoat despite the warmth. He was greeted by our bulls with a gobble of Russian. I realised for the first time that I was being exchanged. One of the nine-to-fives offered me his hand, took my suitcase from me, then turned and accompanied me back through the gate where a solitary khaki-clad officer stood with his hands behind his back. A small group of Tommies stood at ease well to the rear. Somewhere I think I saw a Union Jack. I was on the British side.

I accompanied my clerk to a block of buildings, where he let himself into a small office. He sat down behind the desk, placing my suitcase on top. From a drawer he brought out a bundle of forms and papers and asked me to take a seat opposite. He scribbled for a while then casually asked me a few questions – what prisons had I been in, could I make myself understood in German and Russian, and so on. With the same uninterested air, he opened my suitcase and rummaged around. Even the self-made notebook in which I had written Russian phrases and grammar to help me learn the language only stirred up the slightest interest. He leafed through it without betraying any sign whether he understood it or not. On the whole I found him a pleasant, well-oiled little cog, one of the many hundreds in this great machine which includes from time to time a few cogs greased by the Russians, like Burgess and Maclean.

Bundling the odds and ends back in the suitcase, he smacked the lid shut and gave it back to me. Then he did a short squirrel-like search amongst the papers on the desk and pounced on a form which he passed over to me.

'Please sign this, Mr Pleasants. It is to confirm your promise to pay back to the Home Office the sum of £10, the cost of your fare home.'

For a moment I stared at him in total disbelief. The bureaucratic mind is truly amazing. Then I shrugged my shoulders and signed; neither the money nor the undertaking could possibly have any reality to anyone who had been divorced from such formalities for as long as I had.

Two young fellows of the same type strolled into the room without knocking on the door. Everything about them was casual, their clothes, the way they spoke and moved, but some instinct inside me warned – police! They chatted like old friends with my clerk, who remained sitting behind the desk on which one of the newcomers perched his backside. Nobody had any interest in me any longer. They might well have been a bunch of office workers during their lunch break – which I suppose they probably were. All at once one of them glanced at his watch and said we could catch the 2.15 train. They all stood up and beamed in my direction. I was official business again. One of them asked if I was ready. I nearly said 'After all these years – I should think so!' but instead I just nodded and the two said goodbye to the clerk and strolled out of the door with me keeping close behind, afraid of losing them.

We took a taxi to the station and got into a reserved carriage in a train on the point of leaving. The blinds were pulled down; apparently the ferrets of Fleet Street had caught a whiff of what was going on and were in Berlin in pursuit, but the three of us sat unharried in the now moving train. We hardly spoke. They weren't interested in me nor I in them. After a while, they went out, presumably to the buffet car, leaving me alone in the compartment. I felt relieved to be rid of them for a while and was enjoying the sensation of being unescorted when the door slid open again. A stranger slithered in and sat down opposite me with the furtiveness of a burglar or a policeman on duty.

'I'm a newspaper reporter – when did you arrive in Berlin?'

I liked his nerve so I told him what he wanted to know and was ready to tell him more when one of the escort arrived back and saw the Fleet Street ferret at work on me. He all but physically hauled the poor fellow out of the compartment into the corridor, where I could hear him threatening the reporter with everything short of painful death if he so much as breathed a word of what I might have told him. Meanwhile, the other half of my token escort arrived back on the scene and added his weight. The newsman held his own admirably against the pair of them, finally making a dignified retreat with: 'All right, you pair of angels! I'll say nothing unless you make trouble for me – because if you do I'll let the world know you left that fellow all on his own! Cheerio!'

I sat quietly in the compartment throughout all this, tickled to death by the sight of them all at each other's throats like prison trusties.

I arrived at Calais with the escort sticking to me like leeches: the incident with the news reporter had obviously shaken them. By some roundabout way I was smuggled aboard a cross-Channel boat and this time they must have been sure there was no press on board because I had a cabin to myself. The bunk looked inviting. I stretched out and fell asleep immediately, tired out by the bewildering crush of recent events.

I awoke to the steady vibration of the engines. Getting up, I tried the handle to the cabin door. It was unlocked. I went out on deck to find the boat rocking in the mid-Channel swell. I could see no land astern or forward. Suddenly I felt terribly lonely, naked and insecure – so much space, no fence, no warder or guards, no escort. I hastened back to the cabin. I felt better there in the familiarity of a confined space. Then I realised I was running away from the very thing which I had fought to keep alive for. I made myself go back on deck and this time I looked for my escort.

I finally found my two slaphappy lawmen sitting in the buffet, each with a glass before him. I held nothing against them personally, but all at once I felt a sort of rage creep up inside me and those two squirts were the uniform, the brass, the authority which had lorded it over me for years. The me of years ago stuck his hands in his pockets and strolled over to the pair sipping their drinks and said: 'You know I haven't a brass farthing – which one of you gents is going to buy me a drink?'

I didn't beg, I asked, and I got my drink, a brandy. Picking it up, I walked away from them to an unoccupied table and sat down. I saw them glancing in my direction. The drink was tasteless and the effort had left me shaking, but I felt better than I had for a long time. I swallowed the rest of the brandy and went back to stroll about the deck.

I was standing in the bows when the dark uncompromising outline of the Dover cliffs nosed up through the mist. The sight did nothing for me. There was none of that nostalgia or sentimental sense of homecoming that the sight is supposed to evoke in every returning Englishman. It was raining as we berthed.

One of the escort came over and advised me to stay out of sight of the newspapermen so, having developed a dislike for the cabin, I went below to chat with the engine crew. Nevertheless a letter did get through to me. One thick-skinned newshound had sniffed out my mother in the backwoods of Norfolk and obtained from the bewildered old soul her letter of greetings to me, together with the name of the newspaper offering a large sum for the opportunity to bring me home to her.

'You aren't going to need getting your hands mucked up for a while after this,' grinned one of the engine crew when I eventually said goodbye to them.

Now came more cloak-and-dagger capering to get me ashore into the London-bound train. Only the devil and the Home Office pay clerks know how many policemen were engaged on this. Plain-clothes dicks popped up all over the place until I eventually sat in another reserved compartment with my original escort, who cautiously drew down the blinds and cut out the rain-drenched landscape as we neared London.

A tired, irritable tension crept over me as the train slowed down for its finishing creep into the terminus. Here the escort had either finished its job or failed to carry it out to the full, for as the train ground to a halt the blinds snapped up, the door was ripped open and I stepped down onto the platform blinded by flashing camera lights. A woman reporter with pen and notebook poised barred my way, only to be torn back and nearly trodden on by her gallant colleagues, while others, grasping and clutching, tore my jacket. Somebody with more enterprise than brains grabbed the Soviet trilby from my shorn head. Instinctively I reacted and shot a right fist into his face, tore the hat from his grasp and crammed it securely back onto my naked scalp.

Through the milling hubbub my ears picked up a single familiar voice excitedly shouting my name again and again. I looked around and there, madly waving his arms as he struggled to get to me, was John, the unmistakable blond head bobbing up and down in the tide of people. Then he was swept away and it wasn't until I saw him in Norfolk a few days later that I was able to find out what had happened to him after we had parted in Berlin so long ago. He had in fact made it to Italy but there he had been arrested by the British and brought back to England to stand trial with other members of the British Free Corps. He had been sentenced to three years' imprisonment and had long since completed his term. How he had heard about my impending return I don't know, and as I alighted from the train I scarcely had a chance to do more than wave to him before I was grabbed by two stalwart railway policemen and bundled through a thin part of the mob. Not, as I thought, that this was with the intention of saving me, for I found myself delivered up into the hands of three reporters waiting in a side room. No doubt the pair of railway coppers got their palms well greased for that little bit of manoeuvring.

The three newshounds fired questions at me, offering what were to me astounding sums of money for my story about the British Free Corps and my Russian prison survival. I was hungry, tired and bewildered, but not dizzy enough to agree to anything, but still they were determined to get me home.

They stuck to me all the way, scribbling like mad every time I said anything or remarked on the passing landscape the whole way to the Norfolk village of Rackheath, from where it had all started 17 years ago. They photographed and filmed me at the cottage gate, my mother greeting me, the homecoming embraces, and all the while it sickened me to think that people should be so mawkishly interested in the personal emotions and private comments of others.

At last they were gone. I walked slowly about the cottage, touching the familiar household objects, the few little ornaments kept carefully polished and dusted. It all felt familiar yet alien at the same time. Very little had changed, except that my father's rickety old armchair in the kitchen was empty.

My mother plumped up the cushions on the chair for me but I declined to sit in it. Somehow I didn't feel that I wanted to fill it – it was his, and to me his presence was still a reality. The sense of loss for all that had existed between us didn't hit me until a few weeks later. I was clearing out the attic when I found a large box filled with beautifully made toys – wooden toys, mechanical toys, all carefully and ingeniously fashioned and painted. With them was a yellowing note in my father's hand. They were toys he had made over the years for the children I had never had, and never would have now.

I slept once more in the narrow single bed of my boyhood. A twice-married man with several lifetimes of experience behind me, I lay alone in a boy's narrow bed with a blank world before me. I had arrived in the paradise of which all prisoners dream, and like all dreams of paradise it was a mirage. The problems 'outside' are not so different from those 'inside', only now, perhaps, I had the choice that freedom gives – the freedom to solve these problems as I chose. If I had learnt nothing else over the years, I had learnt that the only reward of life is the living.

The next morning the little old bed, as though reminding me of the habit that two decades of wandering could not destroy, got me up with the sun. For a while I sat outside in the quiet freshness of the early morning, feeling the openness around me. Then I stood up and started walking down the long, empty road back to the city, alone and slightly afraid.

EPILOGUE

Home at last after 16 years of hardship and adventure from one end of war-torn Europe to the other, Eric Pleasants felt little inclination to leave his native Norfolk ever again. Pardoned by the British government on the grounds that he had served his time, he settled back into the home patch of his childhood as a respected neighbour and citizen, working as a physical education instructor in local Norfolk schools and becoming a top martial arts tutor in Norwich, as well as continuing with the wood carving he had learned in prison camp, teaching self-defence to the elderly and qualifying in physiotherapy and massage.

A few years after his return to Norfolk, Eric Pleasants married Pauline, his wife of 30 years. In 1984, Pleasants suffered a massive heart attack, which paralysed him down one side of his body and deprived him of the most basic skills, including the power of speech. But once again his extraordinary steadfastness of spirit prevailed and by sheer will and guts he drove himself back to semi-fitness and in part regained his powers of speech. 'I survived,' he was to say later, 'because I never gave up and was always a little bit stronger than those around me.' He also survived, it should be added, because he had a woman of humour and gentle strength to nurse him back from the darkest abyss in his life – an abyss even more dire than the Berlin sewers and the Inta coal mine.

'Eric was indomitable,' she was to recall. 'I remember that after three months we got a wheelchair and I pushed him outside. Half an hour later, to my horror, I looked out and saw he was out of his chair, dragging his leg and pushing the chair. I've never seen anyone like him. The other day there was this terrific wind and his electric chair had packed up. It was all I could do to keep my moped up, but he biked all the way to Wymondham. You could say Eric's a born fighter.'

In 1998 Eric Pleasants – an anti-war SS trooper under one tyrant and a slave labourer under another – died at the age of 87 in Saxlingham. Though this definitive account of his extraordinary story, as told to Christine Ramble, was written some years before his last illness, only now has the complete, uncensored story of Hitler's self-styled Bastard – the Norfolk country lad, boxing star and champion wrestler, reserve in the British gymnastics team in the 1936 Olympics, one-time bodyguard to the future Queen of England and her sister when both were young princesses, one-time Communist, fascist, pacifist, British SS man, circus strong man and slave labourer in the dreaded Gulag of Stalin's Russia – finally been published in its entirety.

Editors' Notes (Dramatis Personae)

BRITISH FREE CORPS MEMBERS

Aliases

TOMMY ATKINS

Frank Axon: born Crewe. Lance-Corporal in the RASC. Taken prisoner Greece, April 1941.

PETER BUTCHER

Thomas Haller Cooper: born Chiswick, London, 1919. 1938–39, British Union of Fascists. Served in Hitler's bodyguard until LSSAH in Berlin, February to June 1940 and various other Waffen SS units until 1943 when he became an early member of the BFC. Tried by the British for high treason in 1945 and sentenced to death in 1946. Commuted to life imprisonment 1946. Released 1953. Went to Japan. Died late 1990s.

COURLANDER

Roy Nicholas Courlander: served with New Zealand Division in Western Desert and Greece. Captured in Greece, April 1941. Sentenced to 15 years. Served seven years and died in Auckland, 1970.

HANDRUPE

William Charles Britten: a lance-corporal of the Royal Warwickshire Regiment, who was serving in 4 Commando when captured at Duda Bay, Crete, in June 1941. Court-martialled at Colchester in June 1946, he received ten years' imprisonment. Two months later he was found to be suffering from an incurable form of Crohn's disease and was released.

KINGSLEY
Hugh Cowie: a private in the Gordon Highlanders, captured in France in 1940. Made several escape attempts and joined the BFC to avoid court-martial for possession of a clandestine radio while labouring for the Germans in Upper Silesia.

McCARTHY
Francis Paul Maton: Territorial in Royal Artillery. Former member of British Union of Fascists. Captured in Crete while Corporal in 50 (Middle East) commando after being severely wounded in his legs. Surrendered to British troops in Brussels, September 1944.

MILLER
Herbert George Rowlands: born London. Merchant Navy. Fought in and deserted from International Brigade during Spanish Civil War.

MILTON
Alfred Vivian Minchin: a merchant seaman from Surrey, taken PoW after his ship was sunk off Norway.

'TUG' MONTGOMERY
John Eric Wilson: born 1921. One-time senior BFC NCO, he styled himself 'RSM Montgomery, MM'. Served in 1st Armoured Division Provost Company, 1939–40, and later as an RASC driver. Volunteered for 3 Commando in 1943. Captured, escaped and captured again at Bora Manna, Italy. British court-martial sentenced him to ten years' imprisonment.

'LOFTY' NIXON
Although referred to by Pleasants as 'an ex-RAF rear gunner', the alias Nixon was used by Frederick Croft, a bombardier in the Royal Artillery, from Finchley. As a PoW he had escaped five times from his working party before he was put in solitary confinement. He subsequently joined the BFC.

OWENS
Norman Rose: East Surrey Regiment.

PHILLPOTTS
Roy Ralph Futcher: had served as a private in the DCLI. He was not arrested but given a warning as to his future conduct by the military authorities at the end of the war.

'BUCK' ROGERS
Thomas Louis Freeman: was a private in 7 Commando of Lay Force who was recruited by Courlander from Stalag XIIIa in Austria in February 1944. Cleared of any guilt after the war, he had joined the BFC with the object of escaping and sabotaging the

movement. Pleasants' reference to Rogers as a Canadian does not fit Freeman's profile. He may possibly be referring to Edward Barnard Martin, who was known to his BFC associates as 'Bartlett'. Martin was a Canadian from Riverside, Ontario, who served as a private in the Canadian 'Essex Scottish Regiment' and was captured at Dieppe in August 1942. He was sentenced to 25 years at a Canadian court-martial.

'VOYSEY'

Ronald Barker: Australian from Goulburn, NSW. Merchant Navy. Captured on MV *British Advocate* by German rocket battleship *Admiral von Scheer* in Indian Ocean, 1941.

WALTERS

Thomas Perkins: Lance-Corporal in Military Police.

'TEENY WEENY' WOODS

Francis George MacLardy: born Liverpool, 1915. British Union of Fascists,1934–38. Called up in 1940. Joined RAMC in March and captured at Wormhoudt, France, 31 May 1940. Sentenced to life imprisonment at Cheshire court-martial, later reduced to 15 years.

Others

John Amery (1912–1945): son of Churchill's wartime Secretary of State for India and Burma, Leo Amery. John Amery served as a radio propagandist for the sponsored 'British Legion of St George' before briefly running its successor organisation, the British Free Corps. Executed for treason by the British in 1945.

William Joyce (1906–46): British-passport-carrying radio traitor who broadcast propaganda for the Germans during the Second World War. Known to the British as 'Lord Haw Haw', he was tried for treason and executed by the British authorities in 1946.

Otto Skorzeny (1908–75): Austrian-born Nazi commando chief. As an SS lieutenant-colonel he was involved in many daring operations, including the rescue of Mussolini from an Italian mountain in 1943. Acquitted of war crimes, he lived in Spain during the post-war years.

Dr Vivian Stranders (1881–1959): a former captain in the Royal Flying Corps during the First World War. Stranders was responsible for the transfer of the British Free Corps into the Waffen SS. He was nominally head of the BFC from late 1944 to the end of the war. Naturalised as a German citizen in 1933, he was not charged with treason by the British and subsequently settled in North-Rhine, Westphalia, where he died at the age of 78.

Forest Yeo-Thomas (1901–64): British secret agent known as 'The White Rabbit', who was captured by the Germans after parachuting into France. Sent to a concentration camp, he survived the war to be awarded the George Cross.